The Generation of Identity
in Late Medieval
Hagiography

In this interdisciplinary and boundary breaking study, Gail Ashton examines the depiction of female saints in a wide range of medieval texts. She identifies two distinct but equal voices. The first is the controlling masculine voice that defines the identity of its holy subject as saint *and* woman. The second is the concealed, subversive feminine voice articulated through fissures of the surface narrative.

Gail Ashton deploys French feminist theory, primarily that of Luce Irigaray, to illuminate these portrayals of women and to further our understanding both of the lives and deeds of female saints and of their contemporary, and almost always male, attitudes to them.

Gail Ashton is the author of *Chaucer: The Canterbury Tales* (1998).

Routledge Research in Medieval Studies

The Generation of Identity in Late Medieval Hagiography

Speaking the saint

Gail Ashton

London and New York

First published 2000
by Routledge
11 New Fetter Lane, London EC4P 4EE

Simultaneously published in the USA and Canada
by Routledge
29 West 35th Street, New York, NY 10001

Routledge is an imprint of the Taylor & Francis Group

Typeset in Garamond by
BOOK NOW Ltd
Printed and bound in Great Britain by
Biddles Ltd, Guilford and King's Lynn

British Library Cataloguing in Publication Data
A catalogue record for this book is available from the British Library

Library of Congress Cataloging-in-Publication Data
Ashton, Gail, 1957–
    The generation of identity in late medieval hagiography : speaking
the saint / Gail Ashton
        p.   cm.
    Includes bibliographical references and index.
    1. Christian women saints – Biography – History and criticism.
    2. Christian saints – Biography – History and criticism.
    3. Literature, Medieval – History and criticism. 4. Christian
hagiography I. Title.
    BX4656.A85 1999
    235'.2'082 – dc21   98–30700
                                                          CIP

ISBN 0-415-18210-7

Contents

Acknowledgements

I am grateful to the following for their generous permission to use quotations in this work:

'The Council of the Early-English Text Society' for permission to quote from their volumes ES 96, and OS 87, 100 and 206;

Houghton Mifflin Company for permission to cite from *The Riverside Chaucer*, Larry D. Benson (ed.), Third edition (1988).

Penn State University Press for permission to reproduce material from Gail Ashton, 'Griselda and *The Clerk's Tale*', *Chaucer Review* 32(3): 232–235. Copyright 1998 by The Pennsylvania State University. Reproduced by permission of The Pennsylvania State University Press.

In addition I wish to thank my colleagues at the University of Birmingham: Steve Ellis for his good advice and Valerie Edden for both her wisdom and her faith in this project from the start.

Also many thanks indeed to Alison Bullers and Mary Bland for their generous friendship.

And, of course, my gratitude to my sister Jeanette and to Geoff for their love and unfailing support throughout the years.

Abbreviations

ESEL: Carl Horstmann (ed.) *Early South-English Legendary*

GL: William Caxton (ed.) *The Golden Legend*

LHW: Osbern Bokenham, *Legendys of Hooly Wummen*

LKA: John Capgrave, *The Life of St Katherine of Alexandria*

MF: Johannus Mirkus, *Mirk's Festial*

Prosalegenden: Carl Horstmann (ed.) (1885) *Prosalegenden* (anonymous Middle English lives of Elizabeth of Spalbeck, Mary of Oignies, Christina Mirabilis)

SM: Saara Nevanlinna and Irma Taavitsainen (eds) *St Katherine of Alexandria – the late Middle English prose legend in Southwell Minster MS7*

All references are to page numbers throughout with the exception of Chaucer who is cited in the usual manner:

II(B^1): The Man of Law's Tale

IV(E): The Clerk's Tale

VIII(G): The Second Nun's Tale

Actual editions of texts cited are given in the notes

Introduction

Saints' lives: sensationalised, sexualised, saturated by scenes of sado-masochism. Was this the secret of medieval hagiography's popular appeal? Without doubt one of the most striking features of this genre is its extraordinary emphasis upon the body, a body sometimes subject to appalling mortifications of the flesh – flagellation, starvation, self-mutilation; to ritualized torture – severe beatings, immolation in scalding liquids or fiery furnaces, tongues torn out or breasts severed; and to paramystical phenomena and bizarre insignia – levitations, trances, spontaneous song or nonsensical utterance, tears or laughter, mysterious wounds and stigmata. These stories tell of saintly bodies, instrument of divine will, vessel of God's Word, conduit of holy visions and marvellous miracles, of a *corps morcelé* – imitator of Christ's suffering humanity – rendered whole again by the tender care of angels, carried aloft into heaven in a blaze of 'virginal' glory, its earthly corpse simultaneously a leaking receptacle – of light, of fluid, of fragrant odour – and incorruptible flesh, its sanctified relics a site of devoted belief.

What this overview fails to reveal is the problematic nature of a genre that is at once diverse and reductive, its variations of saint multiple, its generic conventions repetitive and restricting. The focus of this study is a frequently neglected series of vernacular texts[1] of medieval female hagiography produced by men during the period 1200–1500 for a range of audiences. Some were intended for a mixed reception, others commissioned for a gendered audience; some for lay pious females or, as in the case of *Mirk's Festial*, for clerics. Together they incorporate the two 'extremes' of saintly life.

The first relates the life of a largely fictional virgin martyr, usually beginning by tracing a noble and pagan genealogy, followed by an account of the saint's childhood, itself marked by early signs of holiness. Subsequently a vow to remain a virgin leads to conversion to Christianity. The climax of such *vitae* is the inevitable confrontation with authority in the shape of a father figure and/or a provost. Continued refusal to renounce the faith permits the hagiographer to record a debate about Christianity, usually in the form of a diatribe against paganism. Torture, miraculous healings and martyrdom complete a reductive structure, each story interchangeable with the previous one. Examples of this type are numerous and include St Katherine, St Agnes, St Agatha, St Lucy and St Dorothy.

The second set of stories – witnessed in the lives of women such as St Clare, Elizabeth of Hungary, St Genevieve, Mary of Oignies or Christina Mirabilis – tends to correspond more closely to a pattern of late medieval piety and affective spirituality where corporeality and the practice of *imitatio Christi* are its defining features. What is emphasised is devotion to the Passion and to Christ's humanity reflected in both voluntary and involuntary bodily imitations of His suffering: asceticism, fleshly mortification, a series of miracles often centred on food (including the Eucharist), on visions or dialogue with Christ. Closely allied to women's mystical writing, these tales retain the format of depicting early childhood with its devotion to Christ and the Holy Family. Where the first set of stories focus on martyrdom and the death of the saint, these emphasise the life of the saint, the practice of sainthood.

What, then, do these saints have in common? In what way might female hagiography differ from stories of male saints? All hagiography exists as an integral part of a cult of saints composed of a faith in deed and word as well as in the actual body of the saint, in the place or site of sanctification when dead. At the same time as the saint's life is recorded in an attempt to ensure sanctity and 'prove' the holy worth of its subject, belief in the various miracles and symbols demonstrating that worth also extends to belief in the *vita* itself. In other words *corpus* (text) and corpse were both saintly relics; the hagiographical text brought together body, book, and the divine Word.[2] The intention of the hagiographer is, therefore, to validate saintly worth and to ensure the veneration of its subject. As such he is bound by contemporaneous notions of what it means to *be* a saint as well as generic convention. In addition, the writer works both as an instrument of the Church – in his impulse to sanction its authority and its teachings by documenting the life of his chosen subject as *exemplum* – and as a craftsman responding to the sometimes conflicting demands of various audiences or shifting notions of piety.[3]

Without doubt hagiography is a textual representation that is ultimately also a cultural and historical construct. An interrogation of this genre is likely to reveal something about late medieval culture, its power relations, its discourse, its ideology. As with any text, what at first sight might appear to be a stable, fixed entity might also be a place where meanings are contested or resisted. That all subjectivity or identity is elided in all saints' lives in preference to a holy identity is not in question, but where this becomes particularly problematic is in the case of female hagiography; representations of saintliness become inextricably mingled with representations of ideal womanliness. Thus, what it means to be a female saint is not quite the same as what it means to be a male saint, for the code of sanctity which the hagiographer must incorporate into his story is subject to different expectations.[4]

At the same time the genre's emphasis upon corporeality raises its own problems. Like Lochrie, I would suggest that the body is an historical as well as a cultural construct. In the case of women, too, the notion privileges flesh rather than the passive body, that which divides unruly human Will from the divine, a pervious and fissured border of potential disruption demanding control,[5] a feminine space repressed via medieval images of the sealed body, that notion of *integritas* witnessed in hagiography, theological treatises, and a wealth of spiritual guides for women[6] as well as prescriptions circumscribing ideal 'womanliness' and behaviour (ideas I discuss in more depth throughout this study but especially in Part II). All of this leads to a gendered psychology of sin where the female was placed in a position of inferiority, redeemable but potentially destabilising and, so, demanding control.

Thus women's imitation of Christ begins from a different position from men's, a difference that immediately lends itself to the theoretical framework I incorporate into this work, that of a French feminist notion of sexual difference. Any discussion of the body implies a gendered body, a gender difference that embraces exemplary standards of behaviour, of what the medieval world constructed as ideal woman. If this ideal extended to a valorisation of silence, then there is a further tension, explored in chapter 3, within the hagiographical genre where virgin martyrology in particular depicts an active, speaking, teaching saint, whose transgressions are contained only through a rhetoric that asserts divine rather than personal authority; the transgression is denied at the same time as it is shown to take place.

Thus, Part I of this study is an attempt to define female hagiography as a genre, to examine its intentions, its conventions, its codes, its discourse and symbols, and also to explore the tensions, ambivalences, and apparent contradictions that might arise from the conflicting demands of those with a vested interest in its production – whether the Church, author, audience cultural shifts in expectations of the pious, or mode of publication (as a compilation, commissioned work, or individual text). The issues raised remain intensely complicated. An individual narrator's personal investment in any text may colour his work while a range of available textual models compounds the issue: *vita* with fictional subject, life of an historical or actual saint, *vita* as living subject, *vita matrum*, virgin martyr, repentant whore, or simply a near-romance story of an holy or an idealised woman. My contention is that the genre itself is far from being the stable, closed, authoritative 'text' by which it is frequently classified; instead it is fissured in the way I shall shortly describe. Equally, despite individual differences, my exploration may well make possible some generalised conclusions concerning the nature of sainthood, the saintly code that it utilises, and the symbols with which it depicts both holiness and womanliness. It is within this complex grid that the voice of the male hagiographer speaks for its subject, the female saint. It is a voice that I term masculine, one that speaks and writes from the heart of patriarchal power structures, simultaneously defining the female as saint and as idealised woman.

For without doubt, whatever the differences within that grid, female hagiography written by men is what the French feminist Cixous terms 'marked writing', a writing 'run by a libidinal and cultural – hence political, typically masculine – economy'.[7] Cixous argues that most writing conforms to a masculine tradition affirming sexual opposition rather than simply difference, thus operating to the benefit of the male by reducing all to his laws.[8] Within what feminism terms the symbolic or the known world, it is a masculine discourse that is prioritised. Within that marked space of writing, women are consistently repressed 'in a manner that is frightening since it's often hidden or adorned with the mystifying charms of fiction', remaining a space 'where woman never has *her* turn to speak'.[9]

Though Cixous is asserting the need for women to write *themselves*, her comments illuminate this study for my approach to my chosen hagiographical texts is a French feminist one largely informed by a framework of ideas provided by Luce Irigaray. These ideas are explored in more detail as and when they are needed in Part II but the question that is immediately raised is how or why is such a contemporary model pertinent to medieval texts? In the first instance my assertion that all hagiography but especially female is a textual and cultural construct is a revealing one. We need to know how (or if) it operates as marked or masculine writing, to identify its rules and the practices of its discourse, to confront what it tells us of attitudes towards medieval women and holiness, and the place of both within a patriarchal power structure, for 'Only through its own techniques can patriarchy be challenged or displaced,'[10] a practice that Irigaray terms 'mimesis' and which I explore in chapter 3. Like many French feminists Cixous insists that 'woman'[11] has always functioned 'within' masculine discourse, a subordinate signifier referring back to its (male) opposite, that which invariably seeks to 'annihilate' that Other.[12] I too wish to challenge 'the authority of the signifier'[13] in this study. Hence Part II is devoted to an exploration of a concealed, possibly subversive, feminine voice, one that exists as a 'necessary outside'[14] to the dominant masculine one of Part I, one that simultaneously affirms a dual identity of saint and ideal woman, yet also subverts and undercuts it, giving rise to an alternative, more humanized subjectivity.

Irigaray asks 'Why only one song, one speech, one text at a time?',[15] a demand that resonates throughout this work and seeks to challenge the right of anyone, man or woman, to speak for others: exactly, of course, what hagiography does. Instead we must address the problem of who speaks for whom, why, and from what position in an effort not to dismantle all systems but to open up what is unsaid, to recognise other viewpoints. Obviously it is not only writers who remain part of that system but critics and readers/listeners too.

My contention is that female hagiographical texts are inherently fissured and unstable texts, the conflicting demands of generic and rhetorical conventions and intentions, plus the imposition of a reductive dual identity of saint and ideal woman, often resulting in texts marked by hesitation, suppression, and ambiguity. In addition, what is contained within them is a doubled discourse, the 'heard' and dominant, intended one – masculine – and a feminine voice that reveals itself *differently* that puts pressure on the masculine generic one, and is as much a part of the *vitae* as that other. It is the male hagiographer's inscription of his own representation of woman and saint that inserts her into a sphere of silence within symbolic discourse. Masculine texts, written by men or women and bound by phallocentric logic, stress singularity, univocality, or, at best, binary opposition, and operate under an unconscious or socialised commitment to patriarchal conventions. Masculine discourse seeks therefore to resolve disparity, to resist contradiction and multiplicity. When Luce Irigaray asks

> How can we speak so as to escape from their compartments, their schemas, their distinctions and oppositions: virginal/deflowered, pure/impure, innocent/experienced . . . How can we shake off the chain of these terms, free ourselves from their categories, rid ourselves of their name?[16]

she raises a fundamental problem. One possible means of discovering alternative identities and evading pre-constructed notions of the feminine might be through the body, itself a target of the medieval female's repression and, as noted earlier, a concept integral to representations of sainthood.

Cixous advocates the body as source, method, and goal of writing, urging women to celebrate it, to 'Write yourself. Your body must be heard', and adding 'Censor the body and you censor breath and speech at the same time.'[17] I would suggest that female hagiography written by men is profoundly implicated in this process of censorship, inscribing its own cultural representations of women in the text, confirming and confining them within its discourse of holiness. Yet, as Irigaray's notion of the two-lips-which-are-not-one indicates, a metaphor crucial to this work, it is possible to hear a feminine voice within that dominant masculine discourse, one springing from jouissance or the chora, those two concepts crucial to French feminism.[18] For it is the multiplicity of both experience and voice intimated in this metaphor of woman's fissured sex, a half-open shape indicating 'inter' and 'enter', two fundamental and only apparently contradictory concepts that privilege this study of equally fissured texts. The notion of space, exemplified in the female genitalia, both 'threshold and reception of exchange' where what exists is 'the mystery of female identity, of its self-contemplation, of that strange word of silence' is crucial.[19] It is this that is explored in chapter 2. Implicit within this metaphor is a privacy and interiority – images and symbols littering the masculine discourse of Part I and themselves indicators of holiness – enabling the saint to come to terms with her chosen path as well as to formulate the beginnings of her identity as a 'self'. In an address to men Irigaray writes that women have

> returned with themselves which must not be understood in the same way as within yourself. They do not have the interiority that you have, the one that you perhaps suppose they have. Within themselves means *within the intimacy of that silent, multiple, diffuse touch*. And if you ask them what they are thinking about, they can only reply: Nothing Everything.[20]

This is the voice that generates a series of feminine identities revealed through a set of images and details that simultaneously affirm holiness and a 'self' that speaks that same experience differently. How then is it spoken?

It is articulated through concepts of space, that psychologically marginal and relational space, both the limit of patriarchy and frontier of the wild beyond it, that is associated in the works of some French feminists with the feminine.[21] Thus women are often linked to marginality, enclosure, and containment, a code corresponding to a notion of *integritas* as seen in Part I, but one that also gives rise to conflicting and sometimes paradoxical interpretations, explored in chapter 2 of Part II. It is spoken, too, in correspondence with Irigaray's representation of women's sexuality which 'gives privilege not to the visual but to the touch' so that another important element of hagiography (again delineated in Part I), a masculine insistence upon sight[22] as a means to knowledge of 'woman', is deconstructed at various points throughout Part II. It is a voice articulated through the metaphor of the two-lips-which-are-not-one, through a multiplicity that fractures a surface text largely devoted to idealising and appropriating the female saint's experiences, inscribing her body as text and vessel and utilising a discourse that contains and reduces all to a single valency. In Part II those same images are identified as multivalent while difference is expressed through the body itself in chapter 4, through representations of the maternal (chapter 2), through the use of silence and speech (chapter 3), and via the presence of a feminine voice articulated in hagiographical terms by details such as heavenly or disembodied voices, tears, sobs, semi-articulate cries or sounds – including singing – which defy classification.

For, as Cixous asserts, what is repressed in women's speech and writing – as in this genre – is song, that 'first music from the first voice of love which is alive in every woman'.[23] It is a song that has its source in the mother and what she inspires – pleasure, laughter, desire, the urge to language, even violence – leaving us with 'Text: my body shot through with streams of song.'[24]

What is important too is the idea of 'woman' as flow or fluent, explored in chapter 4. Irigaray speaks of 'Blood, but also milk, sperm, lymph, spittle, saliva, tears, humours, gases, waves, airs, fire', of a subject identifying himself with/in an almost material consistency which is repelled by all fluence, a masculine fear of the feminine that everything forming part of the symbolic – law of the father, masculine logic – is designed to enclose and protect 'from that indecent contact . . . woman', a fear of contamination informing medieval theology, medical science, hagiographical text, and resulting in that crucial medieval concept *integritas*, the sealed body.[25]

This study then centres upon both voices, the doubled discourse of an unstable and fissured hagiographical text, fissures that appear as tensions, pressures, or paradoxes arising from the conflicting demands of constructing a saint's life within a particularly complex cultural context. As such they cannot be read apart from medieval culture or from its ideology of feminine-as-flesh, its prescriptions for female religious, or modes of literary and theological discourse.[26] Equally such texts may well need to be read in conjunction with recent feminist excursions into that richly rewarding field of female mysticism or feminist perspectives upon body and gender issues, and can only be articulated with other saints' lives, those written in Latin by biographer–confessors, by *amaneunses*, or those few works written by women themselves.

We need to learn to reread these texts, to hear *both* discourses, for if this genre operates as marked – masculine – writing then the feminine remains an integral part of that dominant, apparently closed discourse, of its power, of its cultural ideology. Such a reading might open up understanding of the relationship between author and audience, between men and women, between past and present where the 'I' is not only a sexed universal but has a relationship to two universals, two genders. Though sexual difference may be important, a single gender, or gendered text, is neither absolute nor corresponds to the whole. At the same time as each is itself, it must also recognise an equal other in what Irigaray terms a notion of alterity, symbolized in the angel (discussed in chapter 3), a balance of two, even several, voices or identities all crucial if the 'we' in these stories is to be heard.

It is a search that must look beyond a masculine surface text, one that privileges singleness and closure. It is a search that opens up and multiplies, one that reads and, above all, hears differently for,

> Hers are contradictory words, somewhat mad from the standpoint of reason, inaudible for whoever listens to them with ready-made grids, with a fully elaborated code in hand . . . One would have to listen with another ear.[27]

Notes

1 The only exception to this is William Caxton's *The Golden Legend*, vols 2–7, where I use a translation in preference to the fragmented vernacular original, currently available only on microfiche.

2 For further details on the genre of hagiography see the opening to chapter 1 in this study. In addition see Lochrie 1991b; Petroff 1994; Heffernan 1988; or Elliot 1987.

3 Late medieval lay piety in particular was an affective and somatic experience largely focused on *imitatio Christi* and involving a whole host of ascetic and ecstatic practices designed to imitate Christ's suffering humanity. Christ's body was a central icon, usually depicted as an open, fissured, feminised body with great emphasis upon His blood. This devotion also gave rise to a lay piety that was orientated towards active service in the world especially in the form of charity or healing the sick. See below for differences between men and women's piety. See also Bynum 1984 and 1991.

4 Bynum suggests that it is possible to identify some features specific to women's piety. She suggests that it combined the ecstatic (mystical, full of miracles, stressing union with Christ) with service in the world. Women imitated Christ too in a particular manner emphasising food – especially the Eucharist – illness and disease, extreme suffering and somatic experiences, childhood vocation, and charismatic authority via miracles and prophecies. See Bynum 1984, particularly 'The Mysticism and Asceticism of Medieval Women', 'Women Mystics and Eucharistic Devotion in the Thirteenth Century', and '"And Woman His Humanity" . . . Female Imagery in the Religious Writing of the Later Middle Ages'.

5 See Lochrie 1991: 15–23 for further explication of this notion, plus chapter 4 of this study.

6 I have in mind texts such as *Sawles Warde*, the *Ancrene Wisse* – a guide for anchoresses – or *Holy Maidenhead*. See Bella Millet and Jocelyn Wogan-Browne

(eds) 1990, or Mabel Day (ed.) (1952) *Ancrene Riwle* EETS OS 25. Also John Aylto
and Alexandra Barrett (eds) (1984) Aelred of Rievaulx's *De Institutione Inclusarum*,
EETS OS 287.

7 Cixous (1981b), quotation from 249.

8 ibid. 253.

9 ibid. 249.

10 Elizabeth Grosz commenting on Irigaray in Grosz 1989: 133.

11 Most French feminists insist that 'woman' does not exist as a pre-determined entity
or as anything other than a reductive label. When they speak of 'woman' they are
adopting an ease of reference to a female located in a history of Western discourse;
it is not a universal woman. See for example Cixous 1981b: 245.

12 Cixous 1981b: 257.

13 ibid. 263.

14 For clear and persuasive explication of this concept see Butler 1993, especially her
opening section. The phrase refers to the notion of the female as an inferior or
negative pole in a binary opposition that privileges the male and depicts her only as
lack. Yet, as Irigaray points out, this by its very definition ensures that 'lack' as an
integral part of that opposition serving to affirm the identity of the masculine.
Thus, though apparently outside symbolic discourse and laws, woman is also a
necessary part of it.

15 Irigaray 1985e, quotation on 209.

16 Irigaray 1985e: 212.

17 Cixous 1981b: 250.

18 The term jouissance refers to pleasure. This may be a sexual or sensual pleasure but
also above and beyond that such as the joy experienced in maternity (or paternity).
It is a term widely used by French feminists yet never finally defined. Similarly the
chora is used to depict a notion closely relating to the pre-Oedipal stage in
psychoanalytical terms, before language, where the child remains at one with the
mother. It is seen as a feminine space, full of semi-articulated sounds and cries
(including tears, laughter, song, or humming), often involuntary pulsions that
threaten periodically to break through the symbolic, and something that the
masculine suppresses. Later chapters explore these concepts in more depth.

19 See Irigaray 1985d, especially 175.

20 See Irigaray 1985d: 29.

21 See Cixous 1981, especially 92; also Moi 1985: 167.

22 ibid. 143. See also Irigaray 1985. This is a scathing attack upon visual control
effected through her parody of Freudian psychoanalytical language, and masculine,
scientific discourse where she plays upon the various meanings of 'speculate' and
'speculum' (including the vaginal speculum), the latter in a focus upon the idea of
the mirror said to prompt the Oedipal crisis crucial to the subject's entry into the
symbolic order.

23 Cixous 1981b: 251.

24 ibid. 252.

25 Irigaray 1985e: 64.

26 Karma Lochrie (1991b: 227) makes a similar point concerning women's mystical
texts, Margery Kempe's in particular.

27 Irigaray 1985d: 29.

Part I

Where is she, where is woman in all the spaces he surveys, in all the scenes he stages within the literary enclosure? We know the answers and there are plenty: she is in the shadow. In the shadow he throws on her; in the shadow she is.

(Cixous 1986: 67)

1 Narration and narratorial control

The masculine voice

What, if anything, do a range of tales focusing upon the lives of female saints and largely written in the vernacular somewhere between 1200 and 1500, all by men, have in common? Several of these authors were clerics while others were poets. Some were anonymous. Some too were editors compiling the works of others and, therefore, involved in an entirely different textual process. Of the poets, Bokenham's lives of holy women were commissioned works, a factor undoubtedly influencing decisions about his texts. Immediately apparent is the vast difference between purpose, range, and style of these works. Yet each author was implicated in a process of complicity with the Church. Not only was the text an additional relic in the veneration of the saint but it was also a vehicle for teaching, its story not simply the life of a holy woman but intended as an *exemplum* for others. As such it was usually written in conformation with a specific generic code. What, then, were the features of that code?

Heffernan prefers to term female hagiography 'sacred biography', a narrative of the life of a saint 'written by a member of a community of belief', sanctifying that community, and part of the sacred tradition which it documents. Thus, the text tells of a holy subject worthy of veneration, offers witness to it, and becomes approved by the community as a source of wisdom. It is part of a sacred tradition which implicates writer, text, audience, and a larger community such as the Church.[1]

Equally, such biography is exemplary, designed to teach its listeners to imitate by its focus upon ritual action or *imitatio Christi*, and a series of repetitive, symbolizing structures whose deliberately mimetic nature 'ensured the authenticity of the subject's sanctity'.[2] Hagiography is a received tradition whose continually evolving focus is the changing needs of the community it serves. Heffernan identifies a pattern in hagiographical tales where the act of writing gathers up all the myths and stories surrounding its subjects, whether oral, eyewitness record, or previous, perhaps contradictory, versions of a fictional life, and offers a sanctioned authority which allows all to be brought back into a Christian paradigm. The biographer is concerned not with a chronological record of a human life but to satisfy 'the specific community's traditional understanding of this holy person' and to 'establish the text itself as a document worthy of reverence, as a relic'.[3] As a result, it might be said that the subject's single-minded pursuit of virtue is to achieve union with Christ rather than to perfect self or character.[4] In order for anyone to achieve holiness they must reject the world, including family and children, and renounce the self to ensure a place in Paradise.

This essentially reductive model (later greatly modified by Heffernan) is confirmed to some extent by Alison Goddard Elliot.[5] Her discussion centres upon pre-twelfth-century tales, particularly the virgin martyrs of the fourth and fifth centuries, unlike Heffernan whose prime study is of female hagiography after the twelfth century. Both, however, quite rightly in my opinion, indicate that this textual tradition implicates its audience and remains part of a process involving writer, reader, subject, and the Church or religious community. Elliot points out that hagiographer and audience share an expected and 'common horizon of expectation',[6] so that repetition features heavily within these tales. She also notes,

> The spirit of martyrdom is a social one . . . is a celebration of community, and the values depicted are those of an entire society . . ., the purpose is not the glorification of the individual per se but the affirmation of the ideals for which the saint has given his or her life.[7]

Similarly, it is community which is privileged in the desert tales of the *vitae matrum* where a narrator or questing hero, always male, returns to the community the story he has just discovered:[8] 'As the saint is assimilated into heaven the tale of (his) heroism must be assimilated in society.'[9] In this respect, the role of the biographer in instructing, edifying, and entertaining his often very mixed audience is a crucial one. It is not, however, the sole means of transmission. Other forms of contact might include relics, icons, amulets, or the body itself as the text, so that a saint is authenticated via *corpus* and corpse. Hagiographers' insistence upon text as authority is thus undercut by a complex network of reception.[10]

The aim of this chapter is to explore the ways in which such a model might, at first glance, apply to the texts under consideration: Mirk's *Festial*, Capgrave's *The Life of St. Katherine of Alexandria*, *Early South-English Legendary*, Bokenham's *Legendys of Hooly Wummen*, Caxton's version of *The Golden Legend*, and Chaucer's *Clerk's Tale*, *Second Nun's Tale*, and *Man of Law's Tale* in *The Canterbury Tales* collection. Each focuses upon an idealised female subject whose saintly worth is validated through a series of external, immediately recognisable holy symbols, forming part of a particular code of saintliness – itself arising, in part, from a specific historical and cultural context. It is the imposition of that code, plus the hagiographer's intention to both venerate and offer the saint as *exemplum*, that tends to lead towards a text marked by control, suppression, and closure. Any potential transgressions conflicting with a cultural ideal of womanliness – such as moments of autonomous action or speech – are glossed, and a potentially subversive subject is brought back into the safe confines of hagiographical genre and the Church. This is the masculine voice that dominates in a generalised and universal neglect of any fissures in the text, witnessed at moments of narratorial intervention, and demonstrated in rhetoric emphasising external behaviour designed to sanctify the woman. At the same time the complex relationships between author and subject or author and audience, plus the demands of the hagiographical genre, place further strain upon the text. Thus, these stories are marked texts dominated by a masculine voice that seeks closure, singleness, unity, yet are threatened from within by the very instability of the genre itself. Equally each has a style unique to its author or, as in the case of compilations, its authors. This chapter seeks to identify a common pattern – one later subverted by the feminine voice or discourse explored in Part II – but must never lose sight of the individuality and differences that stamp each of these works.

Mirk's Festial

Mirk's Festial (c. 1382–90) is a collection of homilies in the vernacular, written by the priest John Mirk, prior of Littleshall, Shropshire, for a clerical audience before 1415. Hence, the tone of the collection is sometimes strident and frequently anti-feminist in its warnings against the lechery of women and against adultery, and in its praise of maternity and virginity. The stories within the collection are mainly of men or, more specifically, monks, often devoted to the Virgin Mary. Where women are the subjects, they are either virgin martyrs or sinners. Mirk emphasises the importance of observing Church ritual, especially the keeping of feast or saints' days, an intention reinforced through its organisational principle. Written by a man for a clerical male audience, his intention appears to be a strengthening of belief, a series of orthodox and traditional readings of saints' lives confirming a more general misogyny and mistrust of the feminine's potential for disruption. As such, his renditions make an interesting beginning to this study. The work remains extant in many manuscripts and was reprinted several times well beyond the medieval period.[11]

Mirk's aim is religious instruction. His pattern is to relate a story followed by a sermon or an extraction of its important theological points, with an emphasis upon encouraging all into Church for prayers or confession. His work provides sermon material for other clerics and confirms the role of the priest in all respects.

His handful of female subjects are invariably explicitly holy and the Virgin Mary is privileged as the touchstone of the exemplary femininity delineated. When describing her childhood, Mirk stresses her parents' goodness as well as her own 'choson mekenes.'[*MF*, 15].[12] Both are charitable while Anne is chosen by Joachim for her well-reputed goodness [15]. She is an obedient and dutiful wife who never displeased him 'for þe gret godenes þat was wythyn hur' [15]. One important way that this exemplary and interior goodness is manifested is through her prayer. Obedient to God, she also prays throughout the day in despair of her barrenness, and because her husband appears to have abandoned her [16]. Later Mirk cites one of the Virgin Mary's miracles and concludes with advice to pray to Mary, confirmation of her wider role as intercessor acting upon behalf of men in speaking to God.

Both this pattern and the attitude towards women are exemplified throughout the collection. Mirk is a teacher, a preacher, and a cleric authoritatively speaking the word of patriarchal law, explicating this law to those following its tradition and instructing them in the theology necessary to uphold it. As he prepares to recount the life of St Winifred, Mirk encourages those devoted to this saint to enter Church and worship God as well as listen to the tale of her martyrdom [177]. Worship of God is primary in this text where God is immediately posited as the subject of the *vita*. St Winifred herself is merely the devotional vehicle whereby all are brought into Church; it is the worship of God that comes first in the narrative structure, then the holy maiden. A similar pattern emerges in the life of St Margaret. Mirk reminds his listeners that it is not enough to fast for the love of this saint, advocating that all should come and hear mass 'for scho wyll con you more þonk forto make a masse sayd yn þe worschip of her þen forto fast mony evenes bred and watyr wythout masse' [199]. Clearly here the saint's life is used to manipulate devotion, is bait to call the faithful into Church in its promise to relate part of her life in order to stir devotion. Later, too, Mirk urges all into Church in order to worship Anne, an adoration itself effectively part of a wider devotion, namely worship of the Virgin Mary [213].

Mirk's answer to the threat posed by a late medieval upsurge in lay piety, especially a female lay piety, is to reinforce a sacramental, official worship safely under the umbrella of masculine clerical authority. In an implicit explication of the saint's life, he describes how the function of mass pleases the angels, feeds and comforts purgatorial souls, and succours all on earth. Perhaps anxious to curb the disruptive excesses of some of the female spirituality or mysticism of his time (an area explored further in chapter four), he remarks that fasting is a selfish activity [199]. Mirk's religion is a collective one, confirming male clerical authority as the only authority and denying any other validity to the lives of the women he depicts.

His tales also serve as a vehicle for teaching others, making overt the theological lesson contained within each one. In the life of St Winifred, clarification is made of God's three miracles when she is resurrected [178–9], while Mary Magdalene is used as an example to all sinners, calling for repentance and the regaining of a lost grace [203]. Mirk opens one particular sermon with a clear explanation of its purpose: 'Cristen men and woymen, as ȝe knowyþe well, þys day is called Palme-Sonday. But for bycause þat þe seruyce of þys day is so long, I woll schortly tell you whi þys day is called soo' [114]. Similarly, narration of St Margaret's defeat of the dragon is interrupted in order to clarify the reason for this saint's traditional representation in iconography with the dragon at her feet, and a cross in her hand; it shows how she gained victory over the fiend, not by virtue of her own strength of will or even charismatic saintliness, but by virtue of Christ's cross. The technique is used again during the annunciation of Mary's birth as an example of how to explain the

Immaculate Conception to any ignorant or doubtful listener. He uses the image of a precious stone, 'Onys', clear as crystal which opens to receive one drop of heaven before closing for nine months, free of blemish, leaving the Virgin Mary 'clene as any crystall' until the Holy Ghost opens her heart, and she is born. Closing again, she remains a 'clene mayden as scho was befor' [107]. Thus, a simple and concrete explanation is made, one accessible to all.

Other theological points are articulated during the narration of a variety of lives. Mirk speaks of the active and contemplative life represented by Martha and Mary respectively (a Mary more generally known in hagiography as Mary Magdalene) where implicit in this explication is also a model of exemplary feminine behaviour.[13] Yet, the very model initially contained within the Virgin Mary combines both of these aspects and remains the ultimate *exemplum* for all women as well as the foundation of all Church teaching.

Mirk carefully details how, like Martha receiving Christ into her house, the Virgin Mary is seen to be 'receyuyng hym ynto hur owne body' [231]. The action is intended to imply choice but, at the same time, the maternal is venerated as the passive recipient of the male, and the holy female as the only acceptable female whose body both literally receives the male and meta-phorically accepts his word and teachings. Her privileged status as mother compensates for her true role as other or outsider. Mirk's description reiterates this concept and, by making the male (or Christ) primary, reinforces patriarchal authority. Extending the analogy with Martha who nurtured others, the Virgin Mary feeds Christ with her own hands and breasts, clothes Him, cares for Him in every practical sense, visits Him when imprisoned, heals His sores with milk from her breasts, helps to bury Him and, in short, performs the seven works of mercy so clearly replicated in female hagiography [231]. Similarly, troubled by the world, the Virgin Mary is obliged to take her only son out of one land to another and to witness his crucifixion. The contemplative aspect is revealed through her attention to His preaching and her renunciation of the world after His death [232].

This vital role model is repeatedly replicated. Mirk, in common with so many narrators of female hagiography, presents it as an exemplary ideal and con-tinually affirms its worth. He describes how Mary responds to the angel's annunciation with reverence and meekness, how she greets her cousin Elizabeth 'full mekely' and 'mekely' conducts her leave taking. She also speaks to Joseph 'full mekely' [107]. Mirk draws attention to Mary's virginity, detailing her childhood vow and how Joseph initially fears to marry her until God reminds him that His son must be born in wedlock to prevent Mary's shame, and so that Joseph might witness the truth of her virginity [108].

Thus, woman – meek, virginal and sexually unthreatening, privileged as the passive recipient of the male/God's son and Word – obediently conforms to all social expectations. She is wife and mother or virgin, not a sexual or autonomous self; she is the mirror of the masculine world. What is transcribed onto the text is hagiography's code of sanctity, and that same genre's symbols, such as images of interiority. Yet such a presentation fails to acknowledge that the interiority symbolised within the description of the virgin birth offers a space for dislocation, is a private and self-enclosed area which by its very nature is resistant to masculine 'knowing', a concept explored in later chapters. The paradox inherent within this image is that at the same time as it is lauded, venerated, and rendered acceptable to the masculine world, it is an exclusive place.

Mirk continues to praise such an idealisation of the feminine. Mary Magdalene's scandalising and threateningly disruptive sexuality is partially excused by the narrator's interjection explaining how, after Christ prevented her marriage to John the Evangelist, she gave herself over to destructive lechery, a comment supported by the weight of patriarchal authority 'as mony bokys tellyth' [203]. Christ then exonerated her because of her devotion to His humanity [204]. Unlike Bokenham, Mirk gives no indication of any mutuality in this relationship but uses it to confirm a patriarchal stance. Magdalene, woman-as-other, humbly kneels in silent, passive contrition before Christ, symbol of masculine law and son of a masculine-created God. She speaks not one word, 'saue in hert', receiving in return joy and a 'tendyr loue to Cryst' [204]. Similarly, she is the later recipient of God's protection when, exiled in Marseilles, all flock to hear her preaching, an ability given by the Holy Ghost [205].

Thus, Mirk's women are apparently passive rather than active or transgressive saints. Even the unusual lack of detail surrounding scenes of torture or physical sufferings detracts from the humanity of his subjects whose saintly status is, instead, guaranteed solely by their perfect femininity and an emphasis upon the miraculous or the holy. It is the latter in particular which privileges the hand of God whose timely intervention 'saves' them from torture or proves their worth. Margaret receives a heavenly dove, hears a heavenly voice, and is aided in her vanquishing of the fiend. God answers Katherine's prayers and breaks the wheel, instrument of her impending torture. In return, Margaret converts many onlookers, prays to God, and offers herself up to the greater good of the religious community as she dies. An atypically brief life of St Katherine succeeds in strangling her voice by omitting details of her disputes with the learned men of her time and refusing to allow her to speak directly at all. Ostensibly, all is safely contained within the masculine rhetoric of the biographer.

Mirk's own stance, firmly within the masculine orthodoxy of his time, is amply demonstrated in an anti-feminist diatribe which attributes only destructive power to woman and proposes her as a threat to all order represented both at individual level and at the level of social order, symbolised by the king. Mirk recounts the tale of King Darius who demands of his bodyguards whether wine, woman, or a king is the strongest. 'A king', replies the first, for he commands men and rules lives. 'Wine', says the second, for it can overcome the king and render him helpless. The third indicates 'woman' who keeps the wine and gives the king his heir. Thus, it is traditional female domains – maternal, domestic, nurturing – which give woman her only source of validation. At the same time, the strength of feminine danger is expressed through the additional detail of how the king's mistress slaps his face, how when she laughs so does he, and when he weeps it is because she makes him [287]. Mirk's reminder to his audience of the destructive force of lechery [287] is an indication of a fear of feminine disruption which finds its expression in denigration.

That feminine threat is contained and defused by a theological tradition that Mirk upholds in his extended sermon on the image of woman as a castle. Its moat, symbolising her tears for Christ, is described as a ditch of meekness [228]. The drawbridge to the soul is the bridge of obedience keeping out the fiend [229]. Once again, direct comparison is made to the Virgin Mary who keeps her own counsel, represented by the drawbridge, when she receives the Annunciation. The castle's inner and outer walls symbolise patience, and a virginity that is strengthened by patience and might also be preserved in wedlock or widowhood. Mirk goes on to curse maidens who play, gossip, are flighty, who swear or scold [229], advocating instead a quiet submission in the manner of the Virgin Mary. Though not actually a part of any saint's life, it is this concept which is crucial to any understanding of medieval female hagiography. It is not only a model of feminine behaviour which is idealised here – meek, submissive, patient, passive, virginal. Where these qualities occur in hagiographical texts as images of containment, they mark a cross-over point between social expectations of women and cultural/textual expectations of sanctity, which found expression in the notion of *integritas* highlighted in the Introduction.

Yet, as suggested previously, the model contains an important paradox symbolised in the pearl of virginity and the virgin birth and also in Mirk's castle paradigm. Mirk is typical of a post-twelfth-century textual tradition which emphasises the patient fortitude of a chaste, saintly woman who keeps her own counsel and is frequently meek, frequently passive. Despite this, the achievement of sainthood is a transgressive process requiring *some* speaking out, preaching, action, a visibility which puts its subject at odds with the world she inhabits. The inner and outer walls of the castle (patience and virginity) take on a greater resonance when viewed in conjunction with the interiority of the pearl, marking the site of a conflict between the external and internal, between a public and private notion of self.

The Life of St Katherine of Alexandria

John Capgrave was, like Mirk, an educated priest, and prior at an Austin friary in Lynn, Norfolk. *The Life of St Katherine of Alexandria* is undated and one of only four extant works in the vernacular from this author. Capgrave cites as his source a Latin translation of the original version in Greek written by a local parson Arrek.[14]

The author's purpose appears to be to bring the tale of this saint into the community, into wider public recognition and knowledge. At the same time as he offers Katherine as a model of feminine as well as female holy behaviour, he confirms, probably unintentionally, the problematic nature of her sanctity.

Like Mirk, Capgrave is an upholder of clerical and masculine law. One of the ways in which he achieves this is by emphasising the importance of written, textual authority. In the prologue to the opening book, he relates how the priest Arrek discovered the *vita* hidden in the ground and, before rewriting it, spent many years researching what Capgrave terms the 'facts' of this life. He stayed in Alexandria for twelve years learning Greek in order to translate the original before retelling the story in Latin, the language of power and knowledge. The original writer, Athanasius, was close to Katherine, being her chancellor and secretary as well as her teacher, a pagan whom she later converts. Capgrave takes the second Latin version in order to widen its reception by writing in plain English. Interestingly, Arrek's initial discovery of the text is followed by a dream revelation in which he is instructed to eat the ancient manuscript. When he protests that his mouth is too small, he is ordered to open wide and receive it boldly, and assured that it will taste as sweet as honey.[15]

These details go beyond authentication to confirm what Capgrave perceives as the validation of Katherine's sanctity. Her personal worth may well be revealed but equally resonant is the power of masculine authority and textual tradition. Katherine's story is transmitted via the same masculine line of authority which holds her within its frame of reference. The process of textual dissemination occurs within patriarchy and is mediated solely by men who appropriate her life, retaining it firmly within orthodox law. It is a priest who apparently literally ingests the words of God and a male who disseminates this *corpus* of knowledge. Immediately, however, a source of tension is revealed which confirms the threatening idea of body (both *corpus* of knowledge and Katherine's body or life) as text. The masculine receipt of this body may well be privileged but an underlying tension remains to be later explored.

Thus, Capgrave relates Katherine's life with constant reference to a mascu-line, authoritative voice, the universal voice heard in so many authors. He opens the narration with a reference to what clerks tell us in old stories [16], and similar details abound: 'as seyth our book' [24], 'as seyth Athanas' [48], 'To telle forth our tale as þe cronycles seyn' [26].

Vital to the narration of Katherine's life is the issue of her great learning and the expression of what is a potentially dangerous knowledge. At the same time as this is primarily the way in which this saint is rendered visible and, thus, valorised, it is a behaviour which is unfeminine and threatening to masculine authority. Capgrave neatly attempts to defuse its power, and hence its sub-versive possibilities, by, once again, mediating this learning through men. The initial overseer of her learning is Katherine's original biographer, the chancellor Athanasius. Capgrave accepts the fact of her vast knowledge but adds,

> 'þis was thorow besynes of Athanas þe clerk,
> Wech tended on-to hyr & set hyr thus on werk' [32].

Male influence is confirmed and, indeed, is crucial, for women's nature is ostensibly not inclined towards wisdom. Similarly, Katherine's achievements in this sphere are subtly denigrated, rendered acceptable in the eyes of a patri-archal world. The author remarks that her learning comes from God, a grace specifically given so that she might defeat heretics [32].

Capgrave terms her 'goddys scoler!' and notes how she overcomes heresy and blasphemy throughout the realm [34]. This also simultaneously confirms her holiness by attempting to offer justification for transgressive behaviour. The holy Katherine is permitted her learning because, Capgrave signals, she has an especial role to play in the divine plan. He compares her to the apostles founding the faith, and remarks how God strengthens her with the power of the Holy Ghost [34]. No-one will be able to overcome her learning,

> ffor whan þat hys chyrch was at gret neede,
> he ordeynd þis lady for to ȝeue batayle
> Ageyn all þe werd [34].

Book III details Katherine's miraculous visionary experience in meeting the Virgin Mary and 'marrying' Christ. What this section of the text also offers is a vehicle for Capgrave's own teaching, his clarification of aspects of Christian doctrine. Thus, the subject's own experience is obscured by masculine authority. Capgrave permits Katherine to speak *his* words. She asks how the Virgin Mary might remain a virgin yet be so powerful. The lengthy answer reminds the audience of the fall of Eve and the expulsion from Paradise, and of how the mortal Christ redeems all [200; 206]. Later too, the hermit priest, Adrian, voice of patriarchy, preaches of the Holy Ghost, the Trinity and Articles of Faith [252–7], an education of Katherine which she utilises in her own lengthy debate with philosophers and wise men, exploring such concepts as the Immaculate Conception, the Trinity, the soul and the body, and Christ's humanity [319–20; 322–8; 331–5].

A careful depiction of the actual marriage ceremony Katherine undergoes as the bride of Christ enables Capgrave to confirm the power of male clerics once again. The Virgin Mary informs her that before she can look upon Christ she must be baptised, an office only an earthly priest is allowed to perform. Hence, Adrian, temporarily blinded, enacts this function [237], just as he is made her teacher and author of her life story [239].

Katherine's specially privileged role as a highly educated female is similarly only permitted by her father, whose authority and love shapes her early experiences. It is a learning of which even her biographer is distrustful. Katherine chooses, with her father's permission, solitude and study. Three hundred wise men marvel at her knowledge; when they leave, Katherine is left to her books [42]. Capgrave interrupts his narrative to note,

> . . . stody may not last
> Wyth werdly besynesse ne wyth hys cure,
> þe olde wyse sey þus, I ȝow ensure [38].

Here, Capgrave subtly indicates the anti-social nature of her chosen life, misgivings echoed in the later series of debates and counsels with her own family and subjects. Learning and solitude confer knowledge and power upon

Katherine, and the potential disruption inherent within her story marks the site of a deep fissure which Capgrave struggles to conceal.

He attempts to resolve the problem by emphasising the purpose of his narrative which is to publicise her life and, hence, the martyrdom which awaits her as a result of her difficult choice. Thus, even the potential problem of her pagan background is contained by Capgrave's insistence upon the entire family's explicit, if unintentional, holiness. Capgrave's intent is to affirm the authority of the Church offering his subject's *vita* as an object which is evidence of God's divine working and example to others, an inspiration to belief. The mysterious working of God's providential and marvellous plan is highly praised for, just as the children of Israel were only helped when in despair, Katherine's elderly and childless parents are finally given the gift of a daughter. Her parents are compared to Abraham and Sarah, and to Anne and Joachim, confirming a biblical and, therefore, authoritative precedent [26–9]. At the same time, the narrative's purpose is exemplified as the prologue to Book III vows to spread Katherine's story which was formerly hidden in other lands [172].

Similarly, her holiness is revealed when she foretells the subsequent death of Maxentius, an ability said to be conferred upon her by God, just like her learning [374]. She is compared to Christ, for both correct sin [58]. Even before she is baptised, she is full of virtue affecting the behaviour of others and comforting the sick. She is also 'Godely of her spech' [66]. Capgrave's prologue to Book III informs the audience that just as sparks indicate the proximity of fire, Katherine's holy words and deeds demonstrate the way she unconsciously seeks Christ, as well as suggesting the fire of virginity burning within her [178]. The *vita* ends with a citation of various miracles which occur upon Katherine's death, as well as confirming the healing properties of her tomb, details which publicly advertise her sanctity. That these miracles may be transgressive is ignored as Capgrave highlights the didactic purpose of his text, emphasising the need for faith:

> . . . I wil determyne noo conclusyon
> as in this mater; but fully I beleue
> That hoo-soo myghte see that solenne stacyon,
> he shulde knowe thyng whiche we can not preue [403].

Thus, Capgrave, like Mirk, is a teacher and a preacher. Throughout the tale, he cites at length the words of Katherine's accusers and places into her mouth an explication of orthodox theological thought, or clarifies points of doctrine as she apparently answers the questions posed by pagan philosophers ([321–8] for example). Similarly, her willing martyrdom is an opportunity to underline the transience of worldly vanity when Katherine repudiates as wicked counsel the ostensibly compassionate cries of the crowd who are concerned for her loss of youth and beauty [377]. In the same way, early on, she is obliged to defend her chosen life in the face of complaints from her subjects, comments which highlight and underscore the expectations of feminine, let alone regal, behaviour.

The narrative both points to a valorisation of the saintly choices which inevitably set her apart from ordinary society permitting a certain freedom, and serves to bolster the values of a masculine world. Though it affirms her actions in hagiographical terms, it can only condemn them in social terms as dysfunctional and disruptive. This, then, is the paradox at the heart of all female hagiography, one which is only partially resolved by a biographer's official sanctification at the expense of his subject's autonomy. Capgrave amply demonstrates this dilemma. He places Katherine firmly within a patriarchal framework. At best, he demonstrates the privileged, exclusive status of saint-hood; at worst, the contextual details of her existence pile up in a traditional, unreflective confirmation of masculine-dominated society's values.

Katherine's holiness is proved in the public arena where the full weight of the patriarchal world falls upon her. She is forced to answer her subjects' petition which urges her to marry, to forsake her books, and safeguard the realm. The focus is upon the unnaturalness of her choice, upon the frailty of woman, exemplified in their fear that she will be unable to govern with strength for she is only a maid who will weep if she cuts her finger [98]. They remind her that nature demands the production of heirs and ask her to permit a husband to govern:

'þan may ʒe haue your bokes in your hond
And stody ʒour fille' [114].

Her learning is posited as frivolous as they ignore her reminder that books promote knowledge and form the basis of law and clerical authority [110–12]. She is accused of selfishness and eccentricity [132]. Her refusal to heed even her mother invokes her uncle's authority; speaking for the masculine world, he reminds Katherine of her duty to provide an heir for the realm, and accuses her of wilful and sinful behaviour [144]. Clerical wisdom is similarly utilised [156] while the cumulative effect of these details highlights the extreme yet privileged stance sanctity demands. Paradoxically, it also promulgates an exemplary model of feminine behaviour which the saint apparently rejects.

In many respects, therefore, Katherine, representative of the virgin martyr, contains aspects highly repugnant to her audience. She is anti-social, unnatural, and unfeminine, at the same time as she is holy and virtuous. Where the human details of a subject are unpalatable, the response seems to be to reposition femininity in a way which renders the woman more ideally acceptable, but which stereotypes her as idealised-other and detracts from her as an individualised, autonomous self.

Thus, Capgrave emphasises Katherine's vulnerability in order to elicit sympathy from his audience and retain her as an exemplary feminine figure. His gallant, protective tone, amply demonstrated by his rhetoric and narratorial intervention, conceals his anti-feminist stance. Her father dies leaving 'But a ʒong mayde' as his heir, one who is 'but a woman!' [44] grieving for her beloved and indulgent father. Towards the end, she is beaten 'Soo dispitously that shame it was to see' and, in fact, all turn away 'for reuthe & pytee' [376]. When she faces the wheel, engine of her torture, the narratorial apostrophe gallantly exclaims against such cruelty, stressing the physical weakness of female corporeality. Capgrave asks how she might escape the mighty emperor who has cruelly studied how he might 'Thi virginal body to destroye and shende.' Capgrave offers Katherine and his audience no comfort from temporal authority or jurisdiction but instead refers to

> . . . the courte aboue –
> he wil not fayle the, Ihesu that is thi loue [381],

lines which articulate his story's example under the cover of his chivalrous words.

Even Maxentius initially pities her because of her youth and sex [293] before gaining confidence from the certainty that she, merely 'a woman' [294], will be beaten in any debate. Capgrave continually draws attention to Katherine's gender, both to demonstrate her remarkability as a saint and her vulnerability as a woman. Paradoxically, it also exemplifies the powerlessness of the female subject in a masculine-dominated world. Katherine's uncle terms her 'woman' as he begins his persuasion of her [295]. Pagan authority proclaims that it cannot permit 'a woman' to defame the gods or even allow one to speak. Maxentius is asked how much longer 'this witche' might be protected before he urges them to take 'þis dame' and beat her to death [375]. Even Capgrave's apparently outraged apostrophe begins 'O noble mayde' [381]. Maxentius's fearsome anger is unleashed when a mere woman defeats his philosophers whose knowledge deserts them in the face of 'nature femynyne' [340]. The public outcry against her death sentence, both pitying and accusatory, demands 'What woman are ye that soo despyse' youth and beauty [376]. This reiteration of her sex is clearly a complex and multivalent symbol which indicates a potential fissure in the text. Confirmed as a feeble woman, Katherine also stands for all her gender in her rebellious refusal to accept patriarchal authority, a rebellion which is simultaneously dissolved as it repudiates a specifically *pagan* law.

Similarly, it is woman's troublesome sexuality which threatens masculine order at the same time as it invokes a dangerously unwelcome masculine attention. Maxentius attempts to appeal to Katherine in sexual terms; according to Capgrave, his eloquence is specifically designed to tempt a woman into unchastity [349–51]. Here, although Capgrave assures his audience of Katherine's unblemished virginity, aegis against all temptation, he implicitly acknowledges accepted orthodox assertions concerning the naturally licentious nature of the female which remain unchallenged.

Capgrave also delineates paganism's lack of reason in contrast to Christianity's reasoned control represented in the figure of Katherine. The narrative structure carefully elaborates this fundamental opposition whereby a male emperor is unable to vanquish a female queen precisely as a result of her Christian belief, which permits his defeat against all the odds. Here, too, a link with the vulnerability of Katherine-as-woman is established and Capgrave is able to confirm the power of the Christian faith and its Church embodied in a weak, beautiful virgin. The lesson is clear: if woman, frail flesh and lacking reason, can overcome pagan and temporal authority, no man has any excuse to fail to follow the example. A vessel as weak as the female which succeeds in its rebellion does so through the power of God's love. Indeed, the implausible nature of many of these events, founded as they are on the unlikelihood of a female exercising any public authority, demonstrates the exegesis required in any reading of virgin martyrology, a point Capgrave does not fail to explicate:

> Natur fayleth whan we feyth lere,
> ffor our be-leue standyth so sole,
> Wyth þeis argumentis whech are full of dole
> Wyll sche not medelle be no-maner preue –
> Ther wer no mede þan in our be-leue {212}.

Thus, where Katherine remains calm and reasoned, details of Maxentius's rising vexation accumulate. As he listens to the philosophical debate, the text focuses upon his increasing anger {321–42}. Later, perceiving Katherine restored to health and beauty after her imprisonment, his emotions are uncontrollable {370}, while the miraculous breaking of the wheel designed to kill her leaves him so beside himself {384} that he finally displaces his emotions in the brutal slaughter of his own wife {387}.

Capgrave succeeds in controlling his material, retaining his subject within a clerical and masculine framework which enables him to fulfil his didactic purpose and widely disseminate the crucial lesson inherent within this valuable text. The code of sanctity is further elaborated: the female saint is depicted as a vessel to be filled with holiness or spirituality, a conduit of God's Word. What Capgrave cannot resolve, however, are the ambiguities and tensions contained within a narrative that attempts to deny Katherine as an active speaking subject. Nor is he able to suppress those fissures in his text which reveal themselves as a focus upon the body and gender identity, issues explored in subsequent chapters.

Early South-English Legendary

What makes this early collection of saints' lives particularly problematical is the question of authorial voice. The text was compiled by an anonymous editor or writer as a result of several revisions to produce what is believed to be a 'final' late-thirteenth-century version. Other extant manuscripts preserve fragments of text at different stages of development and suggest the hand of an author other than the original at work. The collection was probably begun at Worcestershire in the 1270s and completed at Gloucester some ten years later.[16] The *corpus* contains a mix of often quite distinct styles indicating the existence of more than one author.[17]

Several scholars do believe, however, that the voice of one particular writer is in evidence throughout much of the manuscript. Although the text lacks an overall shape or unity, simply following the Church calendar and including tales of varying length and style, it might be argued that the anonymous 'main' poet did have an interest in the art of storytelling. Evidence for this is found in individual narratives.[18] This poet's style is identified as light, simple, and repetitive but paying close attention to detail, carefully communicating emotion and employing a highly effective dialogue.[19]

There remains, however, considerable difficulty in assigning a specific narrative voice to this text or identifying one author. This popular and accessible work is filtered through several voices and perspectives, and is neither wholly literary nor a clerical, didactic work. Some evidence of preaching remains, though, together with a generally masculine authorial control over the nature of these disparate narratives. The text seems designed to entertain; instruction is implicit within this process. It is a series of sermons collected for primarily oral transmission during festivals (like *Mirk's Festial*), compiled around the same time as the far more influential *Legenda Aurea* of de Voragine but independent of it. It is a collaborative work stemming from at least two abbeys where only ten from a possible seventy-four tales are of women, and where emphasis is upon a simplistic framework identifying pagan cruelty and Christian courage in the face of horrifically detailed tortures.

Within *Early South-English Legendary* women are held in a framework which grants them little or no autonomy, presents them simply as holy and virginal objects. Lucy is 'Seinte Lucie, þat holie Mayde' [101].[20] Agnes is a 'holi Maide' [181], and Agatha 'þat guode Maide' [193]. In the opening lines of the story of St Fey, she is thrice mentioned as holy and reference to her gender accumulates throughout the narrative ([83–4] for example). This reductive labelling is an addition to the saintly code emerging through this study of hagiographical texts. Holiness and virginity are valorised, both as a religious ideal and a cultural *exemplum* for women through the notion of the sealed body repeated throughout individual legends.[21] Similarly, the narrative focuses upon a literal vulnerability of the female sex as their frail flesh is displayed for all to witness in scenes of public martyrdom. After being stripped naked, St Fey is placed in a furnace, where she gladly embraces her torments [85], the reiteration of 'maide' and 'naked' underlining the point. It is the 'nakede tendre bodi' of Lucy [105] which is the focus of her martyrdom, while a bare Agnes is paraded throughout the city so that everyone can see her lovely form [182].

The paradox inherent in such examples is a disturbing one. The intention is undoubtedly to reiterate the idea that disruptive feminine flesh can be redeemed, for the saints are never actually harmed. What is also affirmed, however, is the female as enticing object of the male gaze, a suggestion explored further in later chapters.

Such rhetoric serves to support the religious intent of these tales. Dangerously beautiful, eloquent, and often learned, these fictional virgin martyrs are merely puppets in a masculine narrative framework which utilises them to articulate certain doctrinal points and drives home their example. St Fey voluntarily offers herself up to a purge of Christians, prays to Christ for inner strength, for divine grace to inspire her, to fill her, passive vessel that she is, with an eloquence that comes only from God [84]. In case anyone misses the lesson contained in the opening of her story, so overt in the repetition of 'holi' and 'maide', it is reiterated at the end. After her beheading, the narrator reminds his listeners that they too might come to joy [86], might receive the crown of martyrdom guaranteeing entry into Paradise. Similarly, St Lucy aptly articulates the teaching implicit in all of these tales when she 'speaks' her biographer's lines:

> 'þe more þat mi bodi a-ȝein mi wille: here defouled is,
> þe clenore is my mayden-hod: and þe more mi mede, I-wis'[104].

She never swerves from the Christian path, her steadfastness symbolised by the inability of her tormentors to move her as they attempt to drag her to a brothel. Despite injuries to her throat, she continues to preach, telling of her forthcoming reward, and, in a neat underlining of masculine authority and clerical precedence, takes the sacrament before she dies [106]. The tale's concluding praise posits her as an intercessor [106]. A female martyr, with no life or humanity of her own, she, typically, exemplifies orthodox Christian thought.

This narrative framework is strengthened throughout the collection. The opening lines of the life of St Agnes carefully articulate authorial teaching, telling how she is martyred for the love of the Redeemer [181]. Offered marriage and wealth beyond her dreams, Agnes declares that her spouse is Christ. She speaks at length of Paradise and the vanity of temporal things [181] and, as her biographer seizes the opportunity for clarification, adds 'Ich am redi for is loue: þat deore me hath i-bouȝt' [182].

St Katherine is the embodiment of exemplary Christian behaviour. The *vita* omits details of her early life to launch immediately into a description of Maxentius's destruction of Christians and their faith, a dramatic opening which pinpoints the edifying intent of the author's material. Katherine is simply a vehicle for this purpose and, thus, the text centres upon her learned disputes or her conversion of others. She mouths clerical preaching when she speaks of Christ's redemptive suffering and cites a range of authorities, from Plato to Balaam, to 'prove' His existence [95] and affirm masculine authority. No-one can believe or accept that a woman might be so eloquent or so learned. The narrator has Katherine tell Maxentius that the Holy Ghost speaks within her [96]. Her body is a passive receptacle filled by Christ which enables her to preach, a powerful skill which results in the baptism of over two hundred onlookers [97].

In the same narrow way, the impassioned incoherence of pagan authority is, once again, opposed to the reasoned eloquence of the Christian voice and further emphasised in the presentation of the female as unorthodoxly active in this role. As suggested earlier, to posit 'woman' as a conquering figure strengthens the power of the faith. Consequently, St Fey's adversary, Dacian, angrily rampages through the region [83–5], while in the life of St Katherine, Maxentius is repeatedly described as being full of 'wroth' [98–9] and so angry that all could hear his loud yelling [99].

Thus, the tales of the virgin martyrs might be generalised as largely sermonising tracts which breathe little humanity into the lives of the women represented, narrated in a repetitive, unreflexive style with scarcely any interruption to the collective lesson embodied in each text. However, this prevailing tendency is undercut by an insistent over-detailing of the virginal body and its torments, a feature which undoubtedly has more far-reaching consequences. Similarly, individual narratives, such as the life of St Cecilia and the tales of repentant prostitutes, though continuing to uphold a narrative and theological tradition to which they are integral, invite a more subtle and problematic response.

Just as the virgin martyr stories exemplify their narrative tradition which places its women firmly and, atypically, in the public arena, the *vitae matrum* tales in *Early South-English Legendary* collection correspond to the private, reflective tone which is part of theirs. Elliot's model for these two genres, which emerged in parallel with each other, remains the most useful I have found. She confirms the evidence offered here, that the 'Passio' saints' lives are binary in structure and linear in action. Confrontation is a public one between saint and tyrant, a dramatic record of events containing much direct speech and many comments from onlookers as Christian and pagan face each other in a climactic interrogation which always results in torture and martyrdom. Virtue and vice are clearly delineated, as a personal identity is submerged into a collective, Christian one. Death is exemplary in every respect.[22]

In contrast, the *vitae matrum* stories focus upon a private and personal struggle to find God, expressed in corresponding images of interiority, and are far less dramatic, far more introspective, in tone. Such tales move from a physical to a spiritual martyrdom, focusing upon the life of the saint rather than her death. They usually involve a journey or a flight from the world, a series of tests, or a miraculous rite of passage. During her time apart from society, the saint is in a 'liminal' or 'transitional' state during which she undergoes a surrogate death or spiritual metamorphosis.[23] The narrative frame, based upon a process of separation – initiation – return, is a story within a story where a second questing hero brings the saint's *vita* back into society.[24] Clearly, this latter model, in particular, is resonant with many of the features designated for exploration in this study, although I would question Elliot's use of the term 'liminal', preferring instead to accept Caroline Walker Bynum's critique of its theory.

On the one hand, it is clear that Elliot is describing a period of escape from society resulting from crisis, or conversion, and presaging reintegration. Equally, too, the *vitae matrum* model takes its example from the desert father paradigm, and, not surprisingly since hagiographers are, on the whole, male writers, the assumption is that female experience is the same as that of the male saint. However, as Bynum suggests, the female desert saint does not undergo liminality in the sense of 'gender or role reversal, or contact with the mystical, interiorised spirituality of a woman saint from whom is gained a powerful humility'. Instead, the female experience is one of continuity,[25] discussed more fully later. Thus, the female desert saint achieves spiritual growth by remaining as she is – a marginalised figure, focused on her body in a series of sexual temptations and food miracles, man's unrecognised other. In this way, she is allowed to be more fully immersed in Christ.

Typically, therefore, the lives of St Mary of Egypt and St Mary Magdalene are far less strident than other female saints' lives in the collection and offer a clear contrast between a former sinful and latterly repentant life which embodies the Christian *exemplum* seen throughout. At the same time, a binary opposition is established which reinforces a prevailing masculine-dominated orthodoxy (demonstrated so admirably in *Mirk's Festial*) that woman is either whore or saint, frail female flesh or holy.

Consequently, St Mary of Egypt's life opens with an emphasis upon her threatening sexuality, rendered even more sinful not solely by her pleasure in it but by the young age at which her life of immorality commenced. What is scandalising is denigrated and suppressed, and contained within a frame which privileges only the exemplary female who, with God's guidance, is able to deny her own subjectivity and retain her place as conforming other within the world. Similarly, the narrative commences not with a history of Mary's birthplace or genealogy, factors which clearly signal her place in patriarchy, but with words which immediately position her as marginal, a source of disruption compounded by the necessity of her flight to the desert within which she 'recognises' the dislocating threat of her own sexuality. It is only this apparent recognition that enables the narrative to move to conceal the fissure which straight away opens within this text.

The story commences with,

> Al hire ȝounge lijf heo liuede: in sunne and in hore.
> Vnneþe heo was tweolf ȝer old: are heo dude folie:
> hire bodi and al hire wille heo dude: to sunne of lecherie [260–1].

Mary refuses no-one be they priest, rich, poor, or married, seducing even those with no real desire or 'wille', a detail which implicitly contains the constant masculine fear of female sexuality. Her role as marginal is reinforced by her active search for satisfaction which takes her far from her homeland, Alexandria [261].

The shocking implications of this for patriarchal society reverberate throughout the series of narratorial interruptions which mark the early section of the tale. The author remarks:

> hit is sunne and schame to ani man: to þenche oþur to wite
> þe fuylþe of þe wrechche sunnes: þat we findeth of hire i-write [261].[26]

His words articulate the extent to which such overt sexuality is intensely problematical and so far outside the protective realm of patriarchal authority that even the written word barely manages to contain its threat. For seventeen years Mary leads a life so foul as the most derided of women [261]. She even uses her body to pay for a journey to Jerusalem, undertaken 'In muche sunne, alas!' [262], an activity so abhorrent to the narrator and so potentially damaging to a masculine universality that its threat can only be contained by a reference to the controlling influence of the divine:

> Iesu, muche is þi merci: and muche þou þoledest þere,
> þat water oþur schip wolde heom bere: þat heo a-dreinte nere! [262].

The depth of her folly is not only articulated by the narratorial voice but apparently by a repentant Mary herself, reflecting upon her former life from the secure vantage of conversion. Scarcely able to credit the depth of her shameful sin, she wonders that the earth did not open up and swallow her [261].

Her punishment is carefully balanced against her former life and it is this balance which informs the narrative frame. Seventeen years as a notorious strumpet is matched by seventeen years of solitude in the wilderness. A further twenty years aids the perfection of her soul before her tale is ready for assimilation, first by a male cleric and then by the wider community, just as her 'life' is narrated by a male author who transmits what is undoubtedly *his* text to a wider audience. This process of dissemination via the masculine is confirmed in Mary's ostensible affirmation of priestly authority; when Zosimus falls to his knees before her, she insists that he rise for a priest should never kneel [268]. Subsequently, Zosimus buries his holy woman and returns to the world the story of her life by writing her *vita* [270]. This initial recorded account is further obfuscated by other male biographers who, in its retelling, still attempt to articulate an authenticity it possibly never had. Nevertheless, in its search for authority the text appropriates its subject's private, inner knowledge claiming to recite words which Mary 'hire-sulfue one heo seide', or 'ase heo hire-sulf gan telle' [261]. Similarly, during her early privations in the desert, her thoughts turn to lechery 'ase heo hire-sulf sede' before she turns to God 'ase hire-sulfue tolde' [264]. Ultimately, it is both Mary's body and the body of her text which are translated and mediated by men and affirmed within a primarily masculine religious community, that of Zosimus's abbey. The female body, site of disruption, is quelled by its utilisation as a vessel containing the Christian 'message'.

The possibly different narrator of Mary Magdalene's story (who typifies the conflation of the figure of Mary as noted earlier) also promotes a contrast between her years as a sexual predator and a passive recipient of Christ's love even though, once again, this alternative is a choice actively made by his subject. Thus Mary too travels far and wide away from her birthplace in search of 'hire flechses wille' [463]. Apparently unable to control her own corporeal impulses, God contains its threat for her.

Though born of a noble, wealthy and well-reputed family, Magdalene profits by her lust as a common prostitute receiving reward from many rich men, according to her biographer [463]. The inherent danger of female beauty is clarified in this misuse of it for the fairer she becomes,

> . . . þe more of hire was prys
> þe more fol womman heo wax: and sunful and unwys

until her reputation is totally destroyed [464]. Subsequently, this problematic loneliness is defused and desexualised in the section detailing her extensive preaching in Marseilles where all are attracted by her fair face now the instrument of God's love [468].

This narrator recognises from the start the necessity of firmly placing his subject within the confines of accepted patriarchal laws and obligations. Thus, her family background is clearly established and her disruptive behaviour posited as an isolated example of foolish femininity. Even her own sister, Martha, upbraids her for her lechery [464], while the tale's opening lines fully explicate the narrative's exemplary intention, calling on all to hear the words of a life

> þat may beo leche: to sunfule men of herte colde:
> A swyþe fol wumman heo bi-cam: and þoruȝ godes grace heo
> was i-brouȝht aȝeyn,
> And nouþe heo is to crist i-come: þe fayre Marie Maudeleyn [462].

The narrative then proceeds to position Magdalene in her proper place by telling of her life, where she was born, and deriving the meaning of her name which earlier sources confirm 'ase þe bok tellez me' [462]. After her conversion, she preaches at great length, voicing

> . . . godes word for to preche
> And of godes lawe with gret wit,

upholding both the masculine and the divine Word, teaching others how to love only goodness [470].

The narrative piles up details concerning her conversion of the Saracen prince, and a lengthy section is devoted to the knowledge he gains from St Peter, a knowledge which this text reiterates and transmits to its audience. This emphasis upon masculine appropriation of knowledge, as well as the tale's didactic purpose, is continued when Magdalene's story, like Mary of Egypt's, is recounted to the hermit who seeks her out in her desert solitude [478], and who, in turn, articulates it to bishop Maximus before the latter prepares her for death, absorbing her life and body back into a community of fellow Christians [480]. Thus, text and body mimic Mary Magdalene's story; as she is sealed within the narration by the bounds of patriarchy, so too, *corpus* and corpse, those instruments of religion, are assimilated into the (clerical) world. The closing lines of the *vita* confirm its function as *exemplum* as the narrator hopes, 'God us schilde fram peyne: and to heouene us bringue!' [480]

This particular text has a clear authorial voice greatly admiring of its subject, praising Mary Magdalene's beauty, wit, and eloquence. She is lauded for her unique relationship with Christ who makes her 'is procuratour: his leof and is hostesse' while she 'louede him with gret honour: in pays and in destresse' [466], a reciprocity echoed in the mutuality of the love between the Saracen prince and his wife which almost dominates the text.[27] This author is anxious that his story is believed; it stems from books, not dreams [474]. He admires his subject, claiming 'To speken of hire ich am wel fous: and it likez me ful murie' [462]. However, far from aiding the authorial process, it is precisely this aspect which renders it problematical as his unintentional affirmation of an autonomous subject, acting in her own admirable right, threatens to fragment his text and reveal the inconsistencies and fissures which mark it. More generally, this widely disseminated collection of saints' lives conforms to the prevailing pattern identified in the previous pair of works, exemplifying the precarious tension between an imposed narrative framework, a textual tradition designed to suppress and control, and the covert danger which threatens it from within.

Legendys of Hooly Wummen

Legendys of Hooly Wummen is a collection of saints' lives unique in its focus upon women. Its author, Bokenham, was an Augustinian friar at Stoke Clare and a doctor of divinity; immediately, he is established as a teacher and a cleric, a potential upholder of Church orthodoxy and patriarchal authority, an assumption confirmed by any reading of his work. According to manuscript evidence, the collection commenced with a commissioned life of St Margaret around 1443 and probably formed part of a much larger work no longer extant.[28]

The production of the text was a complex one believed to have incorporated the work of three different scribes, and, possibly, three distinct sections although the manuscript seems to have been produced piecemeal and not planned for collection.[29] Unlike Chaucer's *The Canterbury Tales*, there is no larger guiding principle or frame but I would suggest that there is a pattern to the text's style and a narrative framework of underlying assumptions which each rendition promotes. Individual narratives appear to have been placed into a larger *corpus* by Thomas Burgh and published around 1447. The text was widely circulated well beyond the local area.[30] Its audience seems to have been, quite uniquely, a female one, designed to satisfy the demands of the swelling number of those pious women excluded from any form of religious institution sanctioned by the Church, with the possible exception of that of anchorite. Thus, Bokenham's natural Augustinian ideals are presented for a female audience ripe for his teaching. At the same time, he is obliged to balance his preaching against the fact of his patronage and ensure that he pleases the range of those, including men, who have commissioned his work.[31]

Bokenham, himself, apparently maintains the balance via a sincere style of courteous modesty full of disclaimers about his own skill. His discourse is flowery and ornate, gallantly emphasising his admiration for the feminine qualities of his idealised subjects, as well as their holiness, piling up lists of their virtues and heaping adjective upon adjective. Donning the chivalrous guise of a lover of all women, Bokenham describes saints who are not only examples of exemplary spirituality but of femininity too. As will be seen, they are passive, pious, silent vessels filled with virtue, itself a gift from God. The pattern to the tales is a crucial framework informing any analysis of the whole text. In typical hagiographical style most begin with a prologue, a preliminary disclaimer and, sometimes, a source reference which confirms a patrilinear dissemination of knowledge. This is often followed by the derivation of name, always a series of exemplary Christian virtues, and a genealogy defined only through the father and which places the saint firmly within the patriarchal world. An epilogue lauds both her holiness and her example to all.

Bokenham's model is a dual one, typical of female hagiography, an imposed generic and explicit holy code plus an idealised femininity which is often difficult to disentangle. In addition, he extends his usually Latin sources to include clear reference to late medieval pious virtues: patience, poverty, charity, and humility. Each model reveals the presence of a narrator who confirms patriarchal power and assumes that the subordinate female is simply an object in the story of her own life.

Bokenham's subjects are ciphers, puppets, which his narrative discourse attempts to control, hence his obsession with labelling. Though ostensibly proudly admiring and gallant, the act of naming signifies the woman and contains her. Repetition of it tightens the frame and reduces her still further. Thus Margaret is 'this blyssyd mayde Margrete' [10], 'thys blyssyd virgyne' [4; 10; 24] or

> . . . blyssyd Margarete,
> Virgine & martyr [3].

Similarly, she is representative of her gender and yet, paradoxically, denuded of sexuality, variants of 'virgin' being repeated throughout [4–7; 26]. Equally Anne is termed 'þat blyssyd virgyne' [40], 'blyssud anne' [44], or 'that blyssyd & holy virgyne' [41], while Agnes is a 'blyssyd uirgin' [111], or, repeatedly, 'Blyssyd Anneys' [113; 115; 118] as well as 'crystys maydyn' [116] and 'þis gemme of iurgynyte' [113]. Dorothy is 'blyssyd dorothye' [135] and 'blyssyd uyrgun, o Dorothye' [136]. Mary Magdalene is termed 'blyssyd lady' [166] and, throughout, 'Blyssyd Mary mawdelyn [139; 144; 145; 158; 160; 162; 165–8]. Examples are too numerous to repeat as the pattern accumulates throughout the collection, amply demonstrating the insistently reductive nature of his terminology.[32]

The references continue, with images of women as vessels of divine grace or enclosed or empowered by the divine. As the vessel of Christ, the child Dorothy is said to be filled with the grace of the Holy Ghost [130]. The praise of Mary Magdalene is fulsome and originates even in the derivation of her name where Bokenham lauds her choice of penitence, contemplation, and eternal life [144–7]. She is portrayed as an example of Christ's forgiveness which enables her to achieve perfection *through* the male, a point underscored by the narratorial intervention:

> Lo, þus may we seen how euere mercyful
> God is, & synners ful besy to saue,
> By þis wumman in specyal [151].

Even her spontaneous act of contrition, as Magdalene anoints the feet of Christ, is denigrated by the reason offered by the text, that the action is prompted because she is 'enflawmyd wyth goostly graas' [155]. The force of her preaching is similarly simultaneously both acknowledged and undercut by the repetitive label of 'apostelesse' [171–2].

That Bokenham's women are first and foremost to be admired for their opposition to and distance from worldly values is the explicit lesson of his text. Katherine's saintly role is equally privileged from the start in its emphasis upon how good works form a chain enabling her to ascend to heaven [172]. The links of this chain are identified as innocence, virginity, a despising of vanity, avoidance of sloth, and lack of cunning in speech [173]. Her explicit holy identity is also affirmed as she prepares to meet Maxentius:

> Hyr cause comendyng to goddys grace
> Wyth crystys cros she merkyd hyr face
> And eek hyr brest [177],

while the rejection of her worldly, public identity is completed during their conversation. She tells how she is a king's daughter, the rightful heir, adding that though royally born and instructed in the liberal arts she sets all 'at nouht for crystys sake' [180]. Her defeat of the philosophers is again, according to Bokenham, a passive victory arising because she

> . . . so is fulfyllyd wyth þe influence
> Of goddys spyryht [186].

In the same way, she remains unharmed in the fire for a specifically holy reason, namely,

> …þe fals byleue for to confounde
> Of þe hethen peple, god thorgh hys grace
> Thys greth myracle shewyd in þat place [186–7].

Equally, Elizabeth of Hungary is commended for active and contemplative life as virgin, wife, and widow while the tale more generally emphasises her holiness, miracles and many examples of perfection [259]. Even as a child, she remains dedicated to God [260]. Praise of Elizabeth borders on the excessive. She is associated with many miraculous events [282–5] and purchases her heavenly reward five times over in Bokenham's opinion [273]. Elizabeth, too, rejects her worldly identity refusing her rightful label of 'lady' or 'mistress' and insisting upon being addressed in the singular rather than the plural, the mark of her rank [281]. She remains truly Christ's (and man's) vessel:

> . . . hyr werkys treuly
> He approuyd & made hyr to be knowe,
> And throgh-out þe werde hyr fame be blowe [258].

Bokenham's narration also depicts his subjects as models of femininity. References to feminine frailty augment holiness and stimulate compassion in his audience. At the same time what is highlighted is the sacrificial nature of suffering, a model of ideal womanly behaviour. Thus, Margaret's torments are pitiable to behold [22] while all weep for her when she is beaten so severely that even the instigator of her torture is unable to witness it [18]. In the same way, Christina's final sufferings are so cruel that 'uerrey pete it was to behold & se' [65], and Agatha's torments arouse similar emotions because they are performed 'Wyth-oute pyte or reuthe, allas!' [234]. Cruel pagan is in sharp contrast to the figure of the Christian martyr, and the pitiless torture the former inflicts upon his vulnerable female victim, once again, offers a valuable lesson to all. Yet, the pagan's attitude towards women in general is shared by the patriarchy he represents. As father of the Law rather than a non-Christian, he speaks on its behalf when Maxentius tells Katherine

> '. . . by natur
> A wumman þou art, & a frele creatur,
> Wych is euere uaryaunth & vnstable,
> Fykyl, fals and deceyuable,
> As we wel knowyn by experyence' [181].

Of particular interest is Bokenham's treatment of the two complementary strands of his narrative framework, namely the holy and the feminine. The pair overlap most clearly in the series of typically late medieval virtues he ascribes to his saints, a code undoubtedly recognised and even demanded by his audience.

As observed earlier, the tales of the virgin martyrs traditionally emphasise a linear, dramatic confrontation where women act aggressively and in an active, almost masculine, manner. The focus of virgin martyrology is an exemplary death rather than an exemplary life, and it is virgin martyrs which form the bulk of Bokenham's collection. In spite of that, his dramas emphasise qualities more often associated with the lives of late medieval historical saints (such as Elizabeth of Hungary whose life he relates), and stress an idealised code of conduct which goes beyond passive endurance of an embraced suffering, instead exemplifying a way of *living*. At the same time, these virtues are lauded as a model of feminine behaviour, and form part of a medieval ideal reiterated throughout a wealth of texts and treatises, as noted in the Introduction. The qualities of patience, humility, meekness, and passivity, this marrying of the active and contemplative lives earlier outlined by Mirk, are privileged throughout Bokenham's text.

Thus, he presents an image of feminine perfection which, at times, is only incidentally holy, and is aptly summarised in his description of Faith as fair and good:

> And in al hir werkys both clene & pure,
> Of contenaunce sad and of chere demure,
> Neythir in worde nere dede wantoun nere nyce [99].[33]

Devout humility, often demonstrated via acts of charity, and patient fortitude are also emphasised. His greatest praise is reserved for the only real-life saint in his collection, Elizabeth of Hungary.

Elizabeth is commended for her charity, perfect faith, and her great patience [258]. Bokenham notes details of her humility, her voluntary poverty, and almost endless list of good deeds. Though of royal rank, she labours with her own hands and gives alms to the poor, one activity from many which are described as 'Exaunple eek to shewyn of mekenesse' [271]. She submits entirely to the will of her confessor with meek obedience [280] while, though her patience is sorely tested after she is widowed, she remains steadfast and merely 'suffryd wyth gladnesse' [275–6]. Similarly, though brought to extreme poverty she remains delighted by the outcome and continues to express contempt for the world, including the love of her children, declaring that she loves nothing but God [280]. Despite her trials, Elizabeth remains 'constaunte to pacyence' and full of 'meke obecyaunce'[280] reminding her followers,

> '. . . whan afflyccyoun
> To us comyth, we owyn wyth mekenesse
> Us to submyt' [281].

Bokenham's lavish praise of his subject is amply demonstrated by his use of key words or concepts – obedience, meekness, patience – and his narratorial intervention.[34] One lengthy interruption in particular summarises this saint's virtues and reveals not only Bokenham's admiration but his full understanding of the generic code, of the rhetoric and images he is required to apply to his subject if she is to achieve a visible holiness and recognised authenticity:

> But of [how] greth deuocyoun & eek reuerence
> To godward she was & of what mekenesse
> And efthsonys of how greth abstynence
> She was to hyr-self, & of what largenesse

And pyte to þe pore, & what tendyrnesse
Of seke men she hadde, & how men in care
To counforte & chere she dede hyr besynesse,
The processys folwynge shul c[l]erely declare [264].

Thus, Bokenham's life of Elizabeth of Hungary is clear demonstration of the narrative pattern he imposes on all the *vitae* which he reworks. His admiring and chivalrous stance ensures that he is distanced from his subject, while his repetitive praise and constant reference to gender simultaneously protect and demean. At the same time, his apologies to his largely female audience, permit him to offer a model of both feminine and holy behaviour for them to emulate. Bokenham reveals an acute understanding of his medieval world, his texts exemplifying all the features of late medieval religious life, in particular those virtues such as patience and humility so prevalent amongst women. Apparently anxious to please an audience which shares this understanding he makes important additions to his Latin sources.

On three occasions Elizabeth is also described as a mirror. Reference is made to 'þis myroure of pacyence, lo!' [267], 'þis myrour of uery obedyence' [268], and during the prologue to the life of Mary Magdalene attention is drawn to the

    . . . holy & blyssyd matrone
    Seynt Elyzabeth, whos lyf alone
    To all wyuys myht a merour be
    Of uery perfeccyoun in sundry degre [138].

The use of this image fully implicates Bokenham in a careful guardianship of patriarchal authority where his saints, and Elizabeth in particular, are offered as perfect reflections of virtuous women; with little or no subjectivity of their own, they function as exemplar, highly praised for their ability to reflect patristic and patriarchal ideals of how this second, inferior sex ought to behave. Bokenham's interjections further highlight this vital component of his narrative framework. Undoubtedly, the clearest example is the incident when Elizabeth uncomplainingly accepts her physical punishment from Conrad, her confessor. This passive reaction leads Bokenham to cry 'O uery mekenesse! O blyssyd obedyence!' [267]. He remarks that few nuns, perfect examples of penitence, would have obeyed so unquestioningly,

    And, to seyn pleyn treuthe, I trowe yt nolde here
    Wyth-owtyn murmur & grucchyng also
    Neythyr prest ner munk, chanoun ner frere [267].

He continues, suggesting that in these days the 'molde' is more wilful, less humble, so that if forced to accept such punishment most 'wolde compleyn & ben euyl apayid' [267]. He adds his own opinion,

And þis ys o greth cause, as I dar wele saye,
That relygyous gouernaunce ys so sore affrayid,
For dew correccyouns ben al put aweye,

before hastily and apologetically recalling his audience and returning to his material:

For perauentur, yf I dyde treuly talke,
Sum folk wolde haue greth indygnacyoun [268].

Once again, this lavish praise of Elizabeth is a narrative voice that also hints at the author's unquestioning support of the society which has made him and which informs the textual tradition he adopts. This stance becomes firmly entrenched when the full implications of this digression are considered and added to the resonant image of the mirror. The plaintive cry concerning the nature of contemporary religious obedience appears to recall another era, to regret a loss of control previously enjoyed by the Church. Quite possibly, this Augustinian friar is displaying his resistance to the fundamental religious tensions surfacing during his lifetime, expressing deep concern over 'heresies' including the Lollard movement or even, somewhat ironically considering his patrons, an upsurge in lay piety which, at its most extreme, surely threatened to fragment traditional clerical roles. For it is masculine clerical power which is privileged in Elizabeth's meek submission to her confessor, a power which is also afforded to the author who has an opportunity to instruct his largely female, lay audience. It is an opportunity which is not lost upon Bokenham despite the narrative voice's typically self-effacing humility and boundless admiration for women. His texts laud the female saint yet diminish the woman. Significantly, they also offer a model of behaviour which has strictly defined parameters. Activity and disruption are only permitted to women if they subscribe to an external framework of both sanctity and femininity imposed by the male and mediated by him. Thus, the text, instrument of clerical authority, contains and controls them.

Another important part of the narrative framework is, once again, the masculine appropriation of the feminine witnessed in the emphasis upon the (masculine) act of writing and a patrilinear dissemination of knowledge. Once again the authorial voice seems to disturb the narrative. Bokenham's eliding of his own power in this act denies the very real authority with which he is almost automatically invested and upon whose maintenance he covertly insists. The prologue to the collection considers the nature of authorship as taught by philosophers [1]. He prefers anonymity hoping that his work will be judged on its merits and not be ridiculed because of his name, for he insists he is no Chaucer [3]. It also avoids the possibility of personal mockery or criticism and encourages a focus upon content instead [6]. Already, the author's edifying and didactic intent is apparent. In spite of this, however, Bokenham himself is a pervasive presence throughout his work.[35]

It is perhaps Mary Magdalene's prologue which contains the key to Boken-ham the author. He insists that he will conform to a Platonic mode of writing as St Austin advises and seek help from God [140] rather than the poetic muses. In fact, he is dismissive of the eloquence of those using subtle conceits or rhetorical devices claiming he is too old to learn this. Thus, he turns to Christ [143], asks for help in translating from Latin into plain English [144], and hopes to clarify his intent of leading all listeners out of sin to follow Magdalene into grace [147].

Here, the didactic intention of his text is clarified and his own credentials as a Christian advertising to a wider, lay audience by writing in the vernacular made entirely plain. Bokenham's role as the humble, clumsy author is yet a further disguise subtly cloaking his authorial aim and deflecting attention from him as an educated proselytiser and cleric. In addition, his numerous references to the literary powers of other notable authors cleverly imply that his own work, simple though it may be, contains an authority or truth denied to theirs precisely because their poetic and rhetorical skill is overly complex, somehow less reliable than words spoken in an everyday style.

Authorial truth is what Bokenham claims for his work throughout in order to fortify his covert preaching and suppress potential disruption by reminding woman of her inferior place. In the opening tale, St Margaret's, he immediately recalls the textual tradition which holds her for

> . . . as hyr legende makyth remembraunnce,
> She steryd the pepyl euere to repentaunce [8].

In addition, he cites a list of virtues recorded in *The Golden Legend* [8] and confirmed by clerical tradition [9]. Similarly, the several pages devoted to St Anne's lineage [41–4] confirm her worth as the mother of the Virgin Mary while all is authenticated by a variety of patristic teaching, 'doctryne of scrip-ture whiche wyl not lye' [41]. Anne's noble pedigree is exhibited as Bokenham closely follows his sources [44], while the virtue inherent in the names of her forefathers is delineated according to the pronouncements of St Austin [43].

Bokenham's source for the life of St Agnes, St Ambrose, is given profuse thanks for writing the original when all appeared lost, and more specifically for edifying the state of virginity, for his instructions on its observance [129; 113]. Here, once again, the didactic nature of hagiography is underlined and patristic authority confirmed. The latter is further enhanced when Faith apparently demonstrates woman's total absorption of this, informing the pagan Dacian,

> 'For, as holy fadrys doctryne doth teche,
> Noht ellis your goddys but deuyllys be' [101].

These saints' lives continually affirm a patrilinear, often clerical, appropriation of the female or her experience.[36]

The life of St Faith apparently confirms a patrilinear transmission of authoritative knowledge. It is a male cleric, a bishop, who translates her body and establishes a monastery at the site of her death [110], while Faith herself has no individuality or humanity, represents only the virtue of her name. The tale focuses upon her torture, her subsequent martyrdom converting onlookers, and, by implication, its audience. In particular, it prompts Caprasius to forsake his mountain hideaway, declare his belief and prepare himself for martyrdom. Thus, the role of the female saint is abundantly clear.

Hearing of her torments, Caprasius prays for knowledge of her reward, and receives a vision of Faith in Paradise which teaches him that patient suffering is the path to eternal life [105]. Knowledge, which springs from the woman, is mediated by the man, indeed, even appears to be solely for *his* instruction, for it is Caprasius who then smites the hill with his hand, and brings forth a well of healing water [105].

The life of St Dorothy hints at an opening fissure which is only contained within the tighter framework of her story. Dorothy herself has no life other than her sufferings and the moment of martyrdom, the main purpose of which appears to be to convert Theophilus by sending him apples and roses from Christ's garden, an action ensuring his praise of Christ [135]. Subsequently, he actively preaches throughout the city gathering up many converts until he himself is martyred [135–6]. For one brief moment, his glorification of Christ, 'god of dorothye', and the means by which he 'so folwyd hys mastrysse dorothye' [136], threatens to shift the balance of the narrative before Bokenham reminds his audience that it is 'of theophyle & of hys deuouth prechyng' that so many are brought to God [135].

The strong narrative frame established by Bokenham does not, however, always succeed in containing or resolving the many fissures and ambiguities surfacing in his text. Though most are discussed more fully in subsequent chapters, several merit exploration here since they suggest very clearly this author's genuine struggle to control his material.

The life of the conflated figure known as Mary Magdalene remains a problematic text. The author takes great care to establish the truth of his version citing numerous authorities in order to verify the exemplary beauty of the repentant Magdalene. He refers to the truth of the gospels throughout, especially John and Luke [146; 147; 151–3]. Other authorities, such as St Austin, are used to strengthen his case [152–3] Mary and Martha are offered as representatives of the contemplative and active lives respectively, proven 'Be þis processe we seen' [152], whilst great emphasis is placed upon the reiteration of the gospel lives of Mary's entire family. The audience is informed of all that is said about Mary, how Christ visits her home, how He raises her brother Lazarus from the dead and cures her sister Martha, or how He appears to her in preference to all others upon resurrection.

Bokenham's careful detailing of such incidents and his reliance upon biblical authority interweave with his undoubted admiration of this saint and her exemplary function. He privileges the exclusive mutuality of her relationship with Christ for it is this special love which contains the kernel of Bokenham's *exemplum*; Christ publicly defends this sinner and so 'proves' God's infinite mercy [151]. Similarly, their meeting after the resurrection highlights this special relationship [157], itself the result of the contrition emphasised earlier, her penitent tears and 'meke obsequyousnesse' [149], a penance whose extent is only realised 'Tyl completly rede be þis story' [146].

What this fervent admiration cannot fully disguise is the subjectivity of the female. Despite the tale's stress upon Mary's life of repentance rather than the sin of her sexuality, the latter cannot be denied. Neither can the fact that, though forgiven by Christ, her contrition is entirely spontaneous and voluntary. Bokenham himself declares that she chose the three best parts, outward penance, inner contemplation, and Paradise [145]. Mary's behaviour stemmed from an active choice, from her own free will. That her first choice, sin, was transgressive and disruptive is scarcely mentioned. At the same time as it is Christ's mercy which permits her repentance [148], it is Mary herself who goes to the house of Simon the Leper and silently weeps as she anoints the feet of her beloved, for by

> . . . þe grethnesse,
> Of hyr herte she shewyd þe corage [149].

Similarly, an autonomous self is revealed by the prologue's repetition of 'ches' or 'chees' [145; 146].

The second part of Bokenham's tale highlights other tensions which, unable to resolve, he simply ignores. This section of Mary Magdalene's life focuses upon her active preaching in Marseilles, an activity which ensures that the exiled Christians are provided for, and which results primarily in the conversion of the Saracen prince and his wife, thus ensuring their safety. The arrival in Marseilles is merely glossed, explicated as divine providence [158], while Magdalene's active and direct intervention to ensure an heir for the Saracens is reduced to a simple trick to prompt the conversion of the all-important male [161]. Similarly, Mary's teaching, which stimulated his initial interest in the Christian faith, apparently requires verification from St Peter whom the prince later visits [161]. In the same way, Peter advises him that the loss of his wife and child is a test in patience [164] and takes him to Jerusalem to establish him in the faith [165]. The subsequent discovery that his family is still alive is regarded as miraculous and Bokenham quickly passes over the disturbing detail that not only has Magdalene herself ensured their survival, but his wife has somehow shared in the enlightenment of his pilgrimage, has been taken to the same places 'in my mende', thanks to her protector, Mary [167].

Such transgressions are swiftly suppressed during the third section of this *vita* which, far from depicting the penance so lauded in the prologue, becomes a vehicle affirming male, clerical power. It is a priest who initially witnesses her miraculous angelic levitations, who discovers her story which is witnessed in the gospels as she herself notes, a story written thirty years previously at the time of her departure from the world [170]. The priest himself is

... þe massager
Of so holy & of so blyssyd mater [170],

transmitting his record to the bishop Maximin who officiates at her final moments, giving her communion and ensuring that both she, and her story, are returned to the patriarchal and narrative structure which defines her. Thus, she is now no longer privileged by the power of choice but simply 'doughtyr', while the bishop is repeatedly termed 'fadyr' [171] in a final underlining of Bokenham's wider message.

St Lucy, too, presents a series of problems which demand a great deal of hard work before her narrator is able to bring her under control. The prologue to her life, once again, stresses masculine authority which enables her to be presented as an example of how unblemished life might bring heavenly reward, itself 'þe entent' of his source, Voragine's writing [244], and similar to all taught by Ambrose [243]. Yet, it is a female saint, Agatha, whose inspirational vision affirms Lucy's goodness and prompts her transgressive action when she cures her mother, urging her to 'yiue ful credence' to the gospel story outlining another woman's healing [246]. Not content with this, Lucy preaches of the vanity of temporal wealth, and she and her mother distribute Lucy's patrimony.

The profound threat implicit in this action is made overt when Lucy's fiancé, deprived of what he perceives as his rightful dowry, accuses her of Christianity. In court, she is reminded that there she speaks on sufferance to a man who is the keeper of the emperor's decree, representative of patriarchy. In contrast, she obeys only God's law and stands accused of the prohibited disposing of her own money as well as sexual immorality [250]. Bokenham declines to explore the resonances inherent in these transgressions, preferring to overlay his reductive narrative framework. Thus, though at the end Lucy declares herself the mediatrix of the city, she is not permitted to die until priests administer the sacrament [256].

The life of St Katherine also struggles to escape the confines of Bokenham's narrative at times. One of his sources is his contemporary Capgrave's much admired recent edition [173], itself a problematical text as indicated earlier. Bokenham elides much of its complexity, however, by beginning from the point of Maxentius's entry into Alexandria and focusing upon Katherine's climactic confrontation with paganism. This conflict is highly dramatic, page after page of words apparently spoken by Katherine herself in defence of her faith. Numerous conversions are effected as a result; she, herself, is a vehicle for the Christian faith declaring that she is ready to sacrifice herself [193]. Similarly, the citation of various miracles [200] augments her holiness.

Despite this, her fortitude demands that Maxentius recognises her as a person in her own right. From the term 'maydyn', he is obliged to move to an acknowledgement of her, and of her identity. In this interesting and isolated example, Bokenham appears unable to perceive the implications of his own discourse where the use of the saint's actual name offers her an autonomous humanity far removed from the irreducible sanctity witnessed elsewhere. Thus

Maxentius addresses her as 'Kateryne' [192], a terminology that becomes repetitive and is consistently echoed by the narrator, a name striking in its absence of other adjectives,[37] and affirmed too by the tale's subject who declares 'kateryne I hycht' [180].

The Golden Legend

Caxton's *The Golden Legend* was a highly popular text reprinted several times and based upon the influential *Legenda Aurea* by Jacobus de Voragine, compiled around 1275. Caxton's version is an English translation of some of these legends, a collection compiled in seven volumes with the first depicting a series of Bible stories, and finished, according to the author himself, in 1483.[38] Caxton's translation is, in fact, based upon an earlier anonymous English text (circa 1450) and a French one, rather than the primary Latin work, and thus filters the original voice of Voragine whose text is marked by a clear didacticism.[39]

Caxton's editorial authority is far less overt. His versions tend to be shorter and, though still plain and simple in style, contain little or no direct intervention unless in the form of an appendix, or else speak in the distinct voice of a separate narrator relating an individual narrative. Though he includes elements of the miraculous and some details of torture, his interest in these areas is a far more limited one. It seems that his intention is simply to allow wider access to these popular tales of Christian edification, to compile a series of devotional, and yet entertaining, texts in the role of translator and compiler rather than preacher. That such a collection contains a number of individual voices, each with its own characteristics, appears of little concern to him.

Caxton appears to assume that his mixed audience is generally already aware of many of his stories and requires only confirmation of their surface details as well as a reiteration of their implicit *exemplum*. Most of the narratives refer to a shared communal understanding of the faith; indeed, it is this collective experience which the *vitae* affirm. Thus, Elizabeth of Hungary prays to 'Our Lord', hears 'Our Lord' speak or, in turn, ensures that 'Our Lord hath heard my voice.' Similarly, she is said to declare 'I love none other thing but our Lord' while her confessor attempts to break her will 'so that she should set all love in our Lord' [Vol. 6, 222–3]. St Clare is described as the 'holy lady and friend of our Lord' [Vol. 6, 186], prepares to receive the host or body of 'our Lord' [173; 176; 180; 182] and is fully implicated in the religious community by a discourse which establishes her as the daughter of clerics and 'dear fair mother' of her followers [176].

In many respects, the *vitae* translated by Caxton reinforce the previously identified features of female hagiography. Certainly, the female subjects of these tales are reduced to powerless mirror images of patriarchal assumption where the only semi-autonomous existence granted to them is associated purely with the holy. Examples are almost too numerous to mention. Agatha is repeatedly described as 'S. Agatha the virgin', 'The holy virgin' [Vol. 3, 33], and other variations [34–9]. Most often, though, she is simply granted an identity as representative of the Church; on numerous occasions she is termed simply 'S. Agatha' [33–5; 38–9]. Similarly, in a guaranteed undermining of her healing, teaching, and political activity, Genevieve is 'S. Genevieve' repeatedly [284; 285; 289; 292; 294; 295; 297], whilst the reductive repetition of 'holy' or 'blessed' insistently calls attention to her gender, her virginity, or her sanctity, permitting her no other life. As with Bokenham, a similar pattern is reiterated throughout the collection.[40] The cumulative effect of this simplistic repetition reaches its zenith in the life of St Clare whose striking individuality and personal struggle on behalf of many women is absorbed into a discourse which hammers home her especial sanctity. She is not only Christ's vessel, but a mere cipher, 'S. Clare', a reference made a staggering eighty-two times within a single narrative.[41]

In the same way, Clare's establishment of the Order of Poor Clares is only acknowledged within a discourse which privileges religious community rather than the self, stresses collective power at the expense of the individual. The narrative places the female subject safely within the confines of the orthodox Church, allows her to exchange her worldly family for one which is united in Christ. Thus, Clare is often described as 'mother' [Vol. 6, 167; 173; 175; 181; 183–4], and the nuns as her 'daughters' [168–9; 174–6; 178–84] or her 'sisters' [166–70; 178–9; 180; 185]. Clare herself is described as the 'especial daughter' of the pope and those cardinals who visit her at Lyons [180], while Bishop Hostence, who comforts her when she is sick, is termed 'her ghostly father' [181].

Throughout, in spite of the individuality of some of these lives, Caxton's work plainly and simply emphasises the holy. This is achieved either by reference to an inscribed generic code, as witnessed earlier, or through direct narratorial intervention which makes explicit a didactic intent. Of the various miracles associated with St Agatha, one involves halting a flow of lava threatening the city, proof of her saintly merit and the efficacy of her intercessory prayers [Vol. 3, 39]. The lesson contained within the *vita* of St Margaret is implicit within the comment that 'she overcame the devil by victory and to the confortation of the spirit of doctrine, for by her doctrine she comforted much people, and converted to the faith of Christ' [Vol. 4, 66]. The tale's focus upon the miraculous ensures that five thousand men are converted [70], while the end of the story indicates both its moral and stresses the masculine, clerical line of its dissemination; a holy man 'writeth' that Margaret is 'full of the dread of God, sad, stable, and worshipful in religion, arrayed with compunction, laudable in honesty, and singular in patience' [71]. In the same way, this addition to the text, presumably made by Caxton himself, functions as a means of objectifying its inherent teaching, of ensuring that it is explicated and firmly fixed in place as authoritative knowledge.

One of the most significant explications of Christian teaching is demonstrated throughout the life of Pauline the widow. The *vita* also delineates those particular virtues of late medieval piety outlined during the earlier discussion of Bokenham's narratorial stance. The strong presence of an anonymous first-person, eye-witness narrator[42] auguments its impact. The author emphasises her glowing example from the very start drawing attention to the way in which her humility surpasses all [Vol. 3, 1]. She is described as 'the pilgrim of Jesu Christ, for the amorous desire that she had to Jesu Christ surmounted the love that she had to her children' [2]. Though a wealthy and influential woman, she rejects the world and leaves for the Holy Land where she later establishes a convent. Pauline 'was the most humble and meek' [3], 'debonair' [3; 4; 5], and admired for her charity. Similarly, she seeks a life of voluntary poverty, weeps penitent tears while the narrator demands 'And what shall I say of chastity in which she was ensample unto all ladies of time past when she was yet secular?' [5]. She is a perfect example of patience as well as an ideal 'mother' to her community whom 'she induced and informed', ensuring a model of both femininity and piety by encouraging silence, mortification of the flesh and hard work [3]. Pauline herself keeps the scriptures in mind at all times [6] and is fully cognisant of spiritual teaching, reading in Hebrew, Greek, Latin, and French [7]. The perfection of her life leads her hagiographer to ask 'Who may recount without weeping the death of this woman?' [7].

Pauline's own charisma, strength of purpose and active subjectivity are denigrated throughout a text which defines her only as holy and subsumes her into a didactism which privileges masculine and clerical power. Thus, her initial renunciation is prompted by the arrival in Rome of the holy Paulinus and the bishop of Cyprus [1], and her faith sealed during visits to the shrines and holy places of Jerusalem, as well as a sojourn with Egyptian monks during which she meets and venerates several ancient fathers [3]. Recounting her personal vision of Christ inspired by His birthplace, the narrator's natural inclination to preach prompts a series of gospel references and a reiteration of biblical revelation of the coming of the Messiah [2]. Similarly, he quotes at length theological teaching to explicate the significance of Pauline's chosen humility for 'by patience is had poverty' [6], adding 'fair Lord God, we mortify ourselves always, and we be reputed as sheep that be brought to death, because that without plaining we mortify our bodies' [7]. In the same way, the lesson of her deathbed penury is contained within his quotation, 'Many give largely for God's sake, but they give not so much but some abideth' [8]. At her death itself the narrator records, not the presence of her community of women as might be expected, but the all-important bastion of 'bishops, priests, clerks, canons, and monks without number' [7].

It is these historical saints, in particular, who most fully demonstrate the reductive extent of a narrative framework whose subject is the female and whose centre is the masculine. St Genevieve's skilled healing and diplomatic personal relationships with both leading churchmen and politicians ensured a privileged position from which she exerted a not inconsiderable influence. Hers was a worldly power as well as a holy one, yet it is the latter which is emphasised in her *vita* to the near-exclusion of the other. Defiantly active, she is, however, diminished in a text whose only acknowledgement of her autonomous self is an implicit one, a discourse permitting only a femininity which is specifically holy and where, notable by its absence, there is no mention of traditional feminine or pious virtues such as patience, poverty or charity.

The biographer mentions that Genevieve is closely linked to St Germain of Auxerre, the bishop of Chartres, St Nicasius the martyr, King Childeric of France and his son Clovis, but the list serves to establish her as an adjunct to these men rather than as their ally or equal, while the opening text reinforces this in its depiction of *their* good deeds [Vol. 3, 284–5]. Similarly, she is chosen by a man in a manner emphasising masculine knowledge and undercutting her own independence. St Germain chooses the child Genevieve and publicly declares that she is 'My daughter', that he 'saw in her a sign celestial I wot not what', giving her a penny signed with a cross as a mark of their mutual alliance [285–6]. Soon after, she is adopted by the bishop of Chartres [288].

Later, too, her virtuous activity ensures that St Germain's return to Paris involves a visit to her house in order to commend her and publicly silence her critics [288]. Upon his death she is defended by the archdeacon of Auxerre who offers Germain's letters as further evidence of her holiness [289], while the commendation of her name, following a patrilinear dissemination of knowledge, reaches the ears of holy Simeon of Antioch who similarly salutes her [294].

Genevieve rallies the Parisians who are besieged in the city, effects the freedom of political prisoners and instigates erection of a church in honour of St Denis, prophesying where the workers will find lime with which to build. Yet all is subsumed into a larger narrative pattern so, for example, the church is established 'By the help of God' and, only secondly, 'of S. Genevieve' [292].

The humanity of Elizabeth of Hungary suffers similarly. Immediately, she is established as a passive vessel, instrument of the divine 'for God hath filled and replenished her with the resplendour of truth, of sweet savour, and of the vigour of the Trinity' [Vol. 6, 213]. She is 'more noble by her faith and religion than by her right noble lineage . . . for the author of nature enhanced her in a manner above nature' [213–14]. Even her marriage is interpreted as a theological act, acceded to, despite her vow of chastity, and 'like as the divine purveyance had ordained because she should bring much people to the love of our Lord, and teach the rude people' [216].

Each separate action is invested with a religious significance that renders Elizabeth explicitly holy, and which allows no room for any further consideration of her strength of will or her struggle to achieve some independence outside the restrictions of either her royal or feminine role. All is performed 'humbly' [216], for 'she was of so great humility' [216; 223], and obediently, her surrender to her confessor showing 'to our Lord that her obedience was more pleasing than the offering of a thousand hosties' [223]. She distributes her own clothing amongst the poor, thus demonstrating 'that the pomp and bobance of the world should be eschewed, and that she conformed her unto the Virgin Mary' [217]. She seeks voluntary poverty, works with her own hands 'so that of her proper labour that she gave to the church, she received glorious fruit, and gave good ensample unto others' [219], and generally 'entended with all her power to the seven works of mercy' [218].

In the same way, 'She had a special grace to weep abundantly tears, for to see celestial visions, and for to inflame the hearts of others to the love of God' [224] while 'It was well showed in the dying of S. Elizabeth of what holiness she was' [227]. A long list of miracles, occurring both after death and during her lifetime, clearly demonstrates her exemplary virtue. Occasionally, the narrator delineates the lesson for his audience; commenting upon the incident of the melodious birdsong which accompanies her death, he remarks how this is a sign Elizabeth is leaving for Paradise, 'and in like wise is showed to cursed men otherwhile their everlasting damnation' [227]. Exactly as in Bokenham's version, other facts are recorded. Elizabeth establishes a hospital where she herself cares for the sick. She dispenses grain during a time of famine. She uses her own money to care for the poor and needy, indeed succeeds in gaining an allowance from her husband for this purpose. With her husband's permission, she both leads the life of a holy woman and successfully performs the duties incumbent upon her role as wife to the Landgrave of Thuringia. Yet, these areas which breathe life into this *vita* are elided, remaining simple observations in a text determined to suppress their potential disruption.

In the same way, St Clare's autonomy is strangled, the loud voice of her hagiographer insistently proclaiming her sanctity which is itself filtered through his univocal assertion of patriarchal authority.[43] Clare closely conforms to a late medieval notion of female piety. Chosen in the womb, she remains 'so composed in all good manners, in port, in maintenance, and in continuance, that all others might take of her fair and good ensample' [Vol. 6, 161]. In every respect she satisfies a code which demands poverty, chastity, patience, and humility. She dresses with modesty, prays, fasts, and performs the miraculous. Her devotion borders on the excessive: 'It is read that from the time on a shere-thursday, the hour of the maundy, unto Easter even the Saturday, she was remembering and thinking on the sufferance of our Lord Jesu Christ so burningly that she was ravished as all drunken in the love of God' [165]. Clare's life and teachings offer 'ensample' to all [174] and she instructs her novitiates by stressing the virtues of chastity, humility, silence, penance, and devotion [177–8].

In this manner, her biographer affirms this saint's holiness, makes her publicly visible and acceptable to society and, perhaps more importantly, to the Church. As a result, the transgressive nature of her struggle to establish an identity for herself, and others, is firmly suppressed; her active power is not personal but stems from the divine and is exercised for the edification of a wider community. The narrator intervenes to remark 'Now it is well reason and right that we say and show of the great marvels *that God showed for S Clare* by her holy prayers' [167, italics mine]. Clare converts her sister Agnes, an action which invokes much hostility and is only achieved with great difficulty, yet the narration points to God as the instigator of her success; Clare merely prays for aid and requests that they might be together, a wish God is said to grant [169–70].

The miraculous is an important element in this tale and one which, once again, privileges divine rather than human endeavour. The narrator notes that

God shows many miracles 'for her' and that when Christ realises how she loves and suffers on His behalf, 'he so illumined and privileged her in such manner that she had power to make tokens and miracles by the cross' [176]. Once, ill and unable to attend a Christmas mass, she claims nevertheless to have experienced it all, a vision the narrator is unable to explain unless 'if God did it not by his courtesy, or if God had not given to her, above all nature of man, force and power to hear it' [173–4].

The power of prayer is also emphasised and regarded as marvellous [172] regardless of the personal influence exerted by Clare in more temporal matters such as her relationships with St Francis and Pope Gregory. Prayer, of course, restricts the female to an intermediary role where the real might is divine, and where she might be seen to act upon behalf of the all-important male.[44] Consequently, it is noted that Pope Gregory relies upon her prayers, a factor recommending Clare's saintliness to the world [172].

Indeed, it is the masculine which is affirmed throughout this *vita*, and which, realistically, is vital if the process of Clare's sanctification and visibility is to be completed. In life, too, her attempt to carve out for herself and her followers a mendicant role akin to the male Franciscan movement was dependent upon a masculine approval which was never forthcoming. Eventually, Clare had to be content with cloistered approval. Text, therefore, mirrors life where the male is primary and his privilege apparent, where it is he who permits the female to act in a manner which contains the threat of her subversion. Thus, Clare's sanctity is dependent upon the permission of men.

All of this is compounded by the hagiographical process which offers final confirmation of public and Church approval. By recording the life of the saint rather than the woman her threat to a masculine-dominated institution is defused by the pen of a skilful biographer. That this narrator is fully aware of the requirements of his craft is abundantly clear.

It is St Francis who provokes Clare's conversion, showing her divine truth. Hearing of his renown, she seeks him out and 'received of him many a holy, sweet, and angelic word' so that, 'informed of S Francis', she flees to a church where she is received by friars who cut off her hair and take her to a convent [162]. This patristic influence continues. Clare accepts the rigours of cloistered life with reluctance; 'if it had not been for the obedience of S Francis, she had never received the sovereignty of them' [163]. In fact, throughout her life, Francis commands her behaviour, informing her of how she must live or conduct herself. On one occasion, Clare is visited by a friar Reynold who advises her of the need for patience, a lesson she claims to have already learned thanks to St Francis [183]; in fact, she declares, everything she knows of Christian grace has been effected by her mentor [184].

Whilst I would not deny the fact of her mentor's crucial formative influence, I would suggest that the text's emphasis upon patriarchal authority has a distorting effect. Nowhere is there acknowledgement of Clare's autonomous self or any recognition that she herself was not only fully aware of a code privileging masculine rather than feminine power but manipulated it to her own advantage. Consequently, St Francis remains dominant and any mutuality in their relationship is denied by the narrative framework. In the same way, the favour of other influential clerics is stressed; the implication is that their recognition reflects upon Clare and reciprocity is absent.[45]

Interestingly, this hagiographer, fully conversant with the techniques of his genre, also intimates that he is aware of its implications in one telling aside. He agrees that the miraculous offers witness to a life of holy perfection but cites John the Baptist as an example of how its lack in no way detracts from sanctity. He remarks that Clare's activity alone ought to be sufficient proof of her sanctity 'if it were not for the people, which have the more great devotion and more greater faith unto the saints when they see the signs and miracles that God showeth for them' [188–9].

It is this isolated example, hinting at an objective awareness of the complicity between author and audience, even text and subject, which perhaps paves the way for the subtle complexities informing the work of the next author.

The Canterbury Tales

The three narratives under consideration are individual works which form a small part of Chaucer's collection of stories known as *The Canterbury Tales*. Only one is a saint's life, the others depicting the lives of what might be termed secular saints or holy women in the style of hagiographical romance. It is their themes of suffering, loss and woman-as-outsider which invite reflection upon the inexplicable, a pattern sometimes best explicated as divine providence. The three stories are entirely separate from one another, each being narrated in its own distinct voice. This problem is immediately compounded by the fact that each also exists within the wider dramatic framework of *The Canterbury Tales*.

Whilst the story of the second nun is an equivocal one, the narratorial figures behind the tales of both the man of law and the clerk are perhaps more clearly delineated. Both appear to attempt to control the stories they relate, frequently interrupting the narrative and orchestrating the readers' or listeners' response, each offering as the subject of the action a helpless, holy and idealised female whose subordination ensures a pitiful array of suffering and tribulation.

The Man of Law's Tale

The man of law himself, as his name suggests, is a fully fledged member of the patriarchy whose values, attitudes and prejudices he articulates. Speaking to the Host, he lauds Chaucer's love of poetry and particularly praises that exemplary wife Alcyone [*11 (B¹)*, 57] before going on to list many more virtuous women.[46] However this list excludes the incestuous Canace [84] and in fact refuses to speak of such unnatural acts [80; 88].

This careful depiction of what constitutes virtue is a reflection of orthodox patriarchal concern, where incest is the greatest threat to social order rupturing the patrilinear exchange of the female. As a lawyer, this character deals with family law and the maintenance of patrilineage. Incest itself is expressly prohibited by the law that this narrator represents. The text, too, may be said to uphold these concerns where the exchange motif is reproduced in the man of law's praise of mercantile trade, at the same time as merchants themselves bring to the Sultan of Syria details of Custance's potential as a bride. Patriarchal organisation, social power, and textual authority are conflated in the assertion that merchants are the

> . . . fadres of tidynges
> And tales [129–30].[47]

The man of law is similarly unable to disguise the profound anti-feminism that might be automatically expected of him; it is this which colours his portrait of his subject and provokes a variety of complexities and ambiguities. He presents the suffering Custance as an object of victimisation, whose idealised woman-hood and saintly qualities simultaneously detract from her humanity and augment a pathos which ostensibly inspires a compassionate and devotional fervour on behalf of his audience. Apparently deeply concerned for the young Custance, his apostrophe underlines his championing of her helplessness, and invokes ill omens and portents of doom [295–315]. The process continues throughout the text.

In many respects, Custance remains a symbol of victimisation and marginal-isation. Separated socially and geographically, she is always defined with reference to others rather than as a figure in her own right. Thus, she is simply daughter of the Emperor [151], news for the merchants, a wife or mother; she is truly man's other. The bond of the family is particularly significant and is discussed more fully later.[48]

The story has prompted many critical readings where often one aspect of the tale is emphasised at the expense of others.[49] These are undoubtedly valuable for the light shed on those particular features, but what they ultimately deny is the rich complexity of this and the subsequent tale. As soon as the narrator establishes control of his story and his subject, fissures appear which the overall frame is unable to contain. At the same time, a multiplicity of perspective and multivalency of symbol (analysed in Part II), together with contrasts and tensions deliberately invoked by the wider dramatic frame of *The Canterbury Tales*, immediately undercut those surface features imposed by the man of law. Thus his *persona*, apparently speaking with the univocal phallocentricity of his kind, remains exactly that, one voice, invoking not, as he believes, the authority of the dominant world but unintentionally offering it up for analysis and criticism. That his remains the final, unmuted voice may well posit Chaucer, despite his apparent sympathy for the female, as a conservative who ultimately upholds order but it does not detract from the fascinating alternatives glimpsed elsewhere.

The man of law's personal investment in the patriarchal and textual auth-ority he upholds is apparent throughout the tale. The beginning offers gallant and admiring praise of Custance whose fame is spread far by a company of merchants trading with Syria and lauding Custance to the Sultan. Masculine discourse speaks Custance who is a 'mirour of alle curteisye' [166], this significant image subsuming her into a patriarchal pattern discussed earlier in connection with Bokenham. Men arrange her marriage [211] and ensure that both countries' laws are accommodated by having the Sultan convert to Christianity [221–6]. Custance is sent far away from friends and family in a public celebration of a political alliance which is, of course, the purpose of marriage, a factor the man of law underscores by suggesting that the tears shed upon her departure surpass those wept when Troy fell or Hannibal attacked Rome [288–93]. Custance exchanges her father's law for her husband's authority. The narrator notes,

> Housbondes been alle goode, and han ben yoore;
> That knowen wyves; I dar sey yow na moore [272–3],

an ambiguous remark that simultaneously implies a chivalric sympathy directed towards woman, and implicitly draws attention to the possibility of an amused conspiracy at the female's expense.

Masculine values are affirmed throughout the text as the tale's speaker portrays feminine vulnerability of his passive, victimised subject, and directs his audience's attention to the pathos of her situation which, in itself, compounds her helplessness. He emphasises the sorrow with which Custance departs for Syria [292] and sympathetically calls

> Allas, what wonder is it thogh she wepte,
> That shal be sent to strange nacioun
> Fro freendes that so tendrely hire kepte,
> And to be bounden under subjeccioun
> Of oon, she knoweth nat his condicioun? [267–71].

Custance departs in highly inauspicious circumstances, a fact recorded by the man of law in a lengthy apostrophe [295–315], and she barely escapes with her life on her wedding night.

Cast adrift and washed up on the Northumberland shore, she is taken in by the constable and his wife who have of her 'so greet pitee' that 'they wepen for routhe' [528–9]. Falsely accused of murder, she attracts the attention of Alla at a time when, an exiled stranger, she is all alone [655], a situation fully explicated by a narrator who is ostensibly compassionate but who, in reality, upholds the patriarchal system and gallantly cries,

> Allas! Custance, thou hast no champioun,
> Ne fighte kanstow noght, so weylaway! [631–2].

Fortunately, Alla responds with compassion and the innocent Custance is spared [682].

Once again, however, faced with the treachery of yet another mother-in-law, one who steals a vital letter from Alla's drunken messenger, the man of law apparently protects his vulnerable charge by interjecting to berate the messenger and vent his chivalrous spleen upon Donegild whom he commends to the devil [771-84]. In this, the second occasion of a narratorial outburst directed against mothers-in-law, the narrator incidentally reveals patriarchy's deep and fearful mistrust of the assertive, independent female. Their shocking evil naturally highlights the virtuous contrast depicted in Custance, but the focus upon their unnaturalness serves to reinforce the idealised femininity, meek and weak, portrayed in their obverse. Thus, the Sultan's mother, 'welle of vices' [323] and slaughterer of Christians is a 'Virago', a 'serpent under femynynytee' and a 'feyned womman' [359–62], while of Donegild he cries,

> Fy, mannysh, fy! – o nay, by God, I lye –
> Fy, feendlych spirit [782–3].

Custance embarks upon her second exile leaving all weeping, takes her child and begs the Virgin Mary for help [835–53] before being forced to leave. Briefly landed under the protection of a heathen castle, a thief attempts to rape her, the man of law again metaphorically rushing to her aid, railing against the sin of lust and demanding to know how a frail woman might defend herself [932–3].

Similarly, he calls attention to the pathos of her final reunion with Alla who weeps for pity while she 'for sorwe, as doumb stant as a tree' [1052–5] until so 'Long was the sobbyng and the bitter peyne' [1065] that the only answer is to affirm a suitably happy ending, 'a blisse' [1075] that elides the tale's tensions and leaves Custance safely within the realms of patriarchy living as a widow under her father's protection 'In vertu and in hooly almus-dede' [1156].

In the same way, the man of law's explicit rendering of Custance as holy retains her within the text and attempts to suppress her subjectivity or individual experience. Custance is full of humility and charity, guided by virtue throughout [164]. She is passive, other, waiting to receive her identity from a world which excludes her. Her heart is described as a chamber of holiness [167], her every virtue authenticated by the masculine voice or, as the man of law describes it, 'And al this voys was sooth, as God is trewe' [169], patriarchal and divine authority being conflated in this line.

It is God whom the narrator calls upon to protect her during her first marriage [245] and Christ whom she commends to all as she departs [318]. Miraculously spared the slaughter of her fellow Christians at the wedding feast, Custance is cast adrift in a rudderless ship bound for 'God woot' where, beseeching the cross of Christ for protection [450–62]. That she somehow survives is directly attributed to God's 'prudent purveiance' [483]. The man of law makes reference to the miracles of Daniel in the lion's den, Jonah in the whale, Mary of Egypt's inexplicable desert survival, and the parable of the loaves and fishes, arguing

God liste to shewe his wonderful myracle
In hire [477–8],

and making explicit Custance's perceived holiness, itself a role which defuses
the possibility of any threatening, independent action.

Offered refuge in Northumberland, Custance thanks God [523] and manages
to convert her protectors, or, to be more precise, God acts through her for it is
Christ 'thurgh his grace' [538] that effects this via the blind man who demands
of Hermengyld his sight 'In name of Crist' [561].

As a result, Custance speaks openly of Christ's might [565–70]. The false
accusation of murder laid at her door is a suffering designed to perfect her will;
the narrator remarks how

Sathan, that evere us waiteth to bigile,
Saugh of Custance al hire perfeccioun,
And caste anon how he myghte quite hir while [582–4].

She enters her trial 'as the lomb toward his deeth is broght' [617], and immediately falls to her knees in prayer, swearing her innocence upon the Bible and
'saved' by a miraculous voice which declares that 'the doghter of holy chirche'
has been slandered [673]. As a result, Alla and many others are converted, and
she marries Alla himself [692].

Religious allusions accumulate. Custance, 'so humble and meke', sits out her
pregnancy 'abidying Cristes wille' [719–21]. Donegild's treacherous letter to
Alla declares his son to be a monster yet he, echoing Custance's goodness,
accepts 'The sonde of Crist' [760]. The pagan evil at work in Alla's mother
ensures her daughter-in-law's downfall and Custance is once more exiled, to the
pity of all. However, she patiently accepts God's will and welcomes the Lord's
dispensation [824–6] trusting to His providence. Her prayer to the Virgin
Mary makes comparison between the mother who witnessed her only child die
on the Cross [844] and herself, anxious for the life of her own innocent child.
Full of holiness [867], she then embarks upon the ship.

There, the narrator emphasises that her survival is due to God's grace [869–
74]. Indeed, he calls upon the help of both God [907] and the Virgin Mary [920]
to protect her against a threatened rape, a prayer that he believes is answered for
'thus hath Crist unwemmed kept Custance' [924]. Explicit comparison is drawn
between her miraculous strength and the courage of David against Goliath or
Judith against Holofernes [934–41] the man of law later remarking:

. . . I seye, for this entente,
That right as God spirit of vigour sente
To hem and saved hem out of meschance,
So sente he myght and vigour to Custance [942–5].

Custance is fortunately rescued by her father's own fleet returning from punishing Syria for Custance's dishonour, an accident entirely due to the Virgin Mary, according to the narrator [950–2; 977]. Safely domiciled with the senator's wife, in reality her aunt, Custance continues to perform holy works [980] while the end of the story reiterates the word 'holy' on three separate occasions [1129; 1149; 1156], as well as implicitly praising her for the maternal care of her son, Maurice, later emperor honouring the Christian Church [1121–7].

All adventures over, Custance returns to Rome, and completes a life of virtue, her timeless sufferings, her journeys, and her exiles all apparently redeemed in a final reunion which confirms that her place is, literally, within the world of men.

The Clerk's Tale

The narrator of *The Clerk's Tale*, though initially far more empathetic to the plight of the female in a masculine-dominated world and a much more ambiguous voice, may well be the complementary twin of the man of law. The latter upholds patriarchal law, the clerk clerical authority; both might be said to participate in a controlling textual tradition which privileges the masculine.

This highly complex tale has prompted a variety of readings; few, if any, appear able to resolve the tensions or difficulties largely stemming from its narrative style. Griselda's life appears to be an exemplary one, despite the protestations of the Envoy, and emphasises virtuous patience, constancy, and silent obedience. Religious allusions abound and some perceive the story as religious fable.[50] Others, such as Jill Mann, identify a paradox of power within the picture of the idealised, passive woman, and perceive suffering as active rather than passive. Griselda maintains her self and is also holy because her will to suffer images Christ. Both her patient suffering and Walter's tyranny represent God.[51]

The role of the masculine narrator remains crucial. Dinshaw argues that both the clerk and the man of law are representative of the double-edge of *translatio* which both creatively reconstructs truth and deliberately edits or distorts. Similarly, both participate in the patriarchal act of telling tales. Dinshaw believes that, in the main, *translatio* is used negatively, but then, surprisingly, suggests that the clerk's response is a positive one for he is allied with the female in the description of him as both a meek, new bride, and a student.[52] Elaine Tuttle Hansen suggests that Chaucer's representation of woman is a revelation of male speakers' anxiety concerning manliness, status or identity, that even where the question of the depiction of woman is addressed by the author, or gender is apparently dissolved, the focus remains man's gendered identity and his relations with other men.[53] My own view remains closest to that of Hansen, that occasionally a feminine voice is heard within Chaucer's work, which is subversive but which is intended as part of a wider focus upon masculine identity.[54] I would go further, however, and suggest that this voice may well have been heard and understood in a way that detracts from its original intention, an idea explored in Part II.

Undoubtedly, Chaucer's presentation of the clerk remains a complex and ambiguous one. Apparently sympathetic narratorial intervention attempts to orchestrate audience response, but this compassion may be deceptive, for the clerk also remains implicated in a masculine conspiracy to deny the female either power or subjectivity. In part, then, the characterisation of the clerk compounds the ambiguity of this tale by disrupting the (masculine) authority of its narration.

His entire appearance is deceiving. Harry Bailly describes him as demure, likens him to a new bride, rails against his sober, quiet study, demanding an exciting tale [*IV(E)*, 1–15], a request to which the clerk obediently accedes [21–4]. Yet the request satisfies only the demand to speak, ignoring the Host's insistent command to speak plainly [19], the clerk removing only a lengthy description of the Italian region in which the tale is set from the high style of his source.

His story, if it is accepted that it offers an *exemplum* at all, contradicts Harry's request to avoid preaching [12]. Though the story of Griselda is far from dull, the clerk's intention is to teach his audience. Similarly, his source is an authoritative one disseminated via the patrilinear; he tells of a story

Lerned at Padowe of a worthy clerk,
As preved by his wordes and his werk [27–8].

Part of his admiration for Griselda stems from her constancy, her patience in the face of adversity, and, in order to highlight this, his narration renders her explicitly holy. At the same time, the clerk typically emphasises Griselda as a creature of pathos, deserving of compassion and gallant protection, a model of femininity. Once again, the narrative focuses upon holiness *and* idealised womanhood.

Thus, Griselda is saintly in her 'vertuous beautee' [211], her hard work, her virginity, her obedience towards her father, and her simple living and poverty [211–31]. As the narrator remarks,

. . . hye God somtyme senden kan
His grace into a litel oxes stalle [206–7].

It is this which attracts Walter though she remains entirely innocent of his intentions [274], fetching water from the well as usual on the day of the marriage and setting down her water pot, again 'in an oxes stalle' [290–1]. Griselda is commended in the narration for her idealised femininity. Newly married and raised from her humble origins, all love her for she is 'So benigne and so digne of reverence' [411]. Walter is praised for his choice in having 'wedded with fortunat honestetee' and this '– nay, but roially –' [421–2]. The clerk agrees remarking that none might detect her humble origins, her birth 'As in a cote or in an oxe-stalle', but, instead, might assume she was 'norissed in an emperoures halle' [396–9].

Equally, references marking Griselda as a passive recipient of arbitrary suffering accumulate. When her first child is taken to its apparent death, she is compared to a meek lamb [538]. She 'mekely' begs the sergeant to bury the child away from wild beasts, kisses her daughter and 'in hire benigne voys' declares how she has blessed the girl with the sign of the father:

> . . . – blessed moote he be! –
> That for us deyde upon a croys of tree [557–60].

Even Walter wonders how she might patiently accept his trials [670]. When Walter decides to take a new wife, Griselda's response remains exemplary. The clerk notes that 'this humble creature' conceals her woe, simply enduring the adversity sent to her by fortune [753–6].

Upon her return to her father's house, the narrator stresses her humility, meekness and 'pacient benyngnytee' [926–31]. His admiration for her is unbounded and seems entirely genuine. He declares how men, clerks in particular, always cite Job as an example of humility, rarely praising women. He is the exception:

> Ther kan no man in humblesse hym acquite
> As womman kan, ne kan been half so trewe
> As wommen been, but it be falle of newe [936–8].

The clerk's reverence is undercut, however, as the narrative moves to its conclusion. Walter's tests have been upon her 'wommanheede' [1075]. That they have been unnecessary has been stressed throughout. Yet it is also their very arbitrariness which ultimately offers testament to the strength of Griselda's fortitude and it is this which the clerk has intended as the lesson of his text. Though 'inportable' as an *exemplum* to wives, Griselda's patience contains a wider lesson; if a mere woman can accept such adversity, then so might a man [1149–52]. All should accept suffering and tribulation, however apparently unjustified, for

> . . . oure beste is al his governaunce.
> Lat us thanne lyve in vertuous suffraunce [1161–2].

The clerk's final words remain ambiguous and, indeed, may not even be spoken by him. They preface the Envoy of Chaucer, a song which takes the audience of the tales as a whole back into its wider dramatic framework and out of the serious material [1175] of Griselda's story. They hint at a masculine disapproval of the disruptive behaviour of the outspoken Wife of Bath and those like her, and disguise a fear of the actively autonomous female she symbolises. Instead, the speaker admires the steadfast purity of a Griselda who is as rare as she is good [1163–9]. Imitation of her example may well be wholly impractical and intolerable but implicit within the text is the clerk's approbation of it. That the passive obedience it advocates even has an alternative is a possibility opened up by both the concluding Envoy and the narrator's glossing of Griselda's terrifyingly perfect 'obeisance' which, apparently, even permits infanticide. Chaucer, hidden behind the mask of his narrator, multiplies possibilities and opens up a series of questions (to which I return in Part II), many of which remain ultimately unanswered.

Thus, as a narrator, the clerk's admiration, and even sympathy, for his subject implicitly denies her personal worth. He duplicates the religious teaching of his profession, ensuring that Griselda is virtuous, holy, and an ideal wife. At the same time, he directs his audience's attention to the needless cruelty of Walter which actually validates his *exemplum* under the aegis of his protective, chivalrous, and increasingly distressed tone, a series of interjections apparently made on Griselda's behalf.[55]

Saint Cecilia: a fissured text

Without doubt, close analysis of the texts under consideration in this study tends to reveal a common narratorial pattern imposed upon female saints' lives by their male biographers. Though each is unique, such texts are authenticated largely by a reductive masculine voice, one confirming patriarchal or clerical authority in every respect, and 'speaking' its subject as saint and/or idealised, exemplary woman. What is continually affirmed is textual authority, a patrilinear dissemination of knowledge. The generic code informing these stories is a closed one designed to venerate the saint and to offer an *exemplum*, in accordance with the rules of its particular piety.

The narrator's task is not simply to reflect the values of a patriarchal world, but to mirror the demands of his time, a movement perhaps most clearly indicated in the life of the minor saint Cecilia. St Cecilia is usually classified as a virgin martyr; certainly, her story ends with a confrontation between herself and the prefect of her time, and is swiftly followed by her death. Yet she is also a wife and one who accepts the marriage ceremony, even if she rejects the sexuality incumbent upon that role. Unlike most other wives in female hagiography, she is neither a mother nor a historical figure. In addition, her widely repeated tale appears as an index of shifting historical movements which lie behind its telling.[56] It seems that an audience's demands made a significant contribution to the textual process. Both author and audience were fully aware of all comprising the saintly code, indeed, were equal participants in its devising. The narrator's role was to ensure that the example of his holy woman was brought into line with the values and expectations of his own culture.

Accordingly, sources required careful revision if an acceptably authoritative new version was to be produced. It is perhaps this delicate balancing act which leaves St Cecilia's life, in particular, prey to the distorting effects of a fissured text. Thus this section concludes with an exploration of several versions of her *vita*, an activity which paves the way for those chapters which follow.

Very early accounts of St Cecilia's life appear to find few tensions which might detract from her Christian example. Written in Latin for a privileged clerical audience, their stress is upon the saint as a teaching aid, a text which supports masculine, and, more specifically, clerical status or prestige.[57] It is Voragine who records the details which begin to open up the text, however, and which apparently prompt some of the difficulties perceived in later versions. At the beginning, he notes the secrecy with which Cecilia approaches her marriage. Privately secure in her personal vow of chastity, she wears a hair shirt beneath her bridal gown, and, with the gospel of Christ 'hidden in her bosom', makes her way to 'the secret silences of the bridal chamber' [469].[58]

It is this private, personal space which affords Cecilia the luxury of asserting her own chosen identity. She is Cecilia, virgin and Christian, and, at heart, this is where she intends to remain. It is this private self, too, which she is later seen to assert when she invites Valerian to share her belief, and it is this initial emphasis upon secrecy that remains unreconciled within later texts. Two distinct Cecilias struggle for prominence. One is gentle, womanly, but fundamentally certain of her private choice. The other is active, strident, an aggressive female martyr, a virago, publicly clashing with male pagan authority. Like all virgin martyrs, her role is to operate as a vehicle for the faith, and, in this respect, she is permitted to preach or actively to convert others.

At the same time, later medieval piety demanded a more abject, humble figure, one patiently enduring suffering, while textual tradition itself, anxious to defuse the threat of the female and idealise a model of femininity, portrayed a reduced, inactive Cecilia, the springboard for later versions. Immediately, her roles as both exemplary wife and holy martyr appear irreconcilable, a split duplicated by a series of authors.

Early South-English Legendary attempts to deactivate a disruptive saint by presenting her as an ideal woman, weak, passive, deserving of compassion. She is an obedient daughter and prepares to become a dutiful wife, retaining only her virginity and joy in God. Richly clad and garlanded, she sings her private song to God and retains a heavenly angel as her warden [*ESEL*, 490].

It is the male who is active, not Cecilia. The tale records what men say to Urban and Maximus, details their explanation of why they are unable to worship idols, and their conversion of Maximus. While the brothers bury dead martyrs, Cecilia, as a wife, must remain at home, says her biographer [493]. She speaks to her husband with gentle courtesy [490], and the narrator's indignant distress interrupts the text as she lies half-dead, chivalrously reducing her to a pitiful, vulnerable victim:

> . . . he was a schrewe!
> Wo dede he þat holy mayde, gulteles hire so to hewe,
> ȝ bi-lefte hire so half a-lyue; welle, wo him be!
> ffor who-so nuste of no doel þer men myȝtte it se:
> þis holy mayde ȝede a-boute, hire heued half of-smyte,
> ȝ was half quik ȝ half ded, þat rewþe it was to wyte;
> ȝe pouere men mechel of hire guode ȝe delde wiþ hire honde –
> It was a wel fair grace of god þat ȝe aut myȝtte stonde [496].

Similarly, all weep for her as she is called upon to debate for her life, their speech emphasising her youth and her beauty [495].

The narrator's interjection confirms her vulnerability, protesting 'hire deþ was bouth to deere!' [495] In the concluding lines, he three times terms her 'holy maid', twice in the space of only three lines [495–6]. The tale's narration is a circular one, ending with the same lack of power, the same passivity Cecilia possessed at the start as simply a good daughter.

What it is unable to complete, however, is its process of reduction. The narrator's inability to control a Cecilia who actively and publicly defends her faith is a more traditional one, and perhaps inextricably bound with the tensions inherent in the genre. She insults her tormentor, calling him a fool [494], publicly rebuking him for his blind worship of wooden images, and declaring him lacking in power [495]. In the flames, she actively preaches [495], thereby converting four hundred onlookers, and, though her throat is half-cut, she teaches those who gather around her [496].

Such activity is entirely permissible in a hagiographical context, for, here, woman representing solely the power of faith is allowed to question authority, for that authority is only a pagan one. What the narrative is unable to suppress are those fissures which arise as a result of that characterisation of Cecilia as active and independent. When the prefect demands knowledge of Cecilia's lineage, she confirms herself as an object in the patriarchal world, declaring that she is the wife of Valerian [494]. Yet, within the privacy of their bridal chamber, she declares her dangerous secret. Though she lavishes endearments upon Valerian [490; 491], her confession stems from a personal belief in the efficacy of her own angelic protector. Significantly, what she desires is a mutuality. She wishes to share 'So gret ioye of our loue schal be þat no tunge ne may telle' [491]. It is a brave initiative on the part of a woman and one which, fortunately, succeeds.

This private space is privileged throughout the opening section of the tale. A converted Valerian returns to her 'chambre', a word repeated for it is the same space to which Tiburce comes to speak to his brother [492], subsequently returning there yet again to meet their angel [493]. Though only a secret, domestic, familial sphere of influence, this private space is, nevertheless, the woman's alone. It is she who invites the male to share it, and it is there, secure in the knowledge of her own identity, that the female is enfolded, creating her own world on the edges of patriarchy. This site of disruption remains in other texts too.

Bokenham also emphasises Cecilia's womanly and holy perfection [*LHW*, 202], for, as usual, his interest in Cecilia is purely as a religious *exemplum*. Though Bokenham utilises material which focuses upon her preaching capacity, it is rendered acceptable to a late medieval audience by delineating contemporary piety. So Cecilia is charitable, busy with good deeds, a passive, even introspective, example of her sex. In fact, her charity consists of nothing more than the sharing of her secret with Valerian. What is important, however, is that she is always busy as a servant of God so that even her active role in conversion is diluted. As Pope Urban supposedly remarks in a prayer of thanks-giving to God, the seed 'Wych Cecyle sowyn hath for þi sake', is brought to fruition in Valerian, a lion transformed into an obedient lamb by Cecilia's actions [206].

As first sight, Bokenham's text confines the female within patriarchal struc-tures, represents her as a feminine ideal, and satisfies the demands of his time by offering a saint whose unacceptably active militancy as a virgin martyr is, in fact, dissolved. Valerian's actual conversion to the Christian faith is effected by the teachings of a male cleric, Pope Urban, in perfect accordance with patri-archal expectations. He is taught how to pray and read the Bible, and receives a vision of an old man who appears with a book of scriptures lettered in gold. He is lifted up, urged to read the text, and to believe it so that he can meet the angel exactly as Cecilia promised [207]. Masculine law is mediated through the male, and affirms clerical authority, the universality of a masculine-dominated religion: 'One Lord, One faith, One baptism', one God, 'fadyr' of all [208].

Yet this surface text conceals an important contradiction, for Valerian's knowledge was prompted not by a man but by a woman. It is Cecilia who is the creative force engendering belief. In order to receive the body of the text, knowledge, Valerian must first surrender his rights over the body of the woman, his wife, and, ultimately, over his own body too, agreeing to her demand for a pact of chastity. In this way, the husband is desexualised, and he is able to receive a garland of roses and lilies from a neuter or non-sexed angel who informs him that so long as each preserves chastity the flowers which symbolise it retain their colour and fragrance, visible only to those who share the faith, share their cleanness of heart and body.

Similarly, Bokenham pays great attention to the section of the text which details Tiburce's conversion. He emphasises the conversational exchange between the brothers, reiterates the sanctioned authority of Pope Urban and all that he represents, and indicates that Cecilia's role is an indirect one, for just as Cecilia saved him from perdition, Valerian might save his brother, an action approved by the angel as good and charitable [209]. Valerian's request is that his beloved brother should recognise the error of his ways, and the converted brothers adopt an active role in the religious community by burying those slain for their faith. Brought before Almachius as a result of this, they declaim at length against the transitory joys of temporal life, their zeal and persuasion converting Maximus and many others [217–18].

These details, designed to uphold masculine authority even within a text devoted to praise of the female saint, are increasingly threatened by an ambiguity which Bokenham is unable to contain. So apparently intent is he upon writing a lengthy life which celebrates the Christian faith and clarifies doctrinal points that he is helpless to deny the driving force behind this series of conversions, which is Cecilia herself. The unspoken instigator of all action is, of course, God. Yet most saints' lives explicitly note the female saint as the conduit of that power. Here, the omission may be a telling one.

It is Cecilia who allays Tiburce's uncertainties when faced with the necessity of association with the exiled Pope Urban. She explains that it is better to lose one's life than to lose Christ, offering a lengthy explication of the power of Christ's redemptive love, and discoursing on the nature of the Trinity [212–14]. The preaching voice behind the surface text is given to Cecilia; Tiburce agrees to be baptised 'Aftyr counsel of my sustyr Cycyle' [214]. It is a counsel which apparently only supports the masculine word, echoes Valerian's earlier persuasions, and is an influence confined to the familial. Nevertheless, its resonant power struggles to escape from the narrative frame until, at the climax of the plot's events, it reaches its own crisis point.

Earlier versions of this *vita* gloss Cecilia's actual death and focus upon the dramatic trial scene preceding it, together with the symbolisation which follows. Later redactions, unable to reconcile her aggressive, heroic stance in defence of her faith with a social climate more comfortable with a patient martyr, tend to stress the torments of a vulnerable, suffering woman. Interestingly, Bokenham chooses to privilege the trial scene but undercuts Cecilia's active participation by returning to his initial depiction of a feminine ideal, and by stressing the greater lesson of her holiness.

Cecilia is brought to trial only because she charitably insists upon burying Maximus and his knights. Her femininity, ideally represented by her high birth and great beauty [219], ensures that the officers sent to demand her presence weep for pity of her. The subjective compassion her passive loveliness incites is extended even to Almachius who, realising she is not to be vanquished, secretly grieves [223]. Unable to face down her unsettling threat [223], he orders her beheading. In one sense Almachius is merely a symbol for all pagans in his inability to recognise Cecilia's holy worth. Yet, as seen earlier, he is also a provost, a father figure, and, hence, representative of the masculine world. So, his insecurity and confusion mirror a phallocentric universe's fear of the feminine, an inability to know and contain the threat of the powerful unknowable, an uneasiness which Bokenham's narrative voice appears to share.

Despite the author's focus upon her saintly example, he cannot firmly resolve an inherent paradox of power, or his Latin source [225], with the demands of his milieu. Thus he details Cecilia's continued preaching despite her impending death, and has her buried by Urban who consecrates the site [224–5], whilst quoting many subsequent miracles as testament to her sanctity and official recognition of her reduction to religious cipher. Yet, the lasting impression is Almachius's unease, and inability to control her in any way; her very corporeality defeats him for she remains unharmed in the fire, and even the maximum number of strokes fails to sever her head [224].

Cecilia's problematical disruption is unconsciously reinforced by Bokenham's insistence upon retaining the forceful figure of Voragine's original in the trial scene in direct contradiction to the quietly gentle, dutiful girl of the opening lines or the passive victim identified by those compassionate officers who weep for her. Gone too is the emphasis upon secret, mutual exchange which characterises the opening scene in her bridal chamber, itself a multivalent symbol.

Once again, it is a potentially disruptive privacy which is stressed at the start. Beneath her clothes of gold, Cecilia wears a hair shirt. As the organs swell during her marriage ceremony, 'couertly in hyr inward mynde', she sings to God [203]. In the quiet of her wedding chamber, 'in her secre sylence', she assures Valerian of her love, offers to divulge a secret 'of greth pryuyte' [204], to share her secret and illicit faith. The diction suggests that Cecilia's *persona* is an introspective, hidden one, fixed not in opposition to her husband or her worldly duties, but upon God. The cumulative effect of other details of privacy confirm her place within a wider Christian community where a stress upon secrecy is merely a protection against a pagan society. Thus Valerian is sworn to silence, sent to seek out Pope Urban, himself in hiding, in order to have himself privately baptised [205]. He is given precise directions, and urged to take Cecilia's blessing to the poor of Appian who will then direct him to the man he seeks [205].

Bokenham, once again, articulates Cecilia's piety, draws attention to the wider lesson of her faith by denoting this secret, collective community of believers. At the same time, however, the strength of Cecilia's own private identity is unintentionally confirmed. The site of potential feminine disruption is, literally, her own space, her bedchamber. It is Cecilia whose identity is so secure that her name is sufficient to guarantee entry to Urban. It is her name and not a man's which is to be recognised by other Christians.

The text closes on a public rather than a private note, Bokenham anxious to hammer home Cecilia's wider exemplarity. Consequently, she is permitted a series of overt, even strident, conversions. She comforts those who shed compassionate tears, utilising their receptive pity actively to demand an audience attentive to her teaching [220]. She converts over four hundred in this way. Urban baptises them, but it is Cecilia who is the leading figure in the suppressed, Christian community to which she originally sent Valerian with the geographical instructions she, ironically, 'wyl þe teche' [205], and she who affirms her own power in the lines

> '. . . for fro me hym to
> Pryuy erandys þou has to do.' [206]

In the same way, her bold and derisive mockery of Almachius exemplifies the transgressive female who breaks the confines of Bokenham's textual structures, and asserts an identity gravely at odds with the passive ideal he wished to represent. Unable to reconcile the dual figure of Cecilia – martyr and humble saint – Bokenham's text remains an unstable one, threatened from within by the very generic code inscribing it.

Equally problematic is Chaucer's Cecilia. Though a contemporary of Bokenham's, she is a far more militant and zealous figure clashing with authority in a text which also privileges her scornful debate with Almachius. She is presented as an active and extreme model of sanctity in spite of the fact that such a depiction was likely to have been entirely unpalatable to a late medieval audience, and perhaps in order to demonstrate the reductive nature of the hagiographical tradition.

Chaucer offers remarkably little background where Cecilia is concerned, and presents possibly the shortest persuasion of Valerian on record. Though she echoes so many other versions in her call to her beloved spouse [*VIII(G)*, 144], the very next line abruptly comes to the point. There is no preparation for the revelation of her dangerous secret; simply, 'ther is a conseil' [145] which he must not betray. Entirely confident of her own powers, Valerian is merely the instrument of her divinely inspired instruction, is 'corrected as God wolde' [162].

Subsequently, patrilinear authority is exemplified, Valerian converting Tiburce, Urban baptising them both, and the angel bringing authoritative proof of one God, one faith, a universality upheld in written text [202–10]. Equally, the brothers convert Maximus who in turn converts many others [404].

This part of the action is, however, relatively brief. What is more important is Cecilia's burying of the corpses, an action which opens the hostilities portrayed in her trial scene. She is contemptuous and derisive throughout, declaring that Almachius speaks in ignorant stupidity [428; 430], scorning his temporal power which is merely an angry vindictive sentence for he knows full well that they are innocent [450; 452]. Her ridicule of him is detailed and eminently public [463–97]. Left to die, she continues to preach the faith [538]. An active, independent Cecilia is the impetus behind the didactic lesson of the text, permitted her role, as usual, because her clash is with pagan authority.

Other details confirm her as an object held within a patriarchal frame in both worldly (holy) and textual terms. She remains a passive vessel carrying Christ's 'gospel in hir mynde' [123], wearing a secret hair shirt, fasting, and praying. Even as the text stresses the crucial aspect of privacy outlined earlier, she remains a model of femininity. Her explication of doctrinal points, admissible only because she contains the Word of God, privileges an almost monotonous reiteration of masculine authority represented in the divine. It is God, not woman or mother, who is the creator. She speaks of what 'Goddes Sone' [324] taught, of all 'That Fadres Sone hath alle thyng ywroght' [326], of teaching 'The Goost, that fro the Fader gan procede' [328], miracles and words of 'Goddes Sone' [330], all of which confirm 'Ther nys but o God' [335], one voice, one law, one authority for all.

Cecilia is a perfect saint and a greatly reduced woman, or so the surface text demonstrates. The tale's narrator, the second nun, fails to appear in the *General Prologue* to Chaucer's collection of tales, indeed rarely makes her presence felt in the story she narrates, and has largely been ignored as a voice. Sherry Reames suggests that there is no irony in this tale for the second nun has no identity while neither the prologue nor the narrative contain any discordant notes. All the *vita* contains is a simple reproduction of ideas prominent in preaching.[59] I would suggest, however, that the text is far more complex than this, since such a reproduction offers itself as a dominant masculine voice determined to control its material.[60]

Chaucer's presentation of Cecilia's story is an interesting one, intensified by the ambiguities raised by a clash between Chaucer's narrative and the narrative voice itself. Close analysis of the prologue tends to confirm that it places its subject firmly within the expected textual tradition. The speaker repeatedly warns against idleness – a key word – and sloth [1–28]. At the same time, Cecilia is associated with activity and good works [98; 105; 116].

Here, the narration points to Cecilia's active ministry which ensures 'she ensample was by good techynge' [93]. The speaker, too, clearly believes she, and other nuns, must remain actively busy in defence of the faith; she remarks 'that feith is deed withouten werkis' [64]. What is also immediately apparent here is that Cecilia is characterised by activity, not the passivity more tradi- tionally associated with the female saint, an activity which the text appears to endorse, and which, I would suggest, takes her beyond the orthodox repre- sentation of the virgin martyr's suffering resistance.

The narrator also makes numerous references to textual sources or patristic authority, in particular implying a written rather than an oral transmission of the tale. The audience is informed that the narration is offered in translation [25], encouraging all to read her story [35]. She prays everyone will read what she records [78], professing herself unable to do the tale justice [80].

Chaucer may well have intended that the life of St Cecilia would be narrated by a male speaker, and the sudden introduction of the second nun stems from a lack of revision, though it would be interesting to explore the possibility of its deliberate intention. However, the text itself points to fissures beneath a self- consciously reductive surface. The narrator is aligned with patriarchal authority as might be expected of one so inextricably part of the orthodox clerical canon. The privileged status of the written record is emphasised where Bernard of Clairvaux, an author of works aimed specifically at male clerics, is cited as an authority [30]. What is offered is a Cecilia active and defiant in public defence of her faith, and an *exemplum* ostensibly confirmed by the speaker's sources. A masculine voice is centred within a patriarchal framework. This speaker con- firms the truth of 'her' authorities, insists upon the validation of the written word in a search for a definitive, didactic version of the saint's *vita*, and trusts in the power of the surface text, carefully copying the original Latin source, and unthinkingly accepting masculine law. Thus it is claimed that Cecilia never ceased to pray, a fact confirmed by written authority [124], that she informs Valerian that he must quote her when speaking to her fellow Christians of the Appian way, and that he does exactly as he has been taught [184]. He is obliged to relay her message to Urban and is only baptised after he receives and reads the book of scriptures from the angel [206; 211]. Similarly, the audience is referred to St Ambrose as the authoritative voice concerning the miracle of the fragrant but invisible garlands [270–83].

However, alternative perspectives and ambiguities mark the body of the narrative. Citing the Virgin Mary during the prologue, praise is lavish and conforms to orthodox presentation of a model of femininity both humble and high [39], full of mercy, goodness, and 'pitee' [51], a 'meeke and blisful faire mayde' [57]. This model is also only a passive receptacle of the divine privileged by the maternal; she is 'Cristes mooder' [70], 'doghter of Thy Sone' [36], a womb where

> Withinne the cloistre blisful of thy sydis
> Took mannes shap the eterneel love and pees [43].

It is the masculine and the divine which is the creative force behind the universe for

> ... thou, Virgine, wemmelees,
> Baar of thy body – and dweltest mayden pure –
> The Creatour of every creature [47–9].

In short, the Virgin Mary is 'the sonne of excellence' [52].

The traditional eliding of Mary's maternal role, where she is mother, daughter, and son and where God is creator, is undercut, however, by the narrator's subsequent reminder of her humanity, of her womanhood which gives birth to a Christ clothed in flesh and blood [42]. She is also the daughter of Anne [70] and here the creativity of the maternal is implied in this small but significant fissure.

Throughout the actual text, too, the militant saintliness which grants permission to Cecilia's active autonomy becomes a multivalent symbol confirming the feminine as a source of power and strength. Once again, the delineation of her secret faith opens up the text; it simultaneously fulfils its surface function and suggests an integrity which is sealed against the masculine world, symbolising the security of a private feminine identity, a site of potential disruption.

Similarly, Cecilia sends Valerian to Urban via those dwelling near the Appian Way [174], where her identity alone is sufficient to guarantee their protection of him. This confirms her representation as a cipher in the story of her own life where, though an active one, her ministry forms part of a wider, collective religious group, but also stresses the significance of a glimpsed female autonomy. Certain of herself, Cecilia instructs Valerian to mention her by name [176] and to repeat word for word all that she tells him [180], while the mere mention of her name prompts Urban's tears.

The ambiguity inherent in her presentation continues. On the one hand, Cecilia is the passive recipient of the Word, is Christ's 'thral' [196] and contains the seed of chastity brought to fruition in the male [197–9]. She is said to be full of God's gift [275], yet, at the same time, the narration points to a womanly figure who is, in fact, primary in the text. The angel offers garlands to Valerian and his wife, but does so first to Cecilia and only afterwards to her husband [222–4]. It is Cecilia whose role in Tiburce's conversion is carefully detailed. She is said to have brought him to bliss [281] and showed him that his idols are false [284]. So delighted is she by Tiburce's acceptance of her words that she kisses him, declaring that he is her ally [292].

Cecilia's influence is at odds with the anticipated patrilinear textual slant. It is she who allays Tiburce's fears concerning association with exiled Christians, teaching him of Christ's redemptive love [342] and other points of doctrine [348]. The narration passes swiftly over the miracles and conversions effected by the brothers [358–9] and, instead, moves to focus upon Cecilia's visit to the imprisoned, newly converted Maximus and his fellow knights. Cecilia urges them on in preparation for a great battle, invoking the traditional imagery of Christian soldiers [379–86]. Equally, she converts those who are ordered to bring her before Almachius.

Though stripped of her femininity in order to dissolve the transgressive power of her militancy and validate her behaviour as holy, Cecilia is so prioritised in this text that the subversive possibilities of her feminine power remain. The life of St Cecilia is only one tale in an entire collection designed to eliminate reductiveness offering unorthodox perspectives and ambiguities, distrustful of all authority, revealing its limitations even if its sceptical author finally retains his conservative stance. The second nun's *vita* apparently confirms the power of masculine, clerical, and textual authority in its accurate parody of a zealous, proselytising saint's life so unfortunately reminiscent of much hagiography. Yet, the narrator's reliance upon the written word, her implicit faith in the univocal and universal phallocentric world uncritically presented, in fact, reveals the limitations of this genre.

For in the fissured texts of female hagiography, a second voice fights to make itself heard, struggles to disrupt surface assumptions and finally articulates itself, however differently, in conjunction *with* the masculine. It is a voice generating identity above and beyond that of saint or *exemplum*, is whispered on margins and at edges. This is the doubled discourse explored in the remaining chapters.

Notes

1 Heffernan 1988 16.
2 ibid. 6.
3 ibid. 35.
4 ibid. 153.
5 Elliot 1987.
6 ibid. 8.
7 ibid. 18.
8 ibid. 76.
9 ibid. 180.
10 Wogan-Browne 1994c: 39–54.
11 Gorlach 1976: 41. Susan Powell traces the development of this collection from its first appearance in the 1380s through to its final revised printing in 1532. She also remarks that its intended use was by uneducated preachers for the purpose of instructing the congregation. See Powell 1991.
12 References throughout are to Johannes Mirkus (John Mirk) Erbe, T. (ed.) 1905.
13 The active life, seen in Martha, focuses upon the 'besynes of þe world', a world which is troublesome and problematic but which is overcome by various activities such as charity to the poor and sick, alms-giving, burying of the dead, and prison visiting, all performed solely for God's sake [MF, 231]. Mary represents the contemplative aspect occupied with spiritual matters such as reading, praying, writing, and contemplation. Mirk urges both men and women to 'voyde from hom'

all worldliness and worldly care [231]. It might be useful at this point to note that the Mary Magdalene presented in hagiographical tales is a construct, a figure who is both an allegorical representation and a conflation of three historical women: Mary Magdalene, Mary of Bethany (sister of Martha), and an anonymous sinner who anoints Christ's head and/or washes His feet. The twelfth-century cult of Mary Magdalene further obfuscates the delineation of this figure, while many works also tend to confuse depictions and representations of Mary and Martha. Mary as Mary Magdalene has three distinct capacities: as a penitent, as a missionary preaching in France, and as an important figure in episodes in the life of Christ. See Constable 1995 'The Interpretation of Mary and Martha'.

14 John Capgrave, Horstmann, C. (ed.) 1893.
15 References throughout are to the edition cited in note 14. There are two versions of this text. As far as possible, I am using Rawlinson Poetry 118 for reasons outlined in Furnivall's foreword. In later chapters, reference is also made to a later, anonymous prose version (referred to as the *Southwell Minster*): Nevanlinna, S. and Taavitsainen, I. (eds) 1993.
16 Other manuscript evidence indicates a wide dissemination of this popular devotional text throughout the second half of the thirteenth century. There is, for example, an East-Midland version, unusually not copied as a largely stable collection but extant in fragmented, individual pieces. See Gorlach 1976.
17 Pickering 1994: 21–37.
18 Pickering (ibid.) discusses this as does Thompson (1991). Pickering suggests that this is the same poet who worked on the *Southern Passion* and its *Expanded Nativity*; his voice is particularly evident in the preaching and sanctorale narratives. See Pickering 1994: 23–4; 27.
19 ibid.: 24.
20 The later 1280s version is used by Charlotte D'Evelyn and Anna J. Mill. I am using the earlier 'Z' Worcestershire text. Reference throughout is to Horstmann, C. (ed.) 1887.
21 Katherine is termed 'Mayde' several times in the opening lines (*ESEL*, 92–3) or else is 'holie maide' or 'maide Katherine'. The word 'maide' is employed thirty times in this version, as well as sixteen in Lucy's life, eighteen in Agatha's, and nineteen for Agnes.
22 Elliot 1987: 18–41.
23 ibid. 170–3.
24 ibid. 177–80 where this is described in detail.
25 Bynum 1991: 27–52, 'Women's Stories and Women's Symbols: a critique of Victor Turner's theory of liminality'. She discusses the ways in which liminality functions for men as well as its different female experience.
26 This is an appendix added to the original by a different hand, probably that of the main redactor.
27 See Thompson 1991: 20–30, where she explores this imbalance.
28 Osbern Bokenham, Serjeantson, M. S. (ed.) 1938: xviii. Reference is to this edition throughout.
29 Edwards 1994: 157–67.
30 ibid.: 167.
31 The set to be accommodated is a mixed one. See *LHW*, xx–xxi for full details.
32 Christina is 'thys blessyd cristyne' [59; 62; 66; 70; 76; 79; 82; 85]. At one point a heavenly voice calls to her 'O blyssyd Crystyne, my doughtir dere' [82], confirming her subordinate identity in social, familial, and divine terms. Katherine is 'blyssyd Kateryne' [173; 200], and Lucy 'blyssyd lucye' [244; 256] or 'nobyl virgyne' [244] as well as 'Lucye, sustyr, & mayde deuouth' [247]. Elizabeth of Hungary is variously referred to as 'blysyd Elyzabeth' [257; 259; 264–5; 268; 286; 288], 'blyssyd matrone' [270], 'thys blyssyd Elyzabeth ful of humylyte' [278], 'thys

blyssyd wumman Elyzabeth' [286], 'Thys holy Elyzabeth' [286], or, 'þis blyssyd creature' [286]. Agatha is 'blyssyd Agas' [229; 242–3], and 'þis holy marytre & blyssyd virgine' [241].

33 Similarly, Bokenham notes of Margaret that 'Greth meknesse she had for cristys sake' [*LHW*, 8], while Agnes replies 'demurely' to all accusations against her [122], and 'To god deuouthly made hyr preyere' [125]. Cast into the flames, her response is to 'demurely' spread her hands [125]. Dorothy answers the prefect 'mekely' [133]. Mary Magdalene enacts her contrition at the feet of Christ 'ful deuouthly', 'dylygently', and 'wyth a deuouth entent' that demonstrates 'meke obsequyousnesse' [149]. Agatha thanks God for her miraculous cure 'wyth deu mekenesse' [237].

34 References to 'deuocyoun' [*LHW*, 260–1; 264; 270; 272; 278–9; 281–3; 285] and 'mekenesse' or 'mekely' [258; 264–7; 271; 278–9] are each repeated thirteen times in this story.

35 The list centres on Boethius, Ovid, Homer, Virgil, Chaucer, Gower, and Lydgate [*LHW*, 12], while in the *vita* of St Anne he again compares himself unfavourably to Gower, Lydgate, and Chaucer, ingenuously describing himself as old and unlearned [38]. In the life of Agnes, Bokenham apologises for his lack of skill adding that prayers for grace and favour are futile, for other great men have arrived ahead of him [111]. In the lengthy prologue to Mary Magdalene's story, he portrays himself as a reluctant, unskilled author, pressurised into accepting his commission [139–40].

36 In the case of Margaret this is literally so. Bokenham recounts at length the translation of her body establishing a masculine line of dissemination [*LHW*, 28–37], which is undercut by his fleeting reference to the fact that John the hermit's knowledge and actions stem from Margaret herself who instructs him in a vision, a transgression permitted only because she is holy (and dead!) and appears to a male cleric.

37 See also *LHW*, 174; 176; 179; 183–4; 186–7; 189–94; 196 and 198.

38 See William Caxton, Ellis, F. S. (ed.) 1900: 277. Reference is to this edition throughout. See also O'Mara (1992) who relates how this edition was compiled, also noting how Caxton himself did not write the legends.

39 de Voragine delineates a simple confrontation between good and evil exemplified in his contrast between pagan and martyr, or the inclusion of futile demonic intervention. His is a voice directly instructing the ignorant. See Jacobus de Voragine, trans. G. Ryan and H. Ripperger 1941.

40 Eugenia is 'the virgin' [*GL*, vol. 5, 145–7], 'blessed virgin' [147; 171] or 'holy virgin' [146]. Justina is 'virgin' [166–9]. Dorothy is 'glorious virgin and martyr S. Dorothy' [vol. 7, 42], 'holy virgin' or 'virgin' [42–7], 'blessed saint Dorothy' [47], and 'S. Dorothy' [42]. Katherine is 'blessed S. Katherine' [28–9], 'holy virgin' or 'virgin' [4; 11–13; 17–18; 20–22; 25; 30] as well as 'blessed virgin' [10–12; 16; 23; 27; 30].

41 Clare is 'this holy saint' [*GL*, vol. 6, 182], 'This sweet saint S. Clare' [187], 'This holy and good Clare' [183], the 'holy' or 'blessed virgin' [184; 186; 192–3], 'a marvellous holy woman' [161], or 'glorious virgin S. Clare' [197–8]. Her role as God's vessel is continuously underlined by the narrator's terminology. She becomes 'this holy lady' [164; 167; 186], 'this holy Clare' [176], 'this blessed S. Clare' [176; 187], 'the holy sweet virgin S. Clare' [171], or 'the handmaid of Jesu Christ' [168]. The repetition of 'S. Clare' is staggering. Reference is made, often more than once, on each of the following pages: 162–72; 176–8; 180–1; 183; 185; 187–98.

42 Possibly the author was Pauline's confessor who records his advice to moderate her almsgiving [*GL*, vol. 3, 5]. Certainly the strong narrative frame privileging the holy indicates that he was a cleric.

43 This is apparently an original version of this saint's life not found elsewhere, and

certainly not present in the original *Legenda Aurea*. Its length alone is testament to interest in it as a devotional vehicle.

44 Paul Strohm has examined the petitionary and intercessory role of the medieval female across a variety of texts, arguing that its presentation confirms patriarchal power, affirms maleness, and supplements a male lack by permitting an alternative female judgement which serves to enhance masculine authority. The prevalence of this role for women is a dupe, a prescription for ideal behaviour, presenting woman as emotional abject, mother, and/or marginal figure endowed with a special spirituality but consistently excluded from authority. See Strohm 1992: ch. 5, especially 95–119. Though I do not fully endorse this argument, the points made here affirm my reading of this aspect of a wider narrative frame.

45 Her prayers support Bishop Hostence, later Pope Gregory, and, as she lies dying, her final moments are delayed by 'Our Lord' in order that she might receive the homage of the pope and his cardinals. Bishop Hostence administers the sacrament, and comforts everyone with sermons. The eloquent preacher-friar Vinberes offers Clare 'much great consolation', and she is revered by the followers of Francis. Pope Innocent V recognises her holiness and honours her with his presence, absolving her of sin and blessing her. Once she is dead, a requiem mass is intoned, Hostence and other prelates preach, and Clare is buried near Francis [see *GL*, vol. 6, 172; 182–4; 187]. This lengthy description confirms Clare's sanctity but offers only the briefest mention of the way she takes advantage of the situation to extract some official recognition of her order, granting 'that her privilege of poverty might be confirmed of the pope and of the cardinals' [181]. Her biographer refuses to relinquish control over the narrative, going on to describe thirteen after-death miracles in overt underscoring of her approved holiness.

46 Reference throughout is to Geoffrey Chaucer, L. D. Benson (ed.) 1988, and to 'The Clerk's Tale', 'The Man of Law's Tale', and 'The Second Nun's Tale' all in *The Canterbury Tales*.

47 For a full explanation of the incest motif see Dinshaw 1989, especially 83–112. Dinshaw's focus is specifically upon this motif which, she argues, is implicit throughout the tale, and which the narrator attempts to suppress because of its direct threat to patriarchal order. She quite rightly identifies a series of tensions and problematical shifts in the tale, but attributes most of them to this particular source.

48 Many critics emphasise the concept of victimisation, most notably Dinshaw (1989), who insists upon a presentation of Custance as exclusively powerless, and Raybin (1990). The latter discusses Custance's historical and dramatic marginal-isation which is representative of Custance's evaluation of the individual in history as well as the place of the female in society. Raybin emphasises crucial images of eternal timelessness which render Custance divine.

49 Some see Custance purely as a vehicle for the faith, a passive symbol of the Church, an example of patient suffering. See Kolve 1984: 297–358, and Raybin 1990.

50 Michaela Grudin (1989) sees the text as politicised, arising from a specific historical context and informed by notions of kingship. Its focus upon Walter's treatment of Griselda, it is argued, reveals a paradox of political power, and, set against medieval theories of rule, as well as Dante's plea for unity and common weal, centres on the place of the individual within an absolute monarchy. Similarly, David Aers (1986) argues in chapter two that Griselda abdicates all moral or religious responsibility, the text thus dramatising the effects of absolution upon both ruler and ruled. Again, David Aers (1980) *Chaucer, Langland, And The Creative Imagination* (London, Routledge and Kegan Paul) uses chapter six to suggest that the tale is ultimately political in its focus upon Griselda's patience, a trait as evil and as absolute as Walter's tyranny. In this way, Aers believes, Chaucer is able to explore absolutism in its political, domestic, and psychological spheres. Others stress that the tale is an

exemplum of one kind or another. Charlotte Morse (1985) examines Griselda's patience declaring that it is this which contains the lesson of the story, an *exemplum* for all women. Priscilla Martin (1990) argues that Griselda is offered as a saint or martyr through the deliberate sacrificial humiliation of her marriage. Elizabeth Salter (1962) emphasises religious fable by exploring the use of key words together with a focus upon the symbolic nature of poverty. She, too, concludes that Griselda's response to Walter is an exemplary one.

51 Jill Mann (1991) suggests that Chaucer presents a female-centred ideal derived from female experience in order to engage with anti-feminism and posit a paradoxically passive power to which the male hero moulds himself. Yet she fails to distinguish between Chaucer-the-author and his fictional narrators. At the same time the poem as a whole makes only passing reference to pregnancy, childbirth, or female sexuality, an apparent sympathy that never challenges its construction. See chapters 1–3 generally and, more specifically, pp. 48; 163–4.

52 Dinshaw 1989.

53 Hansen 1992: 12–17; chapter 4; and 195–205.

54 ibid. 12–17.

55 On three occasions the clerk apparently allies himself with Griselda's example of suffering womanhood, intimating a knowledge of masculine cruelty which he despises [*IV(E)*, 457–62; 620–22; 696–700].

56 Two articles, both by Sherry Reames, focus precisely upon this aspect of the Cecilia text. In the first (1991: 159–89), Reames studies Latin accounts found in office lectionaries and breviaries written in Britain during the Middle Ages. She explores these increasingly abbreviated accounts, arguing for a pattern of near-consensus on certain issues apparently reflecting the shared values and assumptions of its audience. She suggests that later medieval versions produce a far more passive saint, permit merely a private conversion of her husband, and the acquisition of female followers. The second paper (1980) places Chaucer's version of the text in its contextual and textual history, tracing its development from de Voragine, through Aelfric, a popular adaption in the *Northern Homily* cycle, and via Bokenham. She argues that Chaucer portrays the saint as an isolated figure where the ideal of perfection is renunciation rather than personal growth.

57 Aelfric, writing around 996 or 997, directs his work to monks, and is critical of the *Vitae Patrum* for including subtleties the laity ought not to hear. Instead, his intention is to revive a failing faith, and, to this end, Cecilia serves him well. His gentle, reverential tone portrays her as a model of femininity. Largely passive, her final confrontational trial scene is greatly edited, and she is rarely allowed to speak directly. Her role in the conversions of Valerian and Tiburce appears almost incidental. What is emphasised is male power and masculine dissemination of the Word. It is the brothers who debate at length with Almachius, and Urban who buries Cecilia. Cecilia is merely the object prompting the spread of faith. See Aelfric, Skeat, W. (ed.) (1881). A similar situation occurs in both the *Old English Martyrology*, compiled no later than 850, and in de Voragine. See Herzfeld 1899 and Jacobus de Voragine, Ryan, G. and Ripperger, H. (eds) 1941.

58 Jacobus de Voragine, Ryan, G. and Ripperger, H. (eds) 1941: 690.

59 A recent article by Karen Arthur (1998) also argues that Cecilia is a subversive figure, her figuration further problematised by Chaucer's creation of a narrator who, together with an emphasis upon the nurturing aspects of the Virgin Mary outlined in the *Prologue*, destabilises the way in which this text was transmitted by the male. Her concern is with language, gender, and power, and though her interpretation of the *Prologue* is different, we draw attention to similar aspects.

60 Reames (1980).

Part II

Throughout their deafening dumb history they have lived in dreams, embodied but still deadly silent, in silences, in voiceless rebellions.

(Cixous 1986: 95)

2 A concept of space and a notion of identity

The organisation of space, both physical and psychological, almost inevitably involves a series of hierarchies. People enclose, order, divide, dispose of areas belonging to others. Hence, borders or frontiers are established, space is allocated and appropriated. Psychological space functions similarly so that people might be out of place or put in their place, are obliged to conform or risk social sanctions. There is a pattern governing the use of space, where man's space is 'a space of domination, hierarchy and conquest, a sprawling, showy space, a full space'.[1] In contrast, woman is a void and inhabits 'a sort of no man's land which constitutes precisely what men fail to understand of her'.[2]

In hagiographical terms, male narrators locate their female subjects in time and space, detailing a history, a birthplace, a genealogy, an identity derived through religious nomenclature. Literary confirmation of a holy identity is achieved via a narrative focusing upon images of interiority and identifying a series of confining, physical locations – prison, a cell or chamber, a walled space, the heart or soul – or else abandoning the saint to the margins of existence in a desert wilderness. Similarly, such tales emphasise the privileged space of maternity, exemplified in the potent symbol of the Virgin Mary, at exactly the same time as they advocate the rejection of those limiting labels of wife, mother, daughter in favour of an embracing of the spiritual family of Christ, Mary, God.

The void that is woman is appropriated by the male biographer and relocated in a constricting narrative structure in a manner echoing patriarchy's location of her in the imaginary, outside the symbolic order. For Irigaray, the rhythms of masculine sexuality ensure that it is men who establish the limits and boundaries of space and time.[3] It is a space which is external, public, fluid, and yet closed. Above all, it is a place of privilege and power, exclusive of the feminine. Her emptiness is a stillness, involving privacy and interiority. These oppositions are mirrored in a narrative pattern which constructs a set of contrasts of spatial orientation, similar to those identified by Jacques le Goff in his explorations of notions of purgatory. Basing his work on the medieval treatise 'St Patrick's Purgatory', le Goff explores the use of gesture as the knight, Owein, makes his symbolic journey through purgatory, concluding that in theological terms 'high' and 'inside' are positively valued, while 'ascent' and 'internalisation' constitute an ideal.[4]

My intention is to explore the fluid nature of these apparently fixed oppositions, and the means by which they are simultaneously established and dissolved. Irigaray's metaphor of the two-lips intimates that feminine space is both open and closed, a concept firmly tying the notion of space to the body and the arena of sexual difference, to an understanding of selfhood. Undoubtedly, closed is synonymous with power. The Church, symbol of patriarchal domination, represented a fixed, authoritative, public law. Its texts were closed, available only for exegetical manipulation. Hagiographers, emulating this tradition, affirmed a masculine definition of female sanctity. Textually and paradigmatically, women were silenced and enclosed, inscribed by a virginal integrity which was, at times, almost literal, the anchoritic cell intimating the sealed tomb of Christ, or the womb. Yet, such impermeability, outward manifestation of masculine power, contains a paradox, for those same constricting anchoritic walls also conjure images of resurrection, rebirth, and the apertures of all flesh.[5]

Recent, more positive interpretation of the *Ancrene Wisse* text's encouragement of anchoritic life identifies a series of both physical and spiritual enclosures integral to the text's structure. These enclosures, represented by the two windows of the cell, themselves symbolic of the inner and outer 'rules' exemplified in the text, both contain and are containing, each both an entrance and an exit. Wogan-Browne persuasively argues that such a structure takes its model from the body, that both physical and spiritual enclosure become a dynamic where flesh is the border of a sinful body still capable of redemption. I fully agree with her suggestion that other images of holy containment, such as the desert or cell, are similarly ambiguous.[6]

Thus the imposition of closure, be it textual, physical, or psychological, affirms a power vested in the masculine. At the same time, this closed space might well not have spoken of feminine inferiority or unsymbolised emptiness, but offered a more positive identity. The very structures intended to contain were far from inviolable. Neither was this space, privately receptive though it might be, simply a womb, an inner productive space filled by maternity.[7] It is, in fact, this notion of motherhood, so crucial to both male and female identity, which exposes the fundamental ambiguities of hagiographical texts.

The connection between space and identity is, perhaps, most clearly illuminated by a psychoanalytical frame of reference. Kristeva suggests that the notion of emptiness is 'at the root of the human psyche' but most usually assigned to women.[8] It is intrinsic to the beginning of an entry into the symbolic, appearing as a separation between what is not an object and not quite a subject. Emptiness is necessary in order to commence any definition of boundaries or classification of the limits of body, language, or the symbolic world.[9]

Equally, psychoanalysis suggests that for every identity chosen or imposed, there is a shadow self which may be a source of disruption or even psychosis. This psychological split between false and true self is revealed in some hagiographical texts, most notably the life of St Katherine, as will be seen. The psychoanalyst Lomas describes the interchangeability of these two selves, and identifies how an attack upon a false self, in the form of anorexia, breakdown, or illness, features of many holy lives, offers a vital space within which to construct a secure identity.[10] Hagiography, and other medieval patristic texts, imposed a self upon women, defined her in relation only to men. Thus, she is mother, wife, daughter, virgin, or penitent whore. Her holiness, embraced as an alternative and enabling space, is affirmed only by texts denying her a full identity. Privacy and interiority thus become particularly associated with the female.

Saintliness appeared to demand an abnegation of the self. Identity was to be dissolved in preparation for union with the divine. The 'Agnus Dei' of the highly popular vernacular text *The Lay Folks' Mass Book* urges a love of self which precedes love of God.[11] Similarly, *The Cloud of Unknowing* describes the exercise of will crucial to overcoming all that stands between self and the divine, where knowledge of God is gained in darkness, through faith, through the 'cloud of forgetting' which obscures all objects of consciousness.[12] The teachings of Bernard of Clairvaux advocate self-knowledge, an acceptance that humans are defaced images of God who must recognise imperfection and judge the self in humility.[13] Both self-knowledge and the surrender of self are the prerequisites of the divine experience.

This dissolution of self and subjectivity is apparent in female mysticism, ostensibly confirming the role women are given as other, outsider, beyond representation. Mary of Oignies is praised by her eminent biographer, Jacques de Vitry, for forsaking 'hir owne selfe' and considering 'hir–selfe as noghte.' [*Prosalegenden*, 139; 152] The image of the Pauline mirror, mediating between man and God, stresses both human likeness and unlikeness to the divine. At the same time, the Lacanian mirror reflects man. Yet, as Grosz explains, for Irigaray, there is an 'other' mirror, the speculum of her *Speculum of the other woman*, and it is through *this* mirror that an alternative female space is perceived, her identity asserted.[14]

Similarly, the implication of Caroline Walker Bynum's exploration of a theory of liminality applied to hagiography may well be that such stories spoke *differently*, in a manner undercutting the 'masculine' surface intention of the text. Bynum suggests that female saints depicted as models of interiorised spirituality offered an alternative to or critique of masculine power which effectively only bolstered the man. The male saint contacting such a woman (usually a desert mother) returns to the world rejuvenated having appropriated her power, whilst male writers depicting the saint focus upon a series of crises or liminal moments, often involving gender reversal, regardless of the sex of their subject. In contrast, women writing of themselves construct texts marked by continuity which enhance, or continue, ordinary experience and ordinary lives. Thus, 'Women are fully liminal only to men.'[15]

Women, their lives curtailed by domesticity and its space, perceiving themselves in relation to Christ in worldly terms, as mother, daughter, sister, spouse, simply identify themselves as they are. Similarly, when the anchorite withdrew into herself, it was not to sever all worldly connections for the two windows, the inner and outer rules, highlight the impossibility of escaping what is outside.[16]

What may be witnessed then in a feminine 'version' of the hagiographical text is movement, fluidity, and a holiness inextricably bound to and by the world. It is by this that the female saint is marked and not merely by the still interiority usually identifying her.

Psychological space

Hagiographical stories affirm both a religious and worldly identity for their female subjects. The saint is named, labelled, her lineage delineated. Theologically and socially, she is inscribed by a text locating her in patriarchal space and confirming her otherness. However, significant fissures assert themselves throughout providing an opportunity for a re-reading, for the feminine to insert itself into the blank spaces between the lines.

Male hagiographers, representatives of patriarchy, formulate a narrative pattern of female identity which, inevitably, is largely religious. Confirming woman as Mary rather than Eve, their saintly subjects are rendered acceptably visible. Integral to this pattern is an identification of woman acting independently of masculine authority or, indeed, as an authority figure herself. To label woman as virtuous and saintly defuses this fearful transgression. This male anxiety is demonstrated in virgin martyrology where pagan authority, itself a symbol of patriarchal law, insists upon 'knowing' the female saint, demanding that she identify herself in order that masculine power might be reasserted in the public arena of confession, trial, and torture.

Petroff has already described this pattern of unmasking at work in female mysticism where the motif fails to address the disruptive possibility that the female is, in fact, unknowable, the very interiority associated with her a carefully preserved secret self confounding male expectations and impervious to any attempt to classify or contain her.[17] I would suggest that this is the secret contained in the fissured text, extending beyond a concept of space to include motifs explored elsewhere, such as silence and patient, emotionless fortitude; it is the secret self of the metaphorical wall, an idea to which I shall return.

Pagan tormentors demand the identity of their victims. Hagiographers speak for them so that Lucy declares 'I am the handmaid of God' [*GL*, vol. 2, 134], a comment offered as proof of the sanctity promulgated by the text. Faith speaks her own name together with an assertion of her beliefs [*LHW*, 101]. Agatha defines herself as both a gentlewoman and Christ's handmaid [230]. Olybrius asks,

'Sey me, damysel, of what kyn thou art,
And whethyr thou be bonde or ellys fre,'

and Margaret's reply that she is a Christian baffles him in its failure to define herself according to masculine law, to state her position in relation to men as wife or daughter [14–15]. Elizabeth of Hungary is commended for a religious identity surpassing the noble, worldly lineage by which she is contained:

... for she ded magnyfye
Alle hyr kynrede & eek glorify
Wyth manye exaunplys of perfyhtnesse [259].

Yet this holy identity remains inextricably connected to a worldly one. Ultimately, woman is lauded only for her continued residence in a void, man's lack, emphasised by the patrilinear genealogy within which she is located. Once again, it is the Virgin Mary's impossible *exemplum* which informs this notion.

In the Nativity of the Virgin, is outlined, at length, her lineage from Judah through the royal house of David, information taken directly from the gospels but also part of what is termed 'the custom of writing' where 'the generation of women is not showed but of the men' [*GL*, vol. 5, 96]. Bokenham similarly details Joachim's line for, just as Mary's lineage is known by Joseph, it is

The custome of scripture not vsyth, lo,
Of wymmen to wryte the genealogye [*LHW*, 42].

This acknowledgement conveniently excuses the gallant Bokenham before his female audience, but the fact remains that genealogy is delineated according to an inviolable masculine law which takes no account of maternal debt.

The version in Caxton appeals to an authority both temporal and scriptural, witnessed in phrases such as 'after the law he is the son of Eli' [*GL*, vol. 5, 96] and 'by the law he was son of him that was dead, like as it is said in the History Scholastic' [97] enables a containment of the female which ignores all possibility of her selfhood. This masculine order is confirmed throughout its version of Mary's nativity. The author refers to Bede who recounts how Herod tried to gain 'the proofs of lineage' from chests secretly hidden in the temple in order to render himself noble and 'make them believe that his lineage appertained to them of Israel', when, in fact, 'they had learned the order of generation of our Lord, a part of their grandsires' fathers, and a part by some books that they had in their houses and taught them forth as much as they might' [97].

Patristic and theological authority similarly establishes a link between Anne, mother of Mary, James the Greater and John the Evangelist, and her cousin Elizabeth, mother of John the Baptist [98]. All ensures that Christ is established as God, king, and priest [99], but also affirmed is the subordinate place of the female, even within the divine; she exists as wife, mother, or daughter. Thus, saints, fictional or otherwise, must be appropriated by masculine law, fixed in time, place, and history. Virgin martyrs are placed within pagan time or Christian persecution, their tormentors pagan provosts or their own fathers. Many saints are located within a childhood remarkable for its burgeoning spirituality or else, like Katherine or Clare of Assisi, receive an early theological education under the aegis of a male teacher.

Bokenham's fulsome praise of Elizabeth of Hungary affirms a sanctity signalled by her rejection of worldly trappings. She refuses to remarry [*LHW*,

278] or return home to her father when widowed [279], suffers the loss of her beloved childhood retainers, prays for the elimination of maternal love, and declares that she loves no-one and nothing save God Himself [280]. Similarly, she refuses the marks of her royal status, insisting that no-one calls her 'mistress' or 'lady' [281]. Her voluntary embrace of poverty, her self-abnegation, paves the way for union with the divine. However, the unspoken space behind these textual details indicates a repudiation of all the constricting categories within which women are retained by men. Elizabeth's rejection is of all that which classifies her as wife, daughter, mother, princess, friend. Her surrender of self is simultaneously holy and a liberating subversion of masculine values.

Such fissures are revealed elsewhere, most notably in the life of St Katherine. Ostensibly, her response to Maxentius's demand to know her is a satisfactory one; she is learned and she is royal [*LHW*, 180; *SM*, 86]. She is also a Christian while, as queen, she claims that the city belongs to her and her subjects are unlawfully repressed [*LKA*, 291]. Here, Katherine asserts the rights properly bestowed upon her which Maxentius, patriarchal representative, tramples under-foot. Her transgressive role as lone ruler is doubly punished; she is tortured as a Christian and also as an independent female. The holy intention of Bokenham's text is fragmented when he also details her reply 'Kateryne, I hycht' [*LHW*, 180]. This simple naming declares a secure, inward identity which resists all other masculine categorisation, and asserts a positive valence for the feminine self. It is from this strong base that she is able to forsake the safety of her palace for the public arena of martyrdom. Thus, holy and personal identity are inextricably bound in a text which only recognises the former.

Similarly fissured is Chaucer's *The Man of Law's Tale* where, as indicated in chapter one, the narrator's determination to know his subject ensures a series of constricting labels which locate her only as saintly. Custance is defined in rela-tion to the masculine, termed 'the Emperoures doghter, dame Custance' [*11(B¹)*, 151], 'his doghter, dame Custance' [249], 'O Emperoures yonge doghter deere', or simply 'O my Custance' [446–7]. Absorbed into text and society, Custance is in danger of disappearing altogether.

Yet, textual disruption occurs when she recognises herself as the alien out-sider, her marginalisation potentially subversive. Custance demonstrates a sharp awareness of the ways of a male-dominated world. A fearful girl on the point of exchange as a new bride, she ostensibly asserts an acceptance of herself as an object available for masculine appropriation. She calls herself 'child Custance' and 'Custance youre child' [274; 278], subtly alerting the audience to the vulnerability of her youth and reminding her father of his paternal obligation to protect her. The story's circular motion is complete when she is finally reunited with both Alla, her husband, and her father under whose aegis she places herself with the meek declaration 'I am youre doghter, Custance' [1107].

Yet, the subtext whispers of an alternative, true self forged during a series of crises where, as a literal outsider, Custance is forced to use her initiative or die. Cast adrift for the first time, she arrives in Northumberland, her alien status reinforced by her inability to speak the language. Recognising an opportunity to shield herself from danger and discover a new identity, she tells no-one who or what she is, claiming to have lost her memory [524–7]. Adrift for the second time and rescued by her uncle's fleet, she again refuses to identify herself, and is taken back to Rome where she is cared for by her aunt [971–3; 981–2]. This bizarre lack of recognition on behalf of a family whose assured protection Custance effectively declines highlights the way in which she has altered and claimed her identity as an individual in her own right.

This is confirmed by Alla's eventual recognition of her. Here, the textual fissure reveals the significance of the symbol of the face in any assertion of selfhood. Custance's face is always pale. On her original wedding day, she 'Ful pale arist' [265]. Later, on trial for Hermengyld's murder, her pallor is compared to that of the white face which always stands out in a crowd [645]. Such details are designed to evoke pity and emphasise her fear. However, this pale face is also the mark of Custance's identity as an outsider, and the sign, too, of her own self whose features are unique.

Hearing of Alla's pilgrimage to Rome, where Custance and her son now anonymously reside, she sends Maurice to a feast attended by his father. It is through Alla's recognition of the child's face, so like his mother's, that their reunion is effected. Seeing Maurice, Alla recalls his bride [1031–5], at first believing she is only a pale ghost in his head [1037]. When he finally meets Custance, he, unlike her relatives, immediately recognises her as the resourceful outsider he married:

> For at the firste look he on hire sette
> He knew wel verraily that it was she [1053–4].

The emblem is firmly embedded when Custance further manipulates it, this time sending Maurice to her father, who, as 'he looked bisily' upon the child, 'on his doghter thoughte' [1093–7]. Thus, Custance's pale, nearly invisible face, is simultaneously man's other, a family likeness, and her own unique identity. From her marginalised position, Custance stakes a claim for her own space within a world that she manipulates. Apparently supportive of patriarchal law, she finds a quiet space within it from which the concept of woman as absence or lack is negated. The man of law's detailed insistence upon the pathos of the reconciliation scenes cannot obscure what is inadvertently revealed in Alla's comment, 'Maurice my sone, so lyk youre face' [1063]; here, Alla is forced to acknowledge the debt he and his heir owe to the woman.

The face symbol appears elsewhere in hagiography. Though initially resistant to Walter's choice of a lowly bride in *The Clerk's Tale*, his subjects quickly recognise her virtue for all 'that looked on her face' love her true self. What appears as a transformation from Janicula's daughter to Walter's consort earns public approval for a newly-made Griselda, 'another creature' [*IV(E)*, 406–13]. In fact, all fail to perceive that Griselda remains unchanging and true to her self, a point also confirmed by the textual motif of clothing.

Most pagan tormentors are immediately struck by the beauty of their victims.

Dorothy's admires her loveliness but is enraged by her Christian defiance. Defining her purely in physical and sexual terms, he seeks to overcome her integrity, in every sense, by ordering her face to be beaten in with staves 'Tyl of hir face were no semyng' [*LHW*, 133]. Agnes declares of her lover, Christ,

> 'In my face he hath set a specyal merk
> þat noon oþur shuld be louyd but he' [114].

It is both a holy and a specifically feminine, potentially disruptive identity that is established here.

The motif of clothing is an equally ambiguous symbol closely allied to a concept of self. Clothes might be a sign of rank (such as Katherine's royal purple), sexuality, or wealth as in the example of the whore Pelagienne, called Margaret 'for the pomp of my clothing' [*GL*, vol. 5, 236]. Equally, it might denote holiness while lack of it suggests penitence, a return to a pre-Lapsarian innocence presaging a new, holy identity.[18] Masculine disguise indicates a protective covering of self. Even ostentation might function as a sign of spiritual enrichment, a concrete symbol challenging the spiritual impoverishment of a proposed worldly lover, as in the example of Agnes declaring how Christ had clothed her in a golden gown and decked her with jewels [*LHW*, 114]. The contrast between social and religious identity is exemplified in Cecilia's wearing of a hair shirt beneath her bridal dress [*VIII(G)*, 132] while Elizabeth of Hungary asserts her holiness by voluntarily wearing poor clothing or giving away her own [*LHW*, 262; 266; 270].

Such external signals may well deceive. In *The Clerk's Tale* clothing operates as a symbol of Griselda's true self, her covert resistance to masculine appropriation.[19] Walter's secret fabrication of the wedding gown for his chosen bride culminates in his female retainers' reluctant stripping and reclothing of the peasant Griselda. They comb her hair, crown her, 'They clothed han al newe', and suddenly realise her beauty 'Whan she translated was in swich richesse' [*IV(E)*, 253–9; 373–85]. The transformation, which Griselda passively permits, is imposed by Walter as an exercise in patriarchal power. Such a focus upon externals apparently provides Walter with the measure of his bride. His subsequent tests remind her that she is both his subject and his object. The only space permitted is the privilege of maternity, and even that is later removed. Walter reminds how, though he took her 'out of youre povere array' [467], her lowly place as Janicula's daughter cannot be erased [632]. Nevertheless, she accepts her new given identity by taking 'youre clothyng' and her oath of allegiance [657; 650–8].

The text's ambiguities surface when Walter returns her to Janicula's house. At this point, a quietly active Griselda reminds Walter that she brought only faith, nakedness, and her maidenhead as a dowry, that he

> '. . . dide me streepe out of my povre weede,
> And richely me cladden' [863–4].

In a significant gesture she returns those clothes, leaving the palace naked save for a requested smock. Recalled to prepare the palace for her husband's new bride, she wears her old, tattered rags though the world marvels at the dignity belied by her 'povre array' [1020]. Griselda's self, symbolised by her humble clothing, remains clear and unchanged, asserting itself through the fissures of the clerk's tale.

That her selfhood is also unaffected by her experiences is far less clear-cut. Griselda's composure, together with her manipulation of those external signals which Walter misreads, confounds the masculine world represented by her husband. At the same time, she remains Walter's possession for, ultimately, she is once again stripped, reclothed, and recrowned [1114–26]. Her reunion with her children reveals a psychological dislocation as she appears to awaken abruptly from a trance, or a bewildering dream-sleep, weeps, breaks off in mid-sentence, and falls to the ground before composing herself once more [1110; 1060–1]. What is subtly indicated is not solely passive acceptance of patriarchy's final reappropriation, however compassionately depicted, but the grave personal cost of the female's struggle to regain a space and define her self, even though the happy ending then undercuts the tale's tensions to replace Griselda within the reality of her material, gendered powerlessness.[20]

One of the most interesting portrayals of the ambiguity of external signs is witnessed in a set of tales found in Caxton where some saints adopt a masculine disguise in order to flee to the sanctuary of monasterial enclosure. In many cases, flight is prompted less by religious impulse than worldly convenience. Most seek to escape marriage or search for penitential reassurance. However, Marine, a beloved only child, simply accompanies a father unwilling to leave her behind, while Theodora attempts to evade social retribution for her adultery. Many of these women, too, are accused of masculine crimes, namely fathering children, and, thus, the presentation of gender becomes crucial in this special set of stories. Surprisingly, perhaps, it is not that gender identity is dissolved, for the narratorial control of pronouns is remarkable. Usually, 'he' refers to a false accusation or reference to an obvious marker such as a monk's habit which deceives the outer world. There is a sharp division identifying 'she', the holy woman, a subject whom only the male writer apparently truly knows, his narrative demonstrating an awareness of her identity as saint. Beneath this, however, are fissures suggestive of an alternative personal identity, one secure regardless of what the world constructs as gendered.

The double irony of the adulterous Theodora's tale is that so successful is her masculine disguise that she is accused of fornication, and expelled from the monastery. No-one guesses her identity, which is secure beneath her habit. The abbot 'commanded her' in her duties [*GL*, vol. 4, 49] while, readmitted to the monastery, she takes the child which is not her own and 'closed it with her in her cell' [52]. Later when she dies, her husband is allowed to enter 'into the cell of his wife' [53]. So certain is this true self that accusations against her false self, her masculine exterior, refer to 'he': 'he meekly demanded that it might be forgiven him'. The same sentence then switches to 'But he was cast out of the monastery, and took the child upon his shoulder, and so she abode out of the monastery seven years, and nourished the child with the milk of beasts' [50–1].

It is Theodora's maternal role which is conceived as her real self alongside the spiritual mothering denoting her holiness. A new identity is tentatively revealed, however, when her husband meets her outside the monastery, as promised in his dream-vision, and fails to recognise her [50]. Expecting to meet the appendage of former years, he is unprepared for a person who is newly marked by the contemplation of her own guilt.

The narrator of Marine's story subsumes his subject's identity by largely utilising the masculine pronoun. At the end, though, the text fragments, and the structure indicates that 'he' refers to outward appearance, 'she' to an identifiably holy person. Thus, accused of lechery 'He took it all gladly and all things he did patiently and devoutly, and at the last, being full of virtuous life, she died and departed out of this world' [*GL*, vol. 3, 228]. 'She' is allowed out of the monastery to collect wood until the abbot demanded 'of him why he had done so horrible a sin' [227].

These divisions are exemplified elsewhere. Eugenia, disguised as a monk, visits Melancia who attempts to seduce him/her by feigning illness, begging brother 'Eugene' 'that she would lie by her and have to do carnally' [*GL*, vol. 5, 122]. Publicly accused of rape, Eugenia remains silent as Melancia declares that a 'young man . . . would have enforced me' [123]. A disguised Margaret/Pelagien is accused of fathering a child, and the abbot 'condemned him without judgement. And then he was put out' [239]. When other monks 'had enclosed him' in a pit, they leave. It is within *this* space that a self is discovered for, here, 'she was not troubled in any manner' [240]. As death approaches, however, the writer ensures that the only identity finally asserted is a holy one, her appropriately masculine spiritual strength noted, and her virginity presented as the only laudable occupation for women. Margaret is said to write, 'I am a man. I have not lived for to deceive, but I have showed that I have the virtue of a man.' She requests that nuns bury her so 'The women may know that I am a virgin whom they judged for adulterer' [240]. What, for women, is a practical disguise for their own protection, becomes, in the hands of their hagiographers, a double-edged weapon simultaneously asserting sanctity and affirming the masculine cleric as a role model for all.

However, nomenclature points to an important fissure. Uniquely, these women are never termed 'saint' or 'blessed' but simply named, for it is patient fortitude which identifies them as holy rather than a more active martyrdom. Presented as passive, their narrators then fail to comprehend fully that naming involves an assertion of personal as well as religious identity. Some are imposed – brother Marine, brother Eugene. Margaret is both Margaret for virginity, and Pelagienne for the gathering of pain. On trial, 'brother' Eugene reveals 'I am Eugenia, thy daughter' [124], while Pelagienne tells how 'I have been called from my birth Pelagienne, but for the pomp of my clothing men call me Margaret.' She is also brother Pelagien, and, according to the devil, 'Lady Margaret' [236].

What is indicated is that she is, at once, both one, all, and none of these. Though the text approves a single, holy identity, it also presents a multiplicity echoing the diffuseness of the two-lips metaphor. That which is reiterated in order to construct authoritatively, fragments and defies reification. Saints are both saintly and human, holy and secular, themselves and not themselves.

Physical space

As well as its use of physical locations, hagiographical textual structure often establishes a contrast between inner and outer, private and public. The external, public arena is associated with activity, movement, with a travelling, speaking, sometimes sexualised woman facing a crowd or the full weight of the law, and where the transgressions inherent in such independent, disruptive behaviour are contained and diluted by the holiness that this space asserts; this is the legitimised space of trial and martyrdom, of the masculinisation of the female subject. Its opposition is equally holy, but is depicted as still, passive, a female space. It involves interiority, and is denoted by actual or metaphorical enclosure, an anchoritic cell, imprisonment, pregnancy, virginity, even desert solitude.

The imposed linear structure of saints' lives written by men suggests that subjects choose one or other of these arenas, or, at most, move from an interior, private perfection of the soul into the public arena of faith declared. For example, Mary of Egypt's publicly proclaimed sexual appetite ensures she moves from her birthplace in search of other lovers, and it is this jouissance which prevents her entry into the enclosed space of the temple. Inspired to convert, she prays so 'priueliche and stille' in the privacy of the holy rood [*ESEL*, 262–3], before withdrawing to the outer reaches of the desert. Her private story is then brought back into the public arena.

In fact, this division between public and private is far less acute than it appears. There is an unacknowledged fluidity of movement between the two which dissolves the binary opposition constructed by the narrative. Mary Magdalene is an active participant within the world long before she retires into the desert. She remains both within and outside society, and, not surprisingly therefore, her text is important for its fissures, as will be seen. Judith, too, leaves the besieged Israelites in the mountains crossing the plain into the enemy Assyrian camp, before killing Holofernes, and returning to broadcast her success. Yet, it is within the privacy of the chamber that she asserts her independence by cutting off his head [*GL*, vol. 2, 85–9]. The movement of Custance's tale is global and circular as she leaves Rome for Syria, travels to England then Rome then back to England, and, finally, returns to Rome. Such accounts belie the careful, linear movement of the surface structure, and, in this fissure, a feminine rhythm breaks through the narrative-symbolic order.

The concept of imprisonment is significant in hagiography. In this interior, the virgin martyr's faith is perfected, and the theological self-knowledge, prerequisite of divine union, finally achieved. Resonance is added by the use of darkness and light, in the descent intended as a private hell yet where a meta-phorical ascent to heaven is conveyed by miraculous illumination, mystical or angelic apparition, or miracles of feeding and healing. The saint's enclosure echoes the imprisonment of the soul in the body, as well as the sealed tomb of Christ with its intimation of resurrection, or the womb presaging a spiritual rebirth. Here, too, the soul struggles to assert its supremacy over the body, a battle expressed in the private prayers, supernatural illusions, and demonic visitations which fill this time.[21] Holiness is inscribed upon the body itself. The virgin martyr is shut up in darkness after being horrifically tortured; doubly sealed, her wounds are miraculously healed, and starvation has no adverse effects. The tormentor safely contains her, and, though her inscrutable holiness confounds him, her exemplary *integritas* pleases his masculinity. The multi-valency of this space, with both its religious and its patriarchal symbolisation, nevertheless ensures that woman is fully appropriated, for, imprisoned, she exists as the hagiographer's subject and as man's other.

Both male and female saints are imprisoned, thereby confirming the religious value of this symbol. Examples are numerous. Katherine is refused food, cast into darkness, yet later appears 'so shining' [*GL*, vol. 7, 22], so 'fat and round' that her gaolers are accused of feeding her [*ESEL*, 98]. Similarly, after nine days of angelic succour, Dorothy is 'fairer and brighter' [*GL*, vol. 7, 43] than before and, after torture, appears 'all whole and strong without any disease or hurt' [44]. Subsequent torments, and a third imprisonment, render her 'so whole and sound' that she was 'more fairer for to look on than ever she was to fore' [45]. Juliana is brought from her prison cell 'so well guerished, and her visage so fair and so shining' [*GL*, vol. 3, 48]. Katherine embraces her sentence, stepping into her cell 'As a spouse to chaumbre, for hir lordis loue' [*LKA*, 291] while Agatha enters as if to a feast [*ESEL*, 195]. Margaret's spiritual enlightenment sustains her against the dragon, symbol of evil and sexual temptation. She is swallowed by him, metaphorically ingested by both paganism and patriarchy, but the cross she is wearing swells in his mouth and he bursts [*LHW*, 19–21]. So anxious is Agatha to receive her martyr's crown that she refuses to leave though the prison doors are all open [237].

It is during Katherine's second spell of imprisonment that the site exhibits its potential for disruption. The prison, a religious symbol common to both male and female saints, takes on a slightly different resonance in female hagiography. Believing his victim safely enclosed, Maxentius, her pagan oppressor and symbol of the masculine world, visits the borders of his realm, a frontier more usually associated with the outsider-female [188]. The masculine space of prison, closed and powerful, is made her own as, here, she converts Maxentius's queen and her knight Porphyrie in a room blazing with light [188–91].

This textual fissure with its intimations of female assertion sometimes appears when prison becomes a metaphor for oppression. Just as the male writer encloses his holy subject within his hagiographical text, some pagan fathers imprison their Christian daughters within a phallic tower, also a sign of heavenly ascent. The male exercises his power with the key controlling access to the locked door, symbol of purity and control. Details of key, seal, and lock represent chastity and remain the material equivalent of hymeneal sealing.[22]

Thus, Barbara's father hides her in a high, strong tower determined that her great beauty shall be seen by no man [*GL*, vol. 6, 199]. His angry response to the declaration of her faith is vented in a series of tortures which puncture the skin, penetrating the very *integritas* he wished to preserve. The lovely Christina is similarly enclosed by her father who attempts to force worship of his pagan idols [*LHW*, 59]. Her rejection takes a dramatic form. She opens the window, outlook onto a wider world and symbol of her own 'fissured' sex, smashes the idols, and throws them into the street below, whilst covertly worshipping 'god in hyr herte' [64; 61].

The clearest example of the disruptive possibilities of enclosed space is seen in the *vita* of St Katherine, discussed more fully later. However, the symbolisation of *integritas* is exemplified in some of the tortures accompanying imprisonment. Such details, almost unique to women saints, involve interiority and containment. Dorothy is placed in a tub of boiling oil [*GL*, vol. 7, 43; *LHW*, 131], Christine in an iron tub where she 'rocked as a child in a cradle' before spending five days in a fiery furnace dancing and singing with angels [*GL*, vol. 4, 96], and three days in an oven, again, singing [*LHW*, 79]. Cecilia is placed in a bath of flames from where she continues to preach [*VIII(G)*, 514]. Attempts are made to crush Katherine between two wheels or four rotating ones, depending on the source.

Similar images of domestic interiority litter the crucial text of Christina Mirabilis who enacts the pains of purgatorial souls in exchange for their redemption. She creeps into baking ovens or domestic fires, within which she places her hands and feet for so long that all expect them to be burned to cinders. She immerses herself in cauldrons of water pouring the scalding liquid over her exposed limbs, remains in rivers or barrels for six days or more even in the depths of winter, or else crawls into open graves [*Prosalegenden*, 122–3].

This is a peculiarly female domain of ovens, baths, fuel, water, which form the basis of tortures where the masculine aggressor strikes at the heart of femininity in a reminder that this space, in fact, is on loan from him. This is confirmed by male hagiographers who also ensure the validity of their saints by allowing them to overcome miraculously, thanks only to divine intervention. Yet this domestic containment might well have spoken to its medieval audience of a source of disruption. Christina Mirabilis voluntarily chooses her pain; within it is a freedom and a continual movement which, despite, the best efforts of those who attempt to chain her fearing that she is possessed, none can curtail. Equally saint Christina rocks like a child in the flames, voicing her security. Christ's activity on her behalf is imaged as the comforting hand of the mother. What asserts itself in such fissures is the continuity of the familiar, feminine world, a holiness allowing those who sing to speak not only of Christ but from the feminine chora. A violent, masculine assertion of rights undergoes a positive transformation where the closed space of power is imploded, and a personal freedom expressed in the adoption of a religious identity.

At the same time, other texts continue to associate the female with an enclosure and interiority integral to the depiction of her as a passive vessel. In affirmation of sanctity, the male writer comments on what is hidden in his female subject, speaking for her in his assumption that he knows what is secreted within her heart. It is, thus, the image of the heart's chamber filled by virtue, the Word, or the Holy Ghost which resonates throughout these texts. Anne succeeds in pleasing Joachim 'for þe gret godenes þat was wythyn hur' [*MF*, 15]. When Magdalene kneels before Christ 'no word spak scho þat mon myȝht here, saue in hert' [204], while her tears express her secret contrition known only to Christ for He is 'of hertys þe inward knoware' [*LHW*, 149]. Cecilia's religion, too, is private, contained within her heart or her breast.[23] Agatha apparently tells the world, 'I shall have in my heart Jesu Christ as long as I shall live' [*GL*, vol. 3, 37], while Margaret is praised for possession of all the cardinal virtues 'In hyr soule inward endewyd' [*LHW*, 12]. Mary of Oignies, similarly, 'kepte and bare in hir herte wordes of holy writte' [*Prosalegenden*, 163].

Inner contemplation denotes spirituality yet contains a hidden fissure. The secret love of Christ is a knowledge appropriated by the male biographer, and remains his only knowledge of his subject. Yet, this private containment also points towards a wider, more personal space, one which is out of bounds to a male who, in any case, fails to understand it. It is an inner space most evident in the metaphor of the wall informing *The Clerk's Tale*.

Walter's desire to 'know' Griselda is aroused by the sight of one who contains 'in the brest of hire virginitee' a 'rype and sad corage' [*IV(E)*, 219–20]. His tests of her patience are due to his need 'hir sadnesse for to knowe' [452]. Although the narrator criticises this, he has no real knowledge of his subject beyond the holy, ideally feminine patience ostensibly exhibited. Walter watches and waits for change; 'She was ay oon in herte and in visage' [711], exactly as promised. Griselda remains 'ay sad and constant as a wal' [1047], ultimately out of reach of either her husband or the teller of her tale, bricked up within the prison of her inhuman self-control.

This metaphor's physical representation is the cell or chamber. Masculine and clerical approbation of anchoritic life centres upon the entombing of the sealed, silent, hidden woman whose visionary experience is mediated by the male and whose life is subject to theological rules or traditions. Yet this wall or act of self-containment is itself a fissure, seen in earlier discussion of the anchoritic windows. It is a space legitimated by church and hagiographical text, but which remains a fluid link with the world, both entrance and exit. Further, its marginalisation, together with the aperture or window suggestive of the vagina, mark it as a place of dislocation and disruption. It remains a private place of personal concealment, a breathing space for the creation of identity, yet, inextricably part of the symbolic order, of the social world. The *vita* of Catherine of Siena is an excellent example of this concept. Catherine's influential entry into the public domain is not effected until a 'self' has been forged in the privacy of her home. That this is primarily a religious self is abundantly clear from her biographer-confessor's sharp narrative division between these two stages. But, at the same time as her earlier, private life feeds and sustains her religious devotion, her personal will is strengthened. She learns how to protect herself against family disapproval by the construction 'in her mind' of 'a secret cell which she vowed she would never leave for anything.'[24] Deprived of her own bedroom, she simply appropriates her brother's, 'established a desert within the walls of her own home and solitude in the midst of people.'[25]

As discussed earlier, the interiority present in accounts of the life of St. Cecilia, and the significance of her chamber, surface in other texts where always the biographer's intent is to establish holiness. Magdalene's desert solitude is a place of penitence, 'a secret celestial place where no man human might come' [*GL*, vol. 4, 83]. St Francis has Clare enclosed in a cell in order to perfect her soul [*GL*, vol. 6, 163]. Elizabeth of Hungary outwardly performs her public duties and dutifully serves her guests [*LHW*, 267; 269], yet, in the privacy of her chamber, asserts a religious identity by wearing poor clothes, spinning, or having herself scourged [266; 270]. Within this space, she quietly waits so 'that by patience she might possess her soul' [*GL*, vol. 6, 223].

Custance's chamber is both a literal and a metaphorical one with her two lonely exiles in a rudderless ship protected, according to the man of law, only by Christ. The narrator explicitly compares her to Daniel, Jonah, and Mary of Egypt [*II(B¹)*, 470–504] as well as insisting that it is divine intervention protecting her from the threat of rape [920–74]. Despite her passive exterior, the narrative itself inadvertently acknowledges her private strength for, enclosed in her boat, 'in the see she dryveth forth hir weye' or else 'dryveth forth, into oure occian' [875; 505]. Rape is avoided when 'struggling wel and myghtily', she manages to throw her assailant overboard [921–4].

The interweaving strands of spatial orientation are amply clarified in those tales of penitent women. Such saints, usually in masculine disguise, renounce overt expression of their sexuality, and enclose themselves in a cell, a desert, or a monastery. The religious valence of their actions undoubtedly lies with the notion of *integritas*; the ruptured hymen is metaphorically resealed by their physical and moral enclosure.[26] From within this sealed tomb or womb, the repentant female is reborn. The revelation of her true identity is both religious and personal, for it is within this sphere that a notion of self-worth is explored. Such women arouse the admiration of their male biographers who articulate this space as the dissolution of self in preparation for union with Christ. Yet, it is simultaneously an unspoken space from within which the feminine, which has taken invisibility to its limits, might disrupt the symbolic. Accusations of fornication, expressing a masculine fear of a sexually predatory female whose nature is revealed even beneath the habit of her disguise, together with a religious *exemplum* of patience, also conjure the positive symbolisation of the anchoritic window. Total escape from the world is not possible, and there is a fluidity of movement beneath a closed, narrative structure. It is at this frontier that the feminine might speak itself.

Caxton's inclusion of the life of Thaisis is such a fissured text. Doubly legitimised as holy by the abbot Parfuntius, who initiates her conversion, her transgressive sexuality is contained in a framework emphasising repentance. She accepts God's existence, and is so firmly enclosed in a cell where the door is sealed with lead, symbol of her reconstituted *integritas*, that she refuses to leave it, for it is only there that she is able to contemplate the sum of her sins [*GL*, vol. 5, 242–3]. Thaisis is fully located within the masculine. She is instructed to look east, to repeat 'Lord, that hast formed me, have mercy on me' [243], a mantra reiterating that it is *man* who has created her.

The tale's turning point is when Thaisis leads Parfuntius to a place so secret that only God might witness their sexual/spiritual union. Her comment that 'if thou dread him, there is no place that may be hid from him' [241], apparently demonstrates her acknowledgement of the existence of the divine. The surface text asserts the holy identity of this penitent whore, but is barely able to conceal an alternative reading of the events preceding the climactic movement of her recognition and conversion. It is another, hidden space that defines Thaisis the woman.

The privacy of her chamber recalls a secret, sexual pleasure, one which Parfuntius, fearful of temptation, is called upon to punish. She invites him 'into the chamber here within', and ever further inwards 'into divers secret places', until they are on the brink of what Thaisis describes as 'There is within a place where no man entereth, and there shall no man see us but God' [241]. Here, the woman is dominant, the text echoing the rhythms of her jouissance as she draws him ever deeper into a space witnessed only by the divine, a space where, it is assumed, she has formerly unashamedly performed. Even the punishment of her imposed enclosure feels the resonance of this rhythm, for, there, Thaisis herself chooses to remain, faces the 'sum of her sins', and learns the measure of her self.

Theodora's jouissance both prompts her voluntary enclosure and breaks through the order of the narrative pattern. Within her chosen space, she privately grieves over her secret, shaming adultery, and battles with her own conscience, refuting even the tenderness of a concerned, duped husband. She is tormented by demons, and faces a series of sexual temptations. The black and white surface narrative thus reduces this complex tale of personal guilt, so that, in envy of her 'holiness', the devil arranges her lapse [*GL*, vol. 4, 48]. Later, too, because he 'could not suffer her holiness', this 'strumpet' is expelled from the monastery, accused of siring a child [50]. Here, her temptations continue, 'the devil having envy of her much patience' [51].

However, Theodora's is a psychological crisis, a human shame where the devil's words merely mouth her self-assessment: 'thou strumpet above all other, and adulterer, thou hast forsaken thy husband' [50]. She refuses to reveal herself to her husband when they meet, instead speaking to him 'within herself' [50]. Her sexual and erring self remains disguised and unarticulated. Theodora's narrator admires her humility before both man and the divine. Her example lies within the words he awards her when she tells herself 'I will do penance for that I have sinned against thee' [51]. Beyond this is a crisis of identity and self-worth which she alone can resolve, hence the multivalent implication of her incon-solable tears for an aberration committed by her false, adulterous self in a moment of madness nevertheless crucial to self-understanding. Thus, she weeps when, 'returning to herself' [49], she realises the extent of her transgression, a point at which the text's cohesion is fragmented.

St Katherine

It is in accounts of the life of St Katherine that concepts of physical and psycho-logical space mesh most consistently. Spatial orientation is a crucial aspect of the first part of her story. As a young girl, she is given by her father a special study from which to pursue her solitary learning, an activity denoting an indi-viduality later castigated as antisocial folly. Masculine disapprobation of female learning is succinctly expressed in Capgrave's remark:

> . . . stody may not last
> Wyth werdly besynesse ne wyth hys cure,
> þe olde wyse sey þus, I ȝow ensure [*LKA*, 38].

This personal space is described by Caxton as 'her secret study' [*GL*, vol. 7, 10], while Katherine's high rank, virginity, and spiritual elevation are expressed in the symbol of the square or tall tower which contains it.

Some accounts further emphasise the dangerous potential of Katherine's knowledge by noting how her father constructed a walled palace [*LKA*, 36] within which literally to contain all delight in his daughter's wisdom [*SM*, 70]. This space is, in fact, a round garden with many archways through which birds fly in and out. A series of locked gates leads to it, just as in other versions locked doors reach her study. Not only is the walled garden, with its curves, its archways, its natural potency, suggestive of the female sex, it is Katherine who controls access to her own defined place. It is a space marked by fluidity and exchange, for its door and archways lead both in and out, birds freely leave and enter. It is also a space exclusive of masculine power for, though her father constantly changes her tutors, delighting in stimulating the learning he has permitted and which he thinks he controls, it is Katherine who retains the key [*LKA*, 36], moving freely in and out 'at hur owne liberte' [*SM*, 70].

Equally, the garden is walled, and its intimations of Griselda's stonewalling inscrutability underscore the keen sense of identity expressed via Katherine's royal and scholarly privilege. Though part of this identity is holy, the threat of Katherine's knowledge and selfhood simmers beneath the surface text. The sealed, locked door erected by her father represents Katherine's hymen. When this is symbolically breached, it is an action performed by the hermit, Adrian, on behalf of Christ with Katherine's subconscious permission. At the same time, Katherine keeps her own counsel within this space, interacts with the world only on her terms, for she alone permits access to her self and to her own body. This womb-like void nurtures an unspoken identity as a woman, and a realised one as a saint, as well as retaining this child-woman socially, within the bosom of her family.

The narrative's assertion of Katherine's holy validity attempts to defuse her transgressive independence. She metaphorically renounces the privacy of her own world, is led, by Adrian, into the desert, and, there, in visionary splendour, 'marries' Christ. This espousal of Christianity is, of course, effected by a male who himself is supposedly visited by the Virgin Mary and instructed to approach Katherine. Promised that Christ will lead the way, he 'passid fro chambre to chambre tyll he come to the secrete chambre and stody' [*SM*, 76; *LKA*, 190]. There, he finds her, 'In sad stodye, ful solitarie all a-lone' [*LKA*, 192], and reassures her saying Christ has

> . . . leyd hys grete tresour
> Ryght in hyr hert [198].

Thus, the potent symbols of chamber, heart, and interiority are united.

Katherine's conversion is effected, however, at a crucial point. It occurs when grief for the death of her beloved and indulgent father leaves her bereft. Only fourteen years old, newly crowned as queen, she retreats into a protective shell, 'kepyth her chambyr & holdyth hyr þus inne' [62; *SM*, 74]. She is physically and emotionally sealed behind a wall, seeking solace in study until her subjects, fearing her disruptive self-containment, petition her to marry. Her refusal causes a breach in realm and family, and, more significantly, dislocates her sense of self, subsequently re-formed in dramatic, theological terms.

Adrian, representative of the faith, offers consolation in the form of a heavenly family, emotional support, and even power bestowed by Christ in exchange for the surrender of worldly wealth and estate [183–4]. Under intense pressure to conform in a manner abhorrent to her, personal power is precisely what Katherine lacks. Thus, she follows her mentor into the desert 'marred in mynde', and in 'a trauns' [206]. There, her visionary experiences confirm her holy worth as she perceives the false vanity of her former life, and passively accepts the spiritual revelations offered to her. Beneath the surface text, however, a profound fissure fragments narratorial intention. Its focus is the dislocation or splintering of Katherine's self, details ostensibly designed to signal her metamorphosis into saint.

When the Virgin Mary speaks to her, 'she was so much replenished with heavenly joy that she lay as she had been dead' [*GL*, vol. 7, 13]. Married to Christ, 'she fell in a swoon so that she lay still a large hour without any life', reviving to see 'nothing about her save an old cell, and the old man Adrian by her, weeping' [16]. Other versions recount how she 'lay a grete while as ded' [*SM*, 80], 'in trauns' like death [*LKA*, 228], and 'in a sownyng, so þat all the spiritis in hur had lost lyfe by a long space' [*SM*, 84].

What is steadily revealed here is Katherine's human, feminine, and vulnerable self. Her psychological crisis is further deepened when she is informed that, on her return home, she will find her mother dead [*GL*, vol. 7, 15]. The fragmentation of her self is also manifested in the stage-management of a disappearance that ostensibly only presages her sanctification. She is told that the Virgin Mary has 'ordained there one in your stead, that all men ween it were yourself, and when ye come home, she that is there in your stead shall void' [15; *LKA*, 258].

Her personal alienation is also highlighted in other textual details. Katherine's desert vision is of a fabulous monastery [12] within which she is crowned with rose garlands, meets the Virgin Mary, her 'new' mother, and where, reclothed in purple, she is wed to a Christ so lovely that she is 'all ravished in her soul' [11; 12]. This marriage is highly praised, and, with it, Katherine herself [15]. Warmly welcomed by this alternative, holy family she is greeted as 'our dear sister' [11; *SM*, 79], while Mary demands 'Bring me my well beloved daughter', repeatedly terming her 'daughter' [13; *SM*, 80; 81].

When Katherine awakes from her trance, she weeps for 'all the royalty was voided, both monastery and palace, and all the comfortable sights that she had seen' [16]. In its place is the stark, bare cell of Adrian. The opulence of both her own and the visionary realm highlights Katherine's exchange; her decision to convert entails a loss of worldly wealth. At the same time, the parallel between Adrian's cell and her own secret chamber paves the way for her continued learning, her lonely Christian persecution, an isolation similarly augured by the tears shed for the apparent disappearance of her heavenly family.

Thus, a narrative voice reasserts itself. She returns to 'silens syttynge in hir stody' [*LKA*, 275], to her 'chambyr' [258], all 'alone' [*GL*, vol. 7, 17]. Four quiet years elapse, a period elided in all versions. Her seclusion is a metaphorical fortification for a martyrdom yet to come; beyond this, no narrator has any further interest. In this unspoken chora, though she may exist for herself, woman is unrepresentable. Upon Maxentius's arrival Katherine remains,

> fful sore astoyned what hir is beste for to doo.
> If she holde silens, þan is she not truwe
> Of hir beheestes [*LKA*, 277].

Safe within her private sanctuary, a servant urges her to 'Keepe stille youre closet, there is no more to seye' [276]. Finally, she walks out through the palace to publicly reproach Maxentius [278], an activity which secures her saintly crown. Because her 'name is written in the Book of Life' [*GL*, vol. 7, 12; *SM*, 80], she is able to assert her religious self.

Thus, the hagiographers' aim is achieved, despite significant sites of fragmentation. In the private, inscrutable space of her chamber, in the rhythmic jouissance of her own walled garden where Katherine's pleasure is in books and learning, in the personal trauma prompting the ecstatic visions of a surrogate family, the subject of these *vitae* both struggles to assert herself and exemplifies a series of crucial hagiographical motifs. As suggested much earlier in this chapter, Katherine's true identity remains consistent. Her name is Katherine, Christ calls her by this name, and the Virgin Mary's instructions for her baptism contain the demand 'change not her name' [14; *SM*, 81].

Maternity, paternity, and kinship

The saints' model of holy behaviour is intentionally offered as an *exemplum* for all medieval women. What becomes a source of fragmentation in those same texts, however, is their apparent denial of femininity. Sanctity is equated with virginity, and, as part of that concept, inverts the worldly roles constructing women. Thus, in theoretical terms, they deny their own subjectivity or social self, and repudiate a sexual, maternal role, the very thing that is both a site of difference and a potential source of celebration. Yet, this ostensible negation is far from being the full picture.

A French feminist approach to the maternal illuminates the multiplicity created by this fragmentation. Kristeva posits the important body boundary of the pregnant woman as a central notion.[27] The paradox inherent in this un-spoken, pre-Oedipal space, the chora, is that the power of its jouissance is also regulated by patriarchy, for the child must be acknowledged by paternal law.[28] The threat presented by the chora is recoded and stabilised through religion, and, in particular, the icon of the Virgin Mary.[29] The image was particularly popular with male writers, representing nurture, compassion, and affectivity in a complement to their masculine authority. Many reversed female and maternal images so that they applied to men, thus presented as meek, humble, womanly, and holy.[30] Similarly, the concept of maternity touches the response of many female mystics to Christ's Passion, where Christ Himself is feminised in the sense that He is acted upon, submits to the Father, and approves God's power as an exchange object, the human in the divine. This affective response to the humanity and physicality of Jesus remains a highly influential, and complex area.[31] Maternal space is privileged for its procreative function, rather than its jouissance, and is lauded for the restrictions it places upon women, as well as its confirmation of paternal control reflected in hagiographical approval. Masculine fear of the death drive is rearticulated in the symbolic, and displaced onto the mother[32] in a refusal to acknowledge maternal debt. This obliteration of the maternal ensures masculine domination, and, hence, God is the Creator of all life and all genealogy is patrilinear. The highest status afforded to woman, as a result, is as the mother of Christ, or the mother of sons.[33]

Because boys and girls enter the symbolic differently, Irigaray and Kristeva are especially concerned with the relationship between mothers and daughters.[34] Irigaray believes that it is in this space that a feminine self, elided by a mater-nity only equated with reproduction, might be discovered. A masculine defi-nition of maternity as a shelter exiling the daughter, curtailing her expression, and obliterating female history certainly ensures that what is sacrificed is the relationship with self and with all other women. This inability to locate the self, to separate it from the notion of (m)other prompts a hatred of the mother, rivalry between women, emotional dislocation, or even violence. If the only identity offered in the symbolic is a maternal one, the unsymbolisation of woman, to use Irigaray's term, leads to a state of dereliction where she is abandoned without hope, without God.[35] Medieval woman's redefinition of the divine may well have offered some respite from the effects of this masculine ideal.

It is the infinite space between God and self, where women approach but never quite meet the divine,[36] that enables an articulation of an identity which remains holy but does not exactly correspond to the one imposed by male hagiographers.[37] Personal identity is partly formed via social interaction, yet sanctity demands separation, a repudiation of familial and worldly mores. This sacred model places allegiance to God above all else so that what is socially unacceptable is also, according to Heffernan, a sign of election to the divine.[38] This very inversion of worldly values opens up a space which demonstrates what it means to be a woman, not just a saint. At the point of rejection is an abyss reminiscent of the dual valency of the anchoritic window. Rebellion against ties of marriage and kinship merely highlights exactly what restricts women who exchange a worldly label for its corresponding religious one. At the same time, it points towards a continuity of experience which underscores the impossibility of severing such links.

Hagiographical stories are saturated by the patristic and the patriarchal. Theological 'fathers' and a holy family comprised of Christ, Mary, or a host of saints, are recommended as surrogate kin replacing worldly relationships. Male domination continues to reinforce patriarchal law. Thus, the holy hermit, Bueno, is a formative influence upon St Winifred, Adrian upon Katherine, and Conrad upon Elizabeth of Hungary. Parfuntius is a replacement 'father' for Thaisis and Nonnon for Pelagienne. Stories of desert mothers are disseminated only by male clerics, while St Germain's blessing of the child Genevieve, 'daughter' to his 'Holy Father' [*GL*, vol. 3, 286], ensures that, when orphaned, she is protected by various members of the clergy who remind all that 'she was chosen of God in her mother's belly' [289].

Beneath the text's approval of such worldly loss is often a fluidity of movement between the social and the solitary rather than the demarcation intended. Cecilia's public, yet isolated, martyrdom is the crux of all accounts, but is preceded by a secret web of influence affirming the collective and controlled by her. Thus, she is recognised by the Christian community which aids the conversion of her husband and brother-in-law. The text commends such religious bonds, yet elides a social interaction specifically associated with the female which reveals her cooperative and interactive nature.

Similarly, Pauline's love for the divine is said to have 'surmounted the love that she had to her children' [2]. It prevents her attendance at the bedside of a sick child, but allows her to retain a favourite daughter who, influenced by her mother, joins her convent [8]. Dorothy's tormentor fails to account for female persuasion when she reconverts the lapsed sisters sent to effect her renunciation [*GL*, vol. 7, 44]. Aldegonde's rejection of marriage engages the wrath of her mother but is prompted by the conversation of her 'holy sister', with whom she stays as she apparently prepares for her forthcoming wedding [219]. Clare of Assisi is joined in her order by her sister Agnes. Eugenia converts the two male friends with whom she has been studying, and, in disguise, accompanies their entry into a monastery [*GL*, vol. 2, 121]. Searched for by her distraught family, they are not reunited until, accused of lechery and hauled before the provost her father, in order to prove 'that she was a woman and daughter of him that held her in prison' [152] she exposes her breasts declaring 'Thou art my father and Claudia is my mother', names her brothers, and then herself, 'thy daughter' [*GL*, vol. 5, 124]. Justina's conversion of her pagan family is effected through her mother who then tells her father as they lie together in bed [166].

What these examples reveal is an underlying power permitted but not dissolved by the adoption of a holy identity, where positive value is awarded not just to sanctity but to a strength active within a patriarchal world. At the same time, familial and social interaction continues to insinuate itself into a text promulgating the masculine ideal of the 'enclosed' woman, and which is unable to suppress the notion of the female saint-within-the-world, itself prevalent in the practice and reality of late medieval lay piety.

Undoubtedly, this is the fluid marriage revealed in the fissures inherent in accounts of the life of Mary of Bethany, known in hagiographical stories as Mary Magdalene, as well as in Chaucer's *The Man of Law's Tale*. The former remains human and holy, retaining her relationships with her sister Martha and brother Lazarus, influencing a Christian community of exiles and a pagan one with her preaching in Marseilles, as well as establishing a mutuality of love with the humanised Christ. Custance, as already seen, manipulates her worldly identities in a manner which undercuts the helpless passivity emphasised by her narrator, using her own child to prepare her re-entry into the familial, patri- archal world which constructs her. Custance moves from marginalisation and returns to her 'proper' place; speaking from within patriarchy, her voiced awareness of its laws inflicts disruption. She ensures that her father recalls his paternal obligations:

> 'Fader,' she seyde, 'thy wrecched child Custance,
> Thy yonge doghter fostred up so softe,
> And ye, my mooder, my soverayn plesance
> Over alle thyng, out-taken Crist on-lofte,
> Custance youre child hire recomandeth ofte
> Unto youre grace, for I shal to Surrye,
> Ne shal I nevere seen yow moore with ye'
> [*11(B¹)*, 274–80].

Later in the tale, her 'new' self intending to place itself back under her father's protection, she greets him using 'fader' three times in the space of seven lines, determined to identify herself as his daughter, though this is only one identity amongst many [1105–11]. As already indicated, even the shape of this tale, masculine on the surface, remains circular, beginning and ending in Rome, and moving through a series of exchanges as daughter – to bride – to exile – to wife and mother – to exile – and back to wife, mother, and daughter; in this subverting femininity, the tale is fluid, closed yet not closed.

Other tales assert patriarchal law under the guise of a paganism only apparently softened by the adoption of holiness. The cruel, violent tyranny marking these texts ensures a horrified pity for its saintly subjects. However, the paradox is that what pagan men inflict upon their daughters is representative of the patriarchal world itself. Thus, female response to such violence indicates more than holy worth, and its fissure remains an important site of disruption.

Christine's father encloses her in a tower where, seated at the window and with Christ in her heart, she contemplates the cosmos [*LHW*, 59; 61]. As seen, the window itself represents her sexuality, is a site of potential joy, and is implicated in a notion of identity. Christine insists that her father no longer term her 'daughter'. In response, she is beaten, imprisoned, and brought to trial with the threat of being disowned by her father for he is patriarchal in every sense, is both her father and the provost. She smashes his idols, and throws them out of the window [64]. Consequently, her maidens are beheaded before her eyes, and made to mouth patriarchal law in declaration of an innocence which acknowledges their status as victims in a world where the father has 'dominacioun' [65]. Refusing to sacrifice and so assuage her father's sorrow, as well as accept his right to obedience [66], she is tortured, during which she throws a piece of her own flesh into his face declaring 'Haue of þine own' [68], 'take the flesh, which thou hast gotten, and eat it' [*GL*, vol. 4, 95]. In this admirable embrace of Christianity, Christine the woman also declares her abhorrence of patriarchal law. The body which man 'hast gotten' is reappropriated and reinscribed as she takes her own flesh, and, in one defiant gesture, denies the father's claims upon it.

Barbara, similarly, asserts a sense of self which goes beyond a repudiation of the pagan, and becomes a rejection of an identity imposed upon her by the masculine world. She, too, is enclosed in a tower by her father, but leaves it for an unspecified period when he goes abroad [*GL*, vol. 6, 200]. She oversees the building of a fountain originally commissioned by her father, insisting upon a third window to represent the Trinity [200] and possibly the alterity of her feminine self. Returning to the tower, she worships Christ, scratching off the faces carved upon the pagan idols scattered around her room [201], obliterating imposition of an identity defining her as man's other.

Sometimes the relationship between male and female achieves a more overtly positive identification. Alla's acknowledgement to maternal debt in *The Man of Law's Tale* has already been discussed.[39] Anne's human face is glimpsed in a mutuality with Joachim which is an *exemplum* of the holiness of marriage, and yet sounds a personal note of grief. The pair are united not only in wedlock but by the shame of their twenty-year childlessness. Publicly humiliated in the temple where he is informed that the scriptures curse those who are barren, Joachim flees into the wilderness [*LHW*, 46–7]. Anne's inconsolable tears are partially provoked by the words of an insolent maid reminding her,

> 'Thow god thy wombe wyth bareynesse
> Hath shet, & thyn husbonde takyn a-wey,'

while Joachim tells the angel,

> 'I wante þe argumentes of a man;
> & whan men be reknyd I am lefth behynde' [50].

The text recalls that patriarchal and theological law demand fruit from the blessed union of marriage. The unnaturalness of their childless state is emphasised by the natural simplicity of details such as Anne's watching of a sparrow feeding its young [48], and Joachim's description of his vain labour, in spite of his care to tend daily his fields and orchards, or to avoid sowing in gravel [50–1]. Similarly, neither are full participants in society. Joachim spends five months on its fringes in the wilderness, while Anne retires to her chamber. Yet though Joachim outlines his personal failure, there is an indication of the reciprocity of love as he declares his affection for Anne [50]. She, frantic at his disappearance, prays for his return, and, when her prayers are answered, rushes to the city gates to greet him [54]. Those same natural images utilised by the narrator to uphold a divine as well as a social order, speak, too, of human pain.

A similar intent is at work in the life of Elizabeth of Hungary whose implacably virtuous face is only humanised by the reciprocity of her marital alliance. Prevented from displaying his own beliefs, her high-ranking husband gave 'full power to his wife' to effect whatever might be necessary for the good of both their souls [*GL*, vol. 6, 219]. He grants her a small pension, while she submits to the will of her confessor only 'by the consenting of her husband' [217], the narrative voice approving wifely as well as saintly obedience. In return, her husband is spared public and social humiliation.

Elizabeth also influences his decision to embark upon a crusade, a point at which Bokenham asserts the divine *exemplum* contained within. She repeats the narrator's words, declaring herself ready to surrender her husband to Christ. Yet their private love continues to surface, its extent known only to themselves and God [*LHW*, 275]. Later she prays for the return of his body, reminding God of her earthly love, whilst the return of his bones ensures that 'Inwardly in hert she was ful glad' [278], an image more usually associated with a secret Christianity.

In these examples, a reciprocal relationship between a man and a woman is equated with the divine, following the example of Mary Magdalene and Christ. Wifely obedience also confirms patriarchal law, and marital harmony matches both a scriptural portrait of fruitful union and an historical, lay movement towards the practice of married saintliness. However, both Custance and Elizabeth are able to manipulate the protection afforded by their married status. Custance's role as wife and mother ultimately ensures her place in society, despite her status as outsider, while fidelity to her late husband's corpse ensures that Elizabeth successfully evades a remarriage which might hinder her vocation [279].

However, it is in the complex relationships between mothers and their children, especially daughters, that the concept of a fissured text most fully reveals itself. The privileged space of maternity stems from the *exemplum* of the Virgin Mary, vessel of seed, Word, and Law, chosen by the divine to nurture the human Christ who is conceived without lust, and born without pain [*MF*, 109]. Images of the unborn child chosen by God or maternal devotion are frequent in all hagiography. Examples are almost too numerous to quote. St John's mother follows him to Rome fearing his death [148]. St Dunstan's pregnant mother, in church on Candlemas Day when all candles are suddenly extinguished, has hers relit by heaven [60]. Clare's mother hears a voice declaring the chosen grace of her unborn child [*GL*, vol. 6, 161]. Yet this privileged space remains a double-edged sword.

Katherine's arrival after many years to aged, childless parents permits the narrator to make explicit reference to her sanctity in a series of biblical precedents such as Abraham and Sarah, Joachim and Anne [*LKA*, 28]. Capgrave cannot resist highlighting clerical teaching in confirmation of masculine law that, though the maternal space is a legitimised one, the pains of childbirth are holy penance for the sins of Eve inherited and transmitted by all women. He writes of Katherine's mother,

> But þe tyme is come, sche be-gynnyth to grone
> Cryeth & wayleth as do all women –
> ffor of þat penaunce was mary a-lone
> Excused, & nomoo, þus our bokes ken
> Which þat wer wretyn of ful holy men [28].

Typically, it is man's word which is definitive even concerning an activity naturally denied to him. Restricting and restrictive, maternity becomes yet another area of patronisation, a space actually denied to men but immediately appropriated and reinscribed.

In consequence, many hagiographical texts portray mothers acting as agents of patriarchal law against their own daughters, as well as female saints repudiating their mothers. Generally, the appearance of the mother is rare, itself a telling omission, but what it affirms is masculine destruction of a natural bond between women, an insistence that they ally themselves either with men against their own sex, or with the divine.[40] Both refuse to acknowledge maternal debt. Similarly, appeals to the female saint are stereotypically feminine, involving pathetic weeping or renting of clothes, for the mother's response is not to her daughter but to a masculinised aggressor, the saint. Thus, the existence of a genuine reciprocal relationship between mother and daughter is largely suppressed.

This is seen when the pressure on Katherine to marry is both political and familial, and her initial deflection of it leaves her mother angry [*GL*, vol. 7, 7]. She criticises Katherine's learning, and an answer declaring her potential love for Christ. Capgrave agrees, confirming the role of her mother as man's agent, in

> To lyue a-lone in stody, it was neuer seyn
> That ony lady ony tyme dyd so [*LKA*, 74].

In fact, the petition urging marriage arrives with her mother's permission. A tradition of female obedience is asserted alongside a false, masculine notion of female community in the declarations 'Much sorrow be ye like to do me and all yours' [*GL*, vol. 7, 7; *SM*, 73], and 'daughter, leave this folly, and do as your noble elders have done before you' [8; *SM*, 73].

All reasons offered in support of marriage focus upon the vulnerability of the female, and her apparently natural maternal instinct [*LKA*, 100–40], reasons affirming the necessity of patriarchal protection, and the privileged status afforded to the provider of heirs. Katherine's persistent denial of these claims ensures that her mother finally appeals to her uncle, bringing down the full weight of patriarchal law [140–3].

Completely omitted in any version is Katherine's reaction to her mother's death, which occurs during her 'absence' in the desert. Capgrave simply records the fact of her maternal loss [258]. Though both Katherine and her mother weep upon the death of her father [44], there is no emotional response on this occasion for the mother is merely an adjunct of patriarchal law, prompting the finality of Katherine's defection to her new, holy family.

The role of Christine's mother is, similarly, one of agent. She visits her imprisoned daughter, lamenting, tearing her clothes, crying, 'My daughter Christine, the light of my eyes, have pity on me' [*GL*, vol. 4, 94]. She recounts how Christine was carried in her womb for ten months and the torment of her labour. What is most significant, however, is her insistence upon the use of the term 'daughter', which occurs thirteen times in the space of eight lines in Bokenham's account [*LHW*, 66]. Christine is a patriarchal possession with no identity other than that of 'daughter', or, later, 'saint'. The label is firmly rejected, and, on trial, Christine declares that it is God who has given her her name, not her parents, for 'My name I haue of cryst my creatour' [67].

The saint's aggressive and anti-social behaviour is permitted because the pagan family is exchanged for a Christian one. What is simultaneously affirmed, however, is a refusal to acknowledge the debt owed to the maternal for, as suggested by the male hagiographer, it is paternity which is crucial; God or man is the creator and not woman. Even where a maternal bond is delineated in these texts, it is subsumed to the holy. The special relationship between Lucy and her mother is permitted by male writers of her story because the cure prompting her mother's conversion is effected by divine, holy healing powers. At the same time, the main fissure in the tale, occurring when Lucy and her mother dispense her patrimony, is a transgression quickly elided in favour of details of the martyrdom it prompts.

Masculine fear of emotional bonds between women, or between mother and child, is a phallocentric and egotistical one. Its power is defused by rendering it a simple, holy bond. Thus, the story of Juliet and her son Quirine is privileged by holiness, its essential horror emphasised by the purity of the Madonna icon, of the image of the vulnerable child cradled in Juliet's arms as she is called before the provost. Even her child is holy for he 'gave his cries consonant unto his mother as he should have said: And I am also christian' [*GL*, vol. 3, 225].

Mother and son reject paganism in the shape of the provost, and it is this religious valency which the text asserts.

At the same time, the provost remains a representative of masculine law, and it is within this fissure that the boy-child commits the ultimate transgression by refusing to accept his rightful place in the symbolic. The provost takes the child from Juliet, attempting to kiss him when he cries. Quirine turns away his head, scratches the face of the provost, and bites at him in a rejection of his own, masculine identity. In return, the provost demonstrates his power by throwing down the baby so that 'the tender brain fell abroad out of his head upon the steps' [225]. In another version, the child speaks in defence of the faith, and mother and child are dismembered, the pieces scattered far and wide [226].

The portrayal of Griselda in *The Clerk's Tale* is a highly problematical one. In particular, it is her approach to motherhood that many modern readers find especially abhorrent.[41] Detailed examination of her response to Walter's apparent murder of their children indicates a far from simplistic picture.

Griselda's first child is taken whilst she is still breast feeding [*IV(E)*, 450]. Her husband's withdrawal of her children strikes at the very heart of womanhood, and exemplifies not only an exercise of personal power but a manipulation of a privilege, maternity, controlled by the male. She accepts his dominance declaring that both she and her child belong to him to do with as he wishes [502]. Similarly, she is obliged to surrender her second child, Walter's son and heir; here, she is blamed for tainting the line with her peasant blood [625–37]. These forcible removals symbolise the loss that is woman's when her children repudiate her in order to enter the symbolic.

The narrational response to this loss is to underscore its pathos, to call attention to Griselda's imagined distress as the sergeant demands her children. Her patient acceptance of her trials [537–9; 676–9] is indicative of her holiness. The clerk's interjection at these points is almost redundant, and conceals an important ambiguity. He declares, 'Allas! Hir doghter that she loved so' [543], and

> I trowe that to a norice in this cas
> It had been hard this reuthe for to se;
> Wel myghte a mooder thanne had cryd 'allas!' [561–3].

Later too, he specifically asks women what more a husband might choose as a test, knowing that, next to himself, a woman loves her children best [694–700].

This explicit pathos loudly proclaims either the clerk's patronising, chivalric stance or his compassion; both conceal the fact that this is a tale confirming patriarchal law. Beneath a surface sympathy, it incites a fear that the proclaimed power of maternal love hides a fundamental flaw in women constructed by patriarchy. Just as Griselda obediently surrenders her children to infanticide, the mother hands over her children to the father, severing the maternal bond and depriving them of her body. Thus, Walter's cruelty is inverted to become a symbol of protection. Although he initiates the loss,

Griselda's feminine weakness permits a murder which only he has the power to suspend. She even apparently denies the bond, declaring that she has received nothing but sickness, followed by woe and pain [649–52]. In this way masculine fear of the death drive is displaced, and projected onto the female.

The textual ambiguity is compounded by Griselda's response to this loss. The narrator details how she kisses her daughter, lulls her, declaring how she dies for her sake, just as Christ died for all. This allusion to redemptive love, together with the Madonna-like image of the child in her arms, affirms Griselda's saintly qualities, exactly as the narrative intends. Yet, those same details are utilised by a human Griselda to provoke compassion in the sergeant and ensure compliance with her request for a careful burial.

Thus, she calls attention to the vulnerability of her baby in a way which undercuts the clerk's use of pathos, for it inadvertently reveals a paradoxical strength as Griselda imposes upon others her will. Her child's vulnerability is emphasised in the repetition of 'litel' [559; 567; 571] while her request to the sergeant contains an implicit challenge confirmed by her additional comment, unless 'my lord forbad yow' [570]. Here her subservience accepts and confirms the power of patriarchal law, but also manipulates it from within.[42]

Griselda's maternity is far from monstrous. The ending of the tale reveals the depth of a maternal bond which insinuates itself into the text as an example of that which cannot be broken, despite lengthy separation. Gathering up her children in her arms, she weeps 'ful lyk a mooder', and pours out endearments [1082–97]. What is revealed is not the easy option of the happy ending narrated by the clerk but the personal cost to the female of such implacable emotional control. The tale is fully inscribed by patriarchy as the exchange motif is asserted; Janicula surrenders Griselda to Walter who repudiates her in favour of a sham marriage to his own daughter.

Though the daughter replaces the mother, there is no rivalry between them, and, though Griselda surrenders her children, she is not blamed by them for their loss. In this way, the clerk's narration accidentally fractures expectations, and in that dislocated space the feminine might speak itself differently. The privilege of maternity might be bestowed or withdrawn but it cannot be shattered. Griselda's children remain indebted to her, not to Walter, and confirm the power she publicly asserts when she reminds Walter that she is the mother of his children, creator of his heirs, asking for a smock to cover

'. . . the wombe of here
That was youre wyf' [887].

The man of law's narrational intention is similarly undercut by Custance's fragmentation of the patrilinear, as seen earlier. Once again, a male narrator highlights the pathos of the subdued, meek mother praying to the Madonna, child in her arms as she prepares for exile. Custance lulls her child, prays, covers his head, and cries 'O litel child, allas! what is thy gilt' [11 (B¹), 855]. She unsuccessfully attempts to persuade the constable to care for Maurice, before turning to the gathered crowd with words confirming her own passive place but also asserting the significance of that place as mother of Alla's heir. She demands that the constable kiss Maurice goodbye 'in his fadres name!' [861] and declares 'farewel, housbounde routhelees!' [863].[43]

Another disruptive text is the story of Mary Magdalene, whose intercession provides the Saracen prince and his wife with an heir. As a result, the prince makes a pilgrimage to Rome in order to benefit from the teachings of St Peter. When his pregnant wife insists upon accompanying him, her transgression is punished by a storm at sea. Her resulting early labour ensures her death. Her body, together with her newborn baby, is placed beneath a hanging rock upon a nearby island, a place to which the prince returns after two years only to find wife and child alive.

Several strands interweave in this section of Magdalene's *vita*. Accounts largely confirm her sanctity, her intercessory role akin to that of the Virgin Mary. The prince even prays for her help when his wife dies, as well as upon his return to the island [*LHW*, 164; *MF*, 205–7; *ESEL*, 471–6; *GL*, vol. 4, 78–82]. Similarly, Magdalene's role as spiritual or surrogate mother is an important theological concept. While the prince is taken on his pilgrimage, Magdalene leads his wife on a corresponding journey, a pilgrimage of the mind [*LHW*, 167]. The rocky location echoes the solitary barrenness of the desert mothers, while the iconography of the Madonna is evoked as the child creeps beneath his mother's mantle, 'sucking his mother's breast' [*GL*, vol. 4, 81].

The question of how mother and child survive is ignored, but there are indications that it is due to Magdalene's worldly activity on their behalf. Two tales record how the Saracen couple leave 'all their things in the keeping of Mary Magdalene' [79]. Trusted by royalty, it is no surprise that she was able to reach the outlying island, where, the princess insists, Magdalene fed them [*ESEL*, 476], acted as 'min hou(s) wif: mi mayde and mi norice' [474; *LHW*, 167; *GL*, vol. 4, 82].

Interestingly, though all versions emphasise the husband's sorrow, his patient fortitude, and his acquisition of knowledge, the subtext traces a line of female transmission running alongside the patrilinear dissemination asserted by the main narrative. Magdalene effects the Saracens' conversion by twice appearing in a dream-vision to the wife. It is her words which translate the meaning of the prince's dream [469; *LHW*, 159]. With Magdalene's help, the princess survives on the island without husband or kin. The rocky island itself, surrounded by a circle of sea, is transformed into a motif of independence and survival, an exterior location to which the woman is banished. Its effect is a disruptive one.

Magdalene's surrogate motherhood, part of her spiritual valency, is lauded by male writers who permit the partial expression of a maternal instinct. (As a former whore, she is allowed no children of her own, but what is perceived by men as an inherent element of her femininity is allowed expression via this alternative route.) What is not recognised is the unarticulated independence of those exiled women who feed themselves and their 'children', a selfhood which shines through the blank spaces in the text.

Notes

1 Hermann 1981: 169.
2 ibid. 169.
3 Whitford 1991: 162.
4 le Goff 1986: 86–93.
5 A subsequent chapter explores this notion in connection with the body but it might be useful to note here Sarah Beckwith's idea that the inherent paradox in any worship of Christ's body is that it was both closed, exclusive and open, inclusive. Similarly, skin covering that body marked with wounds, may be interpreted as both inside and outside. See Beckwith 1993: especially 44; 61–2.
6 Of particular importance in this area is Linda Georgianna's discussion (1981: 5–6; 33–4; 50–9; 142). Similarly, Wogan-Browne 1994b: 24–52 but especially 27–31.
7 Erik Erikson speaks of a positive identity for woman based upon possession of the womb, both literally and symbolically. He argues that this 'space' is completed only by motherhood. For further discussion see Doyle 1974: 15–40, especially 25–8.
8 Moi 1986: 242.
9 ibid. 244.
10 Lomas describes how the false self develops as a result of oppression or damage to the true self, or innate potential. In order to survive, an apparently adequate false self is constructed until an opportunity to reveal the true self is afforded. Often, this never happens and the subject continues to avoid, deny, reject, or displace, or may seek out alternative experiences in order to make sense of a chosen falseness. An apparently meaningful life might thus be sterile, empty, false. See Lomas 1973: particularly 93–103.
11 Simmons 1878: 51.
12 Hodgson 1944: 1ii–1v.
13 Gilson 1940: 93. More generally, see 70–93.
14 Grosz 1990: 173–4.
15 See Bynum 1991: 27–52; quotation from 49.
16 Georgianna describes the aim of the *Ancrene Wisse* as 'The continuity of internal and external experience' (1981: 142).
17 Petroff 1994. See chap. 2: 25–50, especially 26.
18 When Zosimus first sees Mary of Egypt, he perceives the shadow of a foul person before recognising her as a naked, sunburnt woman prostrate upon the earth (*ESEL*, 143–4).
19 Gilmartin (1979) examines the ways in which clothing functions as a symbol of knowledge in the tale. Walter is deceived by Griselda's clothing which he perceives as a status symbol rather than as a mark of her constancy. In the scene where Griselda asks for a smock to cover her nakedness, the symbol is confused, she argues, so that the request indicates Griselda's fear that she has 'lost' her old self. Wearing her old rags whilst preparing the palace for a new bride signals her final submission to Walter. Whilst interesting, this exploration neglects to perceive that clothing totally deceives Walter, for its symbol is of Griselda's unchanging self.
20 For a similar reading of this incident see Hansen 1992: 192–4.
21 For further exploration of this see Wogan-Browne 1994: especially 179.
22 See Wogan-Browne 1994: 169; 171, for a lucid explanation of the function of this symbol in virgin martyrology.
23 The version in Caxton records that she 'always bare in her breast the gospel hid' [*GL*, vol. 6, 247], whilst during her wedding she sings 'in her heart only to God' [248] or 'To God allone in herte' [*VIII(G)*, 132–40]. Bokenham tells how 'in hyr brest she bare pryuyly/Crystys gospel wyth al hyr myht' [*LHW*, 203] or else sang 'couertly in hyr inward mynde' [203].

24 Raymond of Capua, trans. G. Lamb 1960: 43.

25 ibid.: 77.

26 See Wogan-Browne 1994: 166–9.

27 Kristeva argues that the state is similar to that of abjection, for it is here that woman is both subject and object, identity undefined, and even undermined. See Grosz 1989: 78–82.

28 For Irigaray, the chora is only occupied by women. See Grosz 1990: 173.

29 Many critics have traced the problematical relationship between the ideal of the Madonna and women's experience, not only of motherhood, but of worldly, masculine expectations. See Grosz 1989: 79–85 and Moi 1986: 205–7. A full discussion is offered in Kristeva's influential essay 'Stabat Mater' (1986c) which exposes the paradoxes of the myth. Also useful is Grosz 1989: 120–6, which outlines Irigaray's thoughts upon the subject, and – more generally – Bynum 1984 and Warner 1976.

30 For a delineation of the uses of this imagery, as well as a critical exploration of it, see Heffernan 1988: 189–92, and Bynum 1992: 151–80. Also useful is Bynum 1984 cited previously. A challenging interpretation is by Jill Mann (1991: 182–94), who argues, erroneously in my opinion, that Chaucer integrated both passive and active into one human ideal within which masculine and feminine gender roles were erased. Such a radical suggestion is unsupported throughout Chaucer's work generally, and pays no attention to his frequent use of irony.

31 This humanisation of Christ particularly colours the works of the female mystic Julian of Norwich, and is conveyed through her sensuous and naturalistic writing, full of images of childbirth. The body is especially stressed as part of the intimate relationship between self and God. For further discussion see Tarjei Park 1992: 17–38. Also of interest is the affectivity witnessed in the account of Margery Kempe's life. She weeps as though she is Christ's mother, endures a ghostly, holy labour, sheds tears when she sees male children, and generally considers herself part of an alternative, holy family. Perhaps the best of the extensive work in this area is Beckwith 1986: 34–58, but especially 46–51. Also extremely useful is Lochrie 1991. See too Atkinson 1983.

32 See Whitford 1991: 114–17; 123. Also Kristeva's 'Stabat Mater' 1986c.

33 See Irigaray 1993: 15–22. Also Irigaray 1991: 123–31; 143–4; 151–2; 157–8; 161.

34 See Grosz 1990: 150–3, Irigaray 1993: 46–50, Kristeva 1986: 138–40; 204–5, Whitford 1991: 87; 105–13. Whitford discusses the effect of the Platonic ideal of the cave which ensures that engendering is viewed as a paternal task, the mother merely replicating a reality that is masculine. See also ibid.: 114–17; 142–3; 161.

35 Further details may be found in Grosz 1990: 150–3, Kristeva 1986: 138–40; 180–3; 204–5, and Whitford 1991: 160–1; 76–80; 182. See also Irigaray's discussion of the mother/daughter dislocation and separated women explored via classical mythology in Irigaray 1991: 100–8; 112; 116.

36 Stockton 1994: 50–1.

37 For Irigaray, any reinterpretation of philosophical or cultural material, including literature, might aid the redefinition of women in the symbolic. She remains especially concerned with the concept of the divine, however, which, she argues, provides a space within which women might meet. She quotes the prevalence of late medieval female mystics as an example. See Whitford 1991: 76; 50–1.

38 Heffernan 1988: 230. Also 188.

39 Not only does he recognise his beloved Custance in the face of his son, but earlier, his choice of alien and alienated bride is affirmed by his refusal to reject a child described by his mother as a monster [*11 (B¹)*, 1. 764–7]. When, unknown to him, Custance is exiled, he searches for her night and day, declaring his sorrow and adding, almost as an afterthought, 'and for his child also' [897]. Such details fragment a surface intention to confirm Custance's holy worth.

40 Particularly illuminating in this respect is Chaucer's *The Man of Law's Tale* where Custance's own mother scarcely exists and her mothers-in-law both work to exile her. Many critics argue that the latter are defeminised, adopting male modes of behaviour, participating in a masculine world yet denying their gender. Carolyn Dinshaw (1989: 103–5) suggests that the jealousy exhibited by these women is a manifestation of 'potentially incestuous desires of mothers for their sons'. Eugene Clasby (1979) denounces them as false mothers in contrast to Custance as true. Stephen Manning (1979) adopts a similar stance. Jill Mann (1991) sees them as instruments of the devil, whose power, together with male power, is illusory. In seeking to protect the purity of the line from Custance's foreign and Christian taint, these women, of course, act in a masculine manner. However, their response as women to Custance has been ignored. It seems to me that they are perfect examples of a female failure to accommodate each other or relate to each other as women rather than mothers and rivals, an inevitable result of both patriarchy's system of female exchange and its idealisation of a maternal which only 'exists' as an adjunct to a superior, patrilinear society.

41 David Aers, for example, suggests that Griselda makes no protest against the murder of her children, an assertion that I contest both here and in a subsequent chapter. He argues that she totally surrenders moral and religious responsibility to Walter whom she equates with the divine. His reading of the tale as political, concerning the dangers of absolutism, reduces its subtleties. See Aers 1980: 169–71. Jill Mann notes modern repugnance as Griselda acquiesces in the 'murder' of her children and unprotestingly (again, I take issue with this) allows her own subjection. For her, however, Griselda's passivity is the paradoxical strength of patience which unifies human and divine suffering, even accepts the pains of childbirth and the loss of her children. She argues that for Chaucer, 'The suffering of childbirth is the mirror in which divine patience is reflected.' See Mann 1991: especially 146–52; 163–4; quotation from 164.

42 A similar pattern occurs when she loses her second child. Again, Griselda requests that 'Hir litel sone' is buried where 'His tendre lymes' are protected against wild beasts [*IV(E)*, 681–2].

43 It might be argued that the privileged space of maternity is even suggested in the shape of the verses depicting the silence of Custance's chamber as she awaits Maurice's birth:

> So longe is goon with child, til that stille
> She halt hire chambre, abidyng Cristes wille.

> The tyme is come a knave child she beer [*II(B¹)*, 720–22].

Jill Mann (1991: 162) argues that this textual space is representative of the quiet space where the self is subordinated to the workings of nature. I would suggest that, on the contrary, this blankness echoes the role of woman as a void, as other, a role which remains despite the legitimisation of her maternity. It is a blank space from within which an alternative voice speaks, fragmenting the surface text and the symbolic it represents.

3 Articulating an identity

Speech, silence, and self-disclosure

The question of how language underpins, rather than simply reflects, our perception of the world finds expression in two main areas. The first is a focus upon speech and silence, and, in particular, raises the spectre of women's possible exclusion from certain styles of discourse. The second, largely covered earlier, concerns classification and representation, an integral part of the means by which gender is constructed. The primary concern of this chapter is how to search for an authentic feminine voice within the masculine tradition of hagiography.

A medieval ideal of the silent female was reinforced by a variety of theological and patristic texts. The first Epistle of Timothy, for example, commands, 'Let a woman learn in silence with all submissiveness. I permit no woman to teach or to have authority over men; she is to keep silent' (1 Timothy 2: 11–12). Similarly St Paul urges, 'Let your women keep silence in the churches; for it is not permitted unto them to speak' (1 Corinthians 14: 34).[1]

Public, authoritative speech was, thus, generally denied to women, nor were they permitted an active preaching role. A talkative woman was equated with a threatening sexuality when what was preferred was full integrity, a virginal body unbreached in every way. The *Ancrene Wisse* permitted its anchorites conversation only with their servants, and the sharing of 'edifying stories' or communication when ill or depressed. Expressly forbidden was discussion with men, idle gossip, laughter, jokes, or singing and talking 'in a worldly manner'.[2] At the same time, however, studies of medieval female mystics suggest that their status as visionaries permitted a public voice even where it was mediated or sanctioned by the male. Similarly the rhetoric of male hagiographers masks, but cannot fully deny, the transgressive behaviour of the female saint who often breaks the bounds of propriety by becoming a visible, speaking leader or teacher, albeit expressing divine rather than personal authority.[3] The speaking 'I' of female hagiographical texts effectively belongs both to the writer and to God. The feminine voice itself appears absent or else is silenced. However, closer analysis suggests that this picture is an incomplete one, that silence itself is far less prevalent than might be expected, and may well have been an instrument of power rather than an articulation of powerlessness.

French feminism's premise is that there exists nothing that is not defined by masculinist assumption. A lengthy patriarchal history of philosophy, literature, politics, and the law is articulated by and through the male. This universality ensures that 'The world is man's word. Man is the word of the world.'[4] As a result, all female experience is 'spoken' by men in a particular style of language which presents the 'truth' about women.[5]

French feminists offer several ways to restate this position, and disrupt its univocality. One possibility is to search for hidden voices, listen to 'the unspoken in all discourse', and discover what is repressed or incomprehensible.[6] Kristeva also advocates that women speak and act within patriarchy in order to access it from the inside, in a *different* way.[7] Whilst resisting a definitive notion of 'woman', Irigaray argues for the need to use traditional definitions of her as a lack or absence in discourse in order to exceed or disturb it. It seems that if a feminine voice or discourse is 'to be received as anything other than incomprehensible chatter, she must copy male discourse. The feminine can thus only be read in the blank spaces between the signs and lines of her own mimicry.'[8]

Thus this chapter explores the ways in which women articulate their experiences, through speech, silence, or alternative means of communication, searching for that which lies beneath and between masculine 'truth' or discourse. There is a complex and shifting process at work in female saints' lives. Overshadowing an apparent ideal of silence and meekness is the aggressive, public stance of virgin martyrology. Recent linguistic research suggests that it is possible to identify socially constructed styles of discourse, where feminine speech tends to be cooperative, turn-taking, designed to ensure progressive conversation. In contrast, masculine style is competitive, interruptive, controlling the speech of others by the use of questions or the imposition of silences.[9]

This division is broadly equivalent to French feminist notions of feminine discourse as elliptical, fragmented, open-ended, attempting to articulate drives, pulsions, sensations, even non-language, or what Kristeva terms the split between the symbolic (masculine) and the semiotic. The contrast is, in fact, less crude than it might appear. As indicated earlier, most French feminists resist the idea that feminine discourse 'speaks' a universal 'woman'. Equally, whilst men and women may tend to use the symbolic and the semiotic in different ways, ideally the two will be combined.[10]

What is clear, however, is the reductive nature of the surface text of most female hagiography. The climactic, adversarial debate of virgin martyrology with its stylised and masculinised speech indicates the process by which biographer is also ventriloquist. Male writers allocate words which, they claim, are also divinely inspired, and, thus, render visible a saintly subject who is reduced to a lifeless, patriarchal doll. Yet, concealed within the fissured text are other, differently spoken voices, a feminine style recognised by those with the ability to hear it which fragments a carefully imposed univocality.

Speech and silence

One of the features of feminine speech is its use of gossip described by Deborah Jones, in an open-ended study of the oral culture of women's groups, as a singularly 'female cultural event which springs from and perpetuates the restrictions of the female role, but also gives the comfort of validation'.[11] What is interesting is the absence of this widespread female experience in hagiography. Its absence permits the imposition of an idealised, unthreatening, 'sealed' woman as well as confirming a patriarchal code of exchange which fragments and disrupts female groups, promotes feminine rivalry, and hinders the sharing of a collective identity. The female saint surrenders her identity as a woman in order to enter the masculinised arena of sanctity. What hagiography legitimates, however, may well have been different in practice where even the anchorite was not totally isolated, many saints remained in the world, and, even in the cloister, like-minded and supportive others helped to establish a private, collective space and identity.[12]

Hagiographical textual tradition preferred to confirm the second function of gossip, through its delineation of public opinion. This is a social one, an informed source of information maintaining the values and moral codes of a particular group.[13] In this case, the biographer locates his subject in the wider, Christian community and so validates her as saint. At the same time, this goes beyond the holy and imposes a masculine, univocal stamp upon the world.

This simultaneous affirmation of the religious and the patriarchal is, once again, exemplified throughout. As an ideal, it is promulgated by the anonymous translator of Jacques de Vitry's life of Mary of Oignies who spends much of her time in silence after learning that all gossip is displeasing to the Lord, a decision earning her a place in Paradise [*Prosalegenden*, 148]. In contrast, gossip, or public opinion, which affirms the holy worth of the hagiographical subject is permissible. After some initial reluctance, all adore Griselda and proclaim Walter's choice of bride [*IV(E)*, 400–41]. When she is subsequently rejected, everyone weeps for her [897–8] and later, despite a brief interlude of fickleness against which Chaucer's clerk rails [995–1001], she is praised for her dignity as she greets the wedding guests [1016–26].

Public opinion and narratorial voice again speak as one during Custance's tribulations. No-one can believe her guilty of murder [*II(B¹)*, 621–5], and people weep when she is cast adrift [820]. The mother-in-law who attempts to defame her by switching letters in order to justify her expulsion [724–805] is, therefore, a lone voice whose role merely compounds Custance's virtue. Similarly, those who castigate Mary Magdalene are in opposition to the univocality of the divine, for Christ affirms her worth, His merciful welcome to sinners part of the collective ethos of Christian redemption.[14] The saint's holiness is an example to all. Those who witness Faith's torments are converted, crying

'O vnpetousnesse! o vnryhtful
Domys! & o peruers entent!
To us it semyth ryht vnskylful
That þis seruanth of god, þis innocent
Shuld be slayne wyth swych torment' [*LHW*, 102–3].

They speak for all the Christian community as do those converted by Cecilia who declare their belief 'with o voys' [*VIII(G)*, 420], and those who rail against the treatment of Agatha 'Wyth o voys ful loude' [*LHW*, 239]. That this holy univocality is also the voice of patriarchal order is perhaps best exemplified by those merchants who spread the fame of Custance's virtue as part of the process of patrilinear exchange, offering her as a potential bride to the Sultan of Syria (who, incidentally, converts to Christianity), speaking 'The commune voys of every man' [*II(B¹)*, 155].

This combination of male orthodoxy and masculine control of the text is further reinforced by the power of prayer. In the final moments of her life, the saint hears the siren call of the faith with its promise of heavenly immortality in recompense for earthly pain. The miraculous voice of Christ invites His lovers to join Him after martyrdom. Barbara is told to come and rest in heaven [*GL*, vol. 6, 204], and Margaret is urged to be steadfast in torment for Paradise awaits [*MF*, 202]. Christ calls to His 'dere doughtir' Christine [*LHW*, 71], while Dorothy hears 'Come to me, my dear spouse and true virgin' [*GL*, vol. 7, 46] or 'Come loue, come spouse' [*LHW*, 134]. Katherine is told the gate of heaven is wide open to her [*GL*, vol. 7, 25], and invited in [*ESEL*, 100].

The saint's call for heavenly aid is never refused. Margaret describes herself in the following terms:

'I see me lord, as an innocent sheep
Wyth rauennous wuluys enuyround be' [*LHW*, 14],

mouthing the words of a hagiographer determined to emphasise her vulnerable innocence. He details how the dragon which swallows her is killed by her cross bursting in his mouth [20] for it is a Christian voice which speaks through the text. Thus, Dorothy prays for a sign to sustain her, material proof that God exists [132].

Prayer becomes an important validation of the female saint. This textual detail posits woman as a vessel containing the power of the divine. Woman acts as intercessor, first on her own behalf where the fact that she invariably receives God's help demonstrates her worth, and, second, on behalf of others, as a saint, where Word and body are also text. Narratorial praise of the act of praying is lavish. Clare is lauded for the prayers which both convert and ostensibly save her sister, Agnes, from their family's violent wrath [*GL*, vol. 6, 169–71], while, more generally, her prayers are said to be so efficacious that the pope himself relies upon their intercessory powers [172]. Elizabeth of Hungary's praying 'was of so great ardour that she drew others to good living' [224]. At only five years old, on her knees in church, no-one can drag her away [214]. As a child, she prays in secret [*LHW*, 261], while, as a married woman, she forsakes her husband's bed in order to complete her daily quota, ensuring that if exhaustion should overcome her she is awoken by her maid [264–5; *GL*, vol. 6, 2]. The power of Lucy's prayer is sufficient to cure her mother of a long-standing illness [246–7].

Such numerous examples proclaim not only the holiness of these women but the careful imposition of a voice which speaks of one faith, one God. This strong univocality suppresses all evidence of the living, breathing subject of its text. The only identity acknowledged is a saintly one but a manipulation of that *persona* is evident. Closely allied to a privacy which permits direct access to the divine, a potential site of disruption is established.

Bokenham appropriates Anne's discourse and personal thoughts, carefully noting the words of the prayers she makes to God as she begs for relief from her barrenness. As demonstrated in chapter two, however, those same prayers also articulate the strength of human love, and illustrate the depth of her personal loss as she fears herself abandoned by her husband [47–9].

Similarly, Bokenham attempts to speak for Elizabeth of Hungary when she apparently declares to God her love for both Him and her husband:

'Thow knowyst wel, lorde, thow y hym þe lyuynge
Louyd next þe, yet, lord, for þine honoure
I gladly hym wantyd, & wyth-oute wepynge
To Ierusalem I sent hym . . .' [278].

Threatened with remarriage, she reiterates this love, drawing attention to her personal sacrifice, and asking for help in achieving her desire for voluntary poverty. Bokenham notes that her prayers are granted implying that this is due to her saintly and wifely devotion. He fails to realise the full import of his later detailing of the way in which she ensures her continued widowhood; Elizabeth manipulates her holy identity and singular devotion, receiving her husband's corpse and declaring herself faithful to his memory [278–9]. She makes her own independent choices, and defines a personal identity, an alternative to the religious one imposed by her biographer.

Earlier, I explored Custance's subtle manipulation of her own place within patriarchy. In addition, the prayers described by her narrator in an attempt to portray her as a passive victim deserving of compassion, also call attention to the workings of the law, questioning its power to protect instead of oppress. Expelled from Syria, she prays to Christ begging 'Me fro the feend and fro his clawes kepe' [*II(B¹)*, 454]. The man of law indicates that these prayers are answered, carefully expounding a series of biblical precedents such as Daniel, Joseph, and Mary of Egypt, so that, at last, she is safely brought to the Northumberland shore [470–510]. Then, accused of murder, she once again prays for divine aid [638–44], an activity repeated when she is cast adrift for the second time [826–54].

At the same time as her holy and vulnerable innocence is affirmed, Custance's words fracture the text's univocality. Her analogous reference to the 'white Lamb, that hurt was with a spere' [459] both places herself within a framework of redemption and highlights the injustice of a law that condemned the human Christ. She similarly declares her own innocence at her trial by falling upon her knees, and invoking immortal God who saved Susan 'Fro false blame' [640]. She refers back to this when forced to leave Northumberland, stating her trust in a Christ which has already 'me kepte fro the false blame' [827], and asking of her child, and by implication herself, 'What is thy gilt?' [855]. Her words undermine all notions of earthly justice.

A further feature of hagiographical texts is the masculine fear of a female sexuality requiring careful control. Mary of Egypt's combination of beauty and eloquence seduces many, and she is severely chastised for this improper use of 'faire wordes and fol semblaunt' [*ESEL*, 261]. In the *Early South-English Legendary* version of her life, her narrator interrupts to declare it shame for any man to know the extent of the sins he finds written [261]. Mary, herself, supposedly fears to recount her story to Zosimus for 'Thy holy ears should be made foul of my words, and the air should be full and foul of corruption' [*GL*, vol. 3, 107]. This authoritative, textual tradition inserts Mary into a patristic narrative frame, as outlined in chapter one. It also, however, elides her problematical jouissance whose existence is only briefly acknowledged before being heavily criticised. The bridge between what is the written word, or even the Word of God, and what is apparently spoken by the female is her body. The corporeal and the *corpus* are, thus, inextricably intertwined, opening up the possibility of a female reinscription of that body.

The male narrator's immediate problem is how to close that fissure, how to retain control of a speaking 'I' which threatens to assert itself as teacher, preacher, defender of the faith, man's equal. Consequently, all speech is allocated by the biographer, and though often public discourse, it remains closed, its power springing from writer or God. The controlling voice is a masculine one, inter-rupting, appropriating even the most private of utterances, and asserting 'doctryne of scripture whiche wyl not lye' [*LHW*, 41]. It is not only what is said by the female saint that is important but how it is articulated. Thus a narrative pattern is imposed where women, unless attacking paganism, must adopt a meek, unobtrusive style in deference to the masculine 'word', be that spoken, written, patriarchal, or clerical authority.

Lucy's preaching is legitimate for it is made 'with glade heorte' [*ESEL*, 105]. St Clare matches word and deed for all 'she said with her mouth, she did it in her heart, and gave ensample' [*GL*, vol. 6, 174]. Her teaching is conducted in private. She urges her followers to flee worldly noise, and no cloister is more silent or speech more holy than hers. She, herself, often refrains from conver-sation, and so, by example, restrained others [177]. Similarly, Pauline rules her convent under the edict that 'word sounding to any ordure or filth should never issue out of the mouth of a virgin, for by the words outward is showed the countenance of the heart within' [*GL*, vol. 3, 4]. Any criticism or rebuke is delivered 'debonairly' [3]. Pauline is said to strictly enforce this masculine ideal, remaining 'debonair and courteous unto all' [5]. Dorothy's declaration of faith is, in fact, made 'mekely' [*LHW*, 133], while Elizabeth of Hungary's private words to her husband on the eve of his crusade are appropriated by an omniscient Bokenham who insists that she spoke 'ful wummanly' [275].

In contrast, scathing mockery of pagans is entirely permissible; after all, on such occasions the speaking subject is simply mouthing the masculine textual and theological doctrine so integral to her story. Thus, as Faith summarises in the words to her accuser:

'. . . as holy fadrys doctryne doth teche
Noht ellis your goddys but deuyllys be' [101].

A half-dead Lucy preaches from her furnace of the great joy awaiting her, and those like her, in Paradise [*ESEL*, 105]. Agnes repeats similar words as she too remains unharmed in a fire whose flames are extinguished by the power of the Word [184]. Agatha speaks of Christ at length until the Duke begs her to desist [194]. She is tortured in an attempt to demonstrate that 'þou spillest þi breth' [195] but continues to assert the folly of pagan worship [196].

Typically, in her dying moments Margaret's preaching continues unabated, and converts many [*LHW*, 17]. Dorothy not only converts her entire family but reconverts her lapsed sisters whom she rebuked for their attempt to persuade her to renounce the faith, and informed them by so fair and sweet language of the error of their ways [*GL*, vol. 7, 44–5]. Similarly, Christine iterates her belief despite the outcry of her handmaids who fear patriarchal revenge [*LHW*, 61]. She also declares her love of Christ and worship of the Trinity [63]. When tortured, she expounds paganism's lack of power and foretells the miraculous destruction of the city's idols [76–7].

Thus, the female saint's wise lore is legitimated because of its power to convert others. Bokenham, for example, praises the way in which many are brought to true belief by the mediation of Christine [77]. Agnes is a divine vessel, emboldened before the prefect,

. . . inflammyd wyth grace
And strengthyd wyth gostly stedefastnesse [118].

Agatha scorns her provost, and refutes his foolish idolatry [229; 231]. Lucy explains to Pascas that his belief is mere vanity [250–1]. She insists that her words are not folly as he suggests, for, even under torture, 'goddys wurdys shall neuere cees'. As Christ's handmaid, these words stem not from Lucy but from God. She describes her own body as the temple of the Holy Ghost from within which the divine Word emanates [251].

Here, neither woman's own word nor her body has any overt, personal significance. Instead, patriarchal authority speaks through the hagiographer who inscribes the body of his work in every sense. The female saint is permitted the transgression of public discourse for she is the receptacle of the divine. It is God's Word that overcomes, even though male pagan tormentors attempt to silence it by destroying the female body within which it is contained. Hagiography continually asserts the impossibility of this silence. Inscribed by the male writer, the female body becomes text. Its example is amply demonstrated in the story of Dorothy, scorned by Theophilus who demands visual proof of the roses and apples said to flourish in Christ's garden [*GL*, vol. 7, 45]. He witnesses the destruction of her body, but hears Dorothy articulate the Word before she dies. Subsequently, a corporeal presence, a child, brings to him the promised produce. Converted, Theophilus is also martyred, his body torn into tiny pieces and scattered far and wide for animals to devour [46–7]. All that remains is the Word, disseminated through the story of Dorothy's horrific torture and subsequent death.

This same example also contains an important fissure, however. Dorothy prays for the power to aid women in childbirth, that patience might be granted to those giving credence to the story of her life, that the final sacraments might be guaranteed to all who reside in a place where her story is read or heard [46]. Similarly, Margaret's prayers are offered so that all who read or tell of her martyrdom will receive grace, especially women in labour [*LHW*, 23]. Here, a woman speaks to all, but especially to other women, and particularly to the illiterate. Allied to the cult of relics, and the translation of corpses explored in the final chapter, the saint remains both mediator and active subject whose experiences tell their own story, whose suffering body-as-text speaks its own pain.

At the same time, the spoken response granted by the male writer, the dialogue between saint and pagan tormentor, is, in itself, inherently fissured. The framework of such texts dramatises a confrontation between the holy and the heathen, but it is simultaneously a marginalised, vulnerable woman facing the wrath of the powerful representative of patriarchal law. Under torture, the saint's discourse flows as freely as her blood in validation of her holy worth and the might of textual authority. However, her refusal to be silenced also demonstrates a reinscription of feminine experience for those in the audience aware of what is being said.

One particular detail, that of the sword in the throat of the saint, occurs with alarming frequency. Here is not only a pagan's unsuccessful attempt to assert the inadequacy of Christianity, but a violent male response attempting to quell the threat of an articulate woman. The phallic symbol of the sword penetrates and marks the female body as its own, yet that body continues to articulate itself. On the one hand, it speaks the religious univocality imposed by the hagiographer, and, on the other, it represents the unsuppressable chora. As will be seen, its voice is multiple, whether spoken, tears, or a song, for woman speaks herself from within her two lips, from within *any* fissure of her body.

Thus, Agnes is stabbed in the throat but continues to preach [*ESEL*, 184; *LHW*, 126]. Her parents bury her and receive a heavenly vision in which she is entirely whole, leading other maidens into Paradise, and urging that no-one mourn her [*LHW*, 126–7]. Signalling her holiness, the vision also permits a female to speak to and within a community of women even in death. Lucy preaches from her furnace, and is attacked with a sword 'To bi-nimen hire speche: and hire lijf also' [*ESEL*, 105]. Lucy represents subversive sexuality, and is informed that she talks only of corruption, 'as a ribald' [*GL*, vol. 2, 33]. She refuses to be silenced, and so she is stabbed, 'Hyr sone desyryng to confounde' but still 'she kept hyr speche' [*LHW*, 256]. The use of the word 'sone' (sound) even suggests that her actual words remain unimportant; what is profoundly disturbing is the sound of her voice, the inarticulate chora which urges expression and which even violence cannot contain.

Similarly, Christine's seemingly endless series of tortures culminate in the severing of her tongue; she continues to speak, however, and throws her tongue at her accuser, blinding him in one eye [*GL*, vol. 4, 97]. Here it is the body, sexual difference, which fractures the texts and speaks the feminine. Christine refuses to permit her father, who is also her judge, to call her his daughter [*LHW*, 67] in a denial of her familial and patriarchal role as man's lack or absence. In fact, when female onlookers cry out against the cruelty of placing burning coals upon Christine's head, it seems they too inadvertently speak out against the masculine world:

'. . . o juge, þi decre
Is wroung & wrocht ful vnrychtfully,
For in [þis] mayde als mych as in þe
All wommen þou confoundyst utirly' [75–6].

The suggestion that the powerful male ought to protect his vulnerable other, take better care of his property, indicates that the fundamental phallocentricity of the world remains unchallenged. Beneath this, however, lies a small fragmentation for, masculine 'decre', patriarchal law, *is* challenged by Christine's defiant reinscription of her own body. She spits a piece of her tongue at her tormentor, yet continues to preach [84], throws back her body at the male who supposedly engendered it, and refuses to be vanquished by tyranny.

Ultimately, what cannot be silenced is the divine Word. This is emphasised by texts which reiterate 'word' itself, Bokenham, in particular, making this a key part of his vocabulary as will be seen later in discussion of St Katherine. Pascas tells Lucy that her words are foolish and vainly said, for he alone is keeper of the emperor's decree. She refutes this, but, as noted earlier, Pascas insists she speaks as a strumpet [250]. Her words are permitted to defy him [250–1] because God is superior to heathen law, but Lucy's refusal to be silenced, her cry 'lyst what I seye !' [250] equally threatens the patriarchal law of which her provost is representative.

Similarly, Agatha informs her judge that all his words are mere wind, and have no effect upon either the material world or her faith [229]. The provost is angered by her 'veyn cours of wordys slye' [232], but she reiterates that his words are simply folly [238]. As she scorns his heathen philosophy, she simultaneously challenges him as the guardian of all masculine law, and, thus, with the feminine subtext of her hagiographically imposed, saintly words,

. . . she hym vttyrly confoundyd had
Aforn alle folk euene opynly [232].

On other occasions, fragmentation is threatened by a silence or a blank space in the text. Elizabeth of Hungary persuades her husband to embark upon a crusade, an action affirming her sanctity. Bokenham speaks for his subject, telling of her love overshadowed by the more important need of Christian deliverance. His ventriloquism ensures that she 'says',

> '. . . husbonde, I you counsel & preye
> For soule hele forsake not þis trauayle.'

Exactly what passes between subject and spouse in this private interlude, and at what emotional cost, is unknown and ignored in favour of the action's hagiographical valency. Thus, Elizabeth ensures his agreement simply 'thorgh þese wordys & many mo' [274], while the version in Caxton can only note that whatever is said is appropriately feminine, effected 'by debonair admonishments' [*GL*, vol. 6, 220] which are never detailed.

Similarly, Bokenham writes that Dorothy reconverts her sisters without actually quoting her words [*LHW*, 143]. In contrast, he, like many others, records in detail what saints apparently say to provosts, or how other women, acting on behalf of patriarchy, attempt to deflect the holy one's purpose. Any mutuality of relationship or female collaboration or cooperation is swiftly suppressed for its humanity detracts from hagiographical intention.

Other silences are important, particularly those of the penitent saints, enclosed and in masculine disguise. Their lack of speech is part of their lesson of patience, but equally contains a more personal note denied by the text. Theodora's tears are contrite, but she is also said to speak 'within herself' [*GL*, vol. 4, 50]. Of what she speaks remains unarticulated, a blank space only hinted at through a series of demonic temptations inscribing her as sinful [50–1]. There remains a void, and, within this feminine space, a strong element of fear and sorrow, a dislocation of selfhood. Other saints of this group similarly exemplify the holiness of patience but also, as demonstrated in the previous chapter, forge an identity within their own space; their silence is part of that process.

Equally, Custance refuses to declare her identity when she lands in Northumberland, and, again, when rescued by her Roman relatives. Her silence augments her chances of survival in the first instance, and is part of a lack of recognition prompted by her new self in the second. Granted a breathing space, she breaks that silence when and how she chooses. Similarly, Eugenia, accused of lechery, refuses to declare her gender until she judges that the time is ripe [*GL*, vol. 5, 122]. Her decision to speak out finally articulates Eugenia's sense of identity.

Chaucer's Griselda, often viewed as ideally feminine, meek, and subservient, in fact remains silent less often than might be supposed. What she exemplifies is the fluidity between the two states, speech and silence, and its inextricable connection with the notion of identity. Griselda's moments of silence are highly significant. True to her vow of obedience, she says not one word concerning the apparent death of her daughter, never mentions her name either in jest or seriousness [*IV(E)*, 600; 606–9]. Equally, she remains silent at the loss of her son [708–11]. Repudiated by Walter and returned to her father, she dutifully obeys and 'word ne spak she noon' [900]. Neither word nor deed ever showed that she might be offended or humiliated [920–2].

Here within the silence of a blank, textual space is more than Griselda's acquiescent and virtuous worth; here is her pain. It is an emotional trauma articulated only when her children are eventually restored to her, and, even then, only briefly. Griselda pours out words of endearment [1084–98], swoons as she declares the ambiguous, implicitly critical lines awarded her by the clerk,

> '. . . God of his mercy
> And youre benyngne fader tendrely
> Hath doon yow kept –' [1096–8],

before breaking off because the full horror of Walter's action cannot be told. The scene is followed by the narrator's silence, the imposition of his happy ending, and a return to Griselda's hidden self.

Griselda's discourse is similarly ambiguous and subtle, and is inextricably bound with the implacable emotional control explored in the next section. Ideally feminine, she totally accepts Walter's premarital oath of allegiance, vowing never to contradict or rebuke him [351–64], promising to remain always deferential. This oath is apparently wholly accepted despite hints of possible subversion witnessed in public praise of her diplomacy or comments that she is 'fair of eloquence' [410]. However, the cumulative effect of her dutiful and feminine response is to invert its masculine ideal at precisely the same time as it exemplifies it.

Walter's first test of her obedient patience occurs during the loss of her baby daughter. At this point, Griselda reiterates her vow, assuring Walter that both her body and will belong entirely to him [501–11]. Ostensibly acceding to his wishes, she is able to ensure that all responsibility for his actions is placed firmly upon her husband; infanticide is *his* decision. Similarly, when her son is removed, Griselda reminds Walter that she has agreed to do whatever he likes, and her ambiguous words, that her children are slain 'At youre comandement' [649], simultaneously fulfil the narratorial aim of presenting her as holy and patient whilst, again, calling attention to the extremity of Walter's actions. She continues, describing how her marriage has involved the loss of clothing, will, and liberty. She declares her readiness to die if it might please him, adding

> 'Deth may noght make no comparisoun
> Unto youre love' [666–7].

Once more, beneath surface compliance is implicit attention to the unwelcome imposition of his bizarre form of affection.

Details accumulate in a surreptitious and fissured signalling of Griselda's unchanged, and unchanging, 'corage'. Her public rejection is answered at length in apparently meek and courteous tones. She suggests that she is merely his unworthy servant, privileged by his love, having brought to him only her nakedness and maidenhead. Thus, she returns his clothes and prepares to return home with nothing before requesting a smock to cover her belly; here, she reminds the world that she is the mother of Walter's children, mother to the realm's heirs. Two further lines indicate her implicit criticism of her husband, where her smooth words belie the instinctive underlining of the excesses of his appalling behaviour. Griselda describes herself as 'youre wyf though I unworthy weere' [822], and makes implicit comment on the mismatch between Walter's outward demeanour and inner heart in the following:

> '. . . How gentil and how kynde
> Ye semed by youre speche and youre visage' [852–3].

At this point, the narrator demonstrates the lesson of her saintly fortitude and the submissive, wifely obedience due to all husbands. Yet, Griselda's response also calls attention to the two key areas of word and deed, seen in the key word 'contenaunce' and discussed in the next section. What Walter perceives as an opportunity to gain knowledge of the female by a focus upon external signs, Griselda subverts by demonstrating how that same outward patience is confoundingly deceptive.

The pattern reaches its climax when Griselda is called upon to prepare the palace for her replacement, and is asked how she likes her husband's choice of bride. She praises her for her outward appearance, her beauty, but Griselda's words are also a reminder of her own suffering at the hands of the male; she begs that he never torments his new wife as he has her, since

> 'She koude nat adversitee endure
> As koude a povre fostred creature' [1042–3],

words which finally call a halt to Walter's cruelty.

What is also important is that the narrative structure accumulates images and moments as Griselda speaks, that the ambiguity of her allocated discourse fragments an apparent stillness, and that, as will be seen, the motif of patience may well function beyond and differently from its holy symbolism. Chaucer's subtle opening up of perspective in this tale may well have been designed to shatter notions of textual authority, but is unlikely to have contained an awareness of the depths of other fissures.

Certain saints' lives amply demonstrate the subversive power of a fissuring discourse, at once holy and yet an assertion of identity. Judith's transgressive behaviour, arising from her flaunting of her beauty, fine clothes, eloquence and sexual allure in order to defeat Holofernes, is diluted by her representation as divine instrument, agent of God's chosen people, the Israelites, whom she defends against the pagan Assyrians. Thus, she is allowed to speak publicly in criticism of those countrymen preferring to wait in the mountains rather than act in their own defence [*GL*, vol. 2]. Aided by fair words and fair face, Judith is able to penetrate even the private chamber of Holofernes. She informs him that she alone has access to the Word of God which informs her of His anger against the Israelites, and His promise to deliver them up to their enemy. Judith's words are pleasing, and she is revered by all for a wisdom and beauty [87] which also inflames the lust of Holofernes. Invited into his chamber, she kills him, and then returns home to proclaim what she has done [88–9].

Judith's behaviour is laudably saintly, but what is also exemplified is an assertion of female independence. Once again, outward appearance is deceptive. A highly eloquent sexuality is used to manipulate others, especially men who rely on such visual stimuli to gain knowledge. A feminine self is symbolised in the interiority of Holofernes' chamber, Judith's entry into a masculine, private space, where her enemy, the male, is assassinated before she is able to resume her now redefined place in a world which lauds her for she has behaved 'manly' [92]. Validated as saintly because her transgressive behaviour is legitimated by divine inspiration and aid, Judith's story also fractures expectations, for her enemy is male as well as pagan, and her vanquishing of him is reread as a strike against patriarchy.

The story of Mary Magdalene invariably employs a similar narrative framework which is fragmented by the threat of her sexuality. She is described as speaking 'with a glad visage, a discreet tongue' [*GL*, vol. 4, 76], with 'wordes bolde: with briȝht neb and glade chere' [*ESEL*, 468]. She pronounces only

> ...godes word for to preche
> And of godes lawe with gret wit [47],

and through her words many are brought to God, away from sin, away 'Fram lecherie and hore-dom: þoru schrift, to Ioye and all wunne' [466]. Bokenham remarks on her sweet eloquence, adding that this is no surprise from one who has kissed the feet of Christ [*LHW*, 158]. The account in Caxton reiterates the concept of woman as divine vessel, noting her beauty, reason, and eloquence, and adding that it is no surprise that the mouth of one who kissed the feet of Christ 'should be inspired with the word of God more than the other' [*GL*, vol. 4, 76].

Magdalene's heroic individual action, demonstrated in the previous chapter, remains diluted by such references to divine power. In a similar way, she is placed within the confines of the Christian family, named alongside those others exiled with her, St Maximin and many others [76], as well as the priest who hears her story recounted in her own voice 'Lych þe voys of an aungel clere' [*LHW*, 170]. Yet her eloquence speaks out against masculine law, and criticises the Saracen prince for his lack of care for those washed up on his shores [159–60].

Cecilia's fissured story remains extremely interesting. Her efforts to convert her husband ensure that he is brought within the wider Christian community within which she is a leading participant. Valerian's conversion is effected by her careful manipulation of a feminine ideal, and, consequently, she is unfailingly courteous in all versions of her life. She speaks gently, with 'chere demure' [204], calling him 'sweetheart' and 'lover' [*ESEL*, 490–1]. She says, 'O, my best beloved and sweet husband, I have a counsel to tell thee, if so be that thou wilt keep it a secret and swear that ye shall bewray it to no man' [*GL*, vol. 6, 248]. Using the language of patriarchy and speaking from within its centre, she is prepared to share all for 'So gret ioye of oure loue schal be þat no tunge ne may telle' [*ESEL*, 491]. In the powerful, interior space of her chamber, Cecilia asserts her own identity, sharing the religious element of that self with her heathen husband. Though the manner of that sharing is meekly submissive, as befits medieval wife and saint, it is also expedient, for the secret announced is a dangerous one.

Cecilia's awareness of the need to retain her role within the world, utilise its discourse and manipulate its ideals, is similarly demonstrated in the consistently strong focus upon her public visibility as a saint. Undoubtedly, it is a sanctioned holiness which, once again, legitimates her public discourse. She never ceases from prayer or holy talk [*LHW*, 202], and preaches to her brother-in-law of the futility of idolatry [*VIII(G)*, 284–7]. Called before the prefect Almachius, she speaks 'boldely' [319], and scorns his beliefs [449–511; *LHW*, 212–14]. She remains 'ful bisily to preche' [342], and, visiting those imprisoned and awaiting martyrdom, spends the night speaking to them of holy things [*LHW*, 218].

More importantly, yet again, the saint's body becomes text. Though her head is half-severed, Cecilia continues to preach [*VIII(G)*, 5331–9; *ESEL*, 495–6], and her body, inscribed by torture, is a source of holy validation. What is spoken is the Word which is mediated through the vessel of the female body. At the same time, however, that body is reinscribed in a manner fissuring the literary text, for it is also *her* voice, *her* body speaking itself, from within and against patriarchy. Cecilia's defiance is levelled against a male pagan, representative of masculine law. Though her insubordination is a voice conferred by her religious identity, it, nevertheless, remains subversive. Thus, when Valerian is told by the angel to read the scriptural text [*LHW*, 207], to surrender himself to martyrdom in exchange for the Word, it is Cecilia who acts as a driving force, instructing him to go to Urban and to declare to him 'the wordes whiche I to yow tolde' [*VIII(G)*, 180], to repeat 'Wurd for wurd al my sentence' [*LHW*, 206] in order to gain entry into the secret faith.

Patient control: a mimesis

A crucial aspect of late medieval piety was the concept of patient fortitude, and its close ally patient poverty. The anonymous fourteenth-century *Patience* poem transforms the story of Jonah and the Whale into a lesson on the necessity of unquestioning acceptance of God's providential plan, the need to submit and silently accept suffering which brings its own heavenly reward.[15] It recounts how poverty and patience are inextricably linked,[16] as well as encouraging the virtues of pity, penance, meekness, mercy, chastity, and peace.

A wealth of other texts similarly iterate the significance of this admirable trait. Interestingly, such meek submission to tribulation was far less passive than might initially appear. In Langland's *Piers Plowman*, the figure of Patience instructs and guides the dreamer and Activa Vita concerning the true nature of patient poverty, and voluntary submission to the will of God. If patience is a special form of earthly purgatory guaranteeing a place in Paradise, it is also a virtue leading to freedom.[17] In Passus XV of the poem, Patience guides the dreamer and shows how his spiritual food should be the scriptures and other patristic authorities, urging him to eat the text and swallow the Word.[18] Similarly, in Passus XVI, Patience talks to the figure of Free Will advocating patient poverty as the only path to Christ,[19] while Passus XII involves a debate on the nature of poverty.[20]

Patience invokes images of interiority for it is carried 'in thy bosom',[21] but its expression is active and demonstrated through meekness, mildness, and charity. He who has patience,

> Ne neuere hete ne hayl ne hell – pouke hym greue
> Noþer fuyr ne floed, ne be aferd of enemye [22]

for, ultimately, '*Pacientes vincunt*'.[23]

In many respects, however, the representation of patience remains problematical, not least in the *Piers Plowman* text. Though the figure of Patience offers an important spiritual ideal, the tensions created by this remain unresolved in this crucial poem, and, possibly, in life.[24] Whilst the medieval notion of active patience seemed to permit a paradoxical power, the implacable control vital for its practice may well have ensured the further isolation of a saint whose affective piety led to bizarre and extreme forms of behaviour.

My concern is with a patience which not only marks the female saint as holy, but provides an opportunity for the secret nurturing of a hidden, masked self. The concealment of such a personal identity is, at once, protective and confounding, and its practice a mimicry that demonstrates the extent to which the female has learned the rules of a patriarchal world which has constructed her.

The ventriloquism of female hagiography ensures that a frequently masculinised saint participates in adversarial debate. Both her stylised speech and her moments of silence, as already seen, conform to a masculine ideal. Yet, it is that same speech, that silence, and a meek manner of speaking that undermines male power. It passes well beyond the depiction of patience and emotional control as simply holy, and surpasses too an Anglo-American strand of feminism, championed by Elaine Showalter, which depicts the existence of dominant (male) and muted (female) groups, where the latter's style of hesitant, cooperative, less assertive discourse signifies not its difference but a correspondence to its subservient, oppressed social position.[25]

Instead, Irigaray posits the notion of mimesis, an active mimicry based upon the Freudian delineation of the 'hysterical' female whose dysfunctional miming of a passive and seductive femininity, itself defined by the male, is an unconscious response to a patriarchal world which involves a repression of her own sexuality.[26] Irigaray offers the option of remaining close to but inverting this notion of hysteria, so that the female stays in touch with her own body and still confined within a masculine orthodoxy.

This option involves a refusal rather than a repression of heterosexuality.[27] It resists, or refuses, all conformation to masculine expectations. It operates by using a desired passivity in active but covert defiance of masculine law and the female's own social position. Female behaviour apparently reflects all that is ideal but is not reduced by it; it is, instead, a mimicry.[28] What hysterics do unconsciously Irigaray does deliberately, thus disrupting the present system in order to initiate a new one. The result is the opposite of the compliance suggested, and throws back to the world 'what it cannot accept about its own operations'.[29] It is a process also articulated by Kristeva who believes that women are often restricted to the margins of society, are made foreign to themselves. Yet, in this state of both separation and self-knowledge, they are able to keep a vigil, to prevent groups from closing and oppressing, to act, in fact, in a manner similar to that of Irigaray's self-aware hysteric.[30]

Clearly, male hagiographers were not participants in a process of mimesis, whilst, for their female, largely fictional, characters there can be no question of conscious choice. However, 'it is the *political context* of such mimicry that is surely always decisive'.[31] The female saint's life is appropriated by a male writer who operates a controlling textual tradition on behalf of a masculine world. He attempts to annihilate his subject in order to advance her sanctity and retain her transgressions within the reductive framework of his genre. Her patience is, therefore, offered as part of her holy worth. At the same time, his depiction of recognisably feminine behaviour satisfies his audience, and accounts for her female mystique by dissolving the threat of her sometimes silent, interiorised, and confounding response. The paradox is that the saint's behaviour triumphs, and to those who recognise *themselves* in the depiction of her ideal meekness a different truth is spoken. Irigaray's term to describe this self-conscious parody of the ideal is sometimes translated as 'mimeticism'. Here she means 'camouflage' or 'protective colouring', and suggests that women tend to adopt such behaviour in order to deflect the worst excesses of a masculine economy.[32] I would suggest that this is the process at work in the fissures of female hagiography, where the presentation of emotional control has both a surface and an underlying meaning.

Chapter 1 introduced Mirk's depiction of the castle with its walls of patience and chastity, paradigm of ideal and holy femininity, while, later, Griselda's response to Walter 'as a wal' was seen to be an integral part of a more private expression of individuality or identity. Allied too is a concept of *integritas* which extends to the stemming or sealing of natural emotions – talk, joy, laughter, pleasure, pain, sexuality, tears – and their expression. What is not controlled is threatening according to the male world; only divinely inspired emotion seems acceptable.

Saint Faith is praised, for not only is she clean and pure but

Of contenaunce sad and of chere demure,
Neythir in worde nere dede wantoun nere nyce [*LHW*, 99].

Clare teaches her fellow converts to put away all flesh, all emotion [*GL*, vol. 6, 177]. Neither flattery nor terror of pain alters the universal rule of the holy martyr demonstrated in Agnes who, brought before the provost,

... wyth o chere in contenaunce perseuerently
Be-forn hym she stode fresh of coloure [*LHW*, 116].

It is an example taken directly from the Virgin Mary who, at only three years old, is surrendered to the temple, but never cries, 'ne chaunged no chere as oþer chyldyr don' [*MF*, 246]. Christine is badly beaten but,

She chaungid neythir hir colour ne hir chere
For fulfyllyd she was wyth heuynly solace [*LHW*, 166].

Christine, immolated in the furnace, retains 'a glad semblant' [*GL*, vol. 7, 45], while Dorothy, placed in a vessel of boiling oil, is 'As mery & glade' as if anointed with sweet balm [*LHW*, 131]. Agatha enters her prison 'wyth a sturdy chere' or goes 'as myryly' as if to a feast [232]. This patient, indeed confounding, response to torture is crucial to martyrdom, and is demonstrated in the voice summoning Christine to heaven, reward for the fact that she has been patient in adversity [184]. Similarly, its holy nature is exemplified in Margaret's rejection of the tears of those onlookers who urge her to sacrifice and save herself; she calls them 'o ye wykkyd counselours' [17].

The lesson of patience reverberates throughout these texts. Clare of Assisi bears sickness and pain during which time 'she was so sweetly visited of God that it seemed unto all them that saw her that she had no pain ne disease' [*GL*, vol. 6, 166], while her dying moments affirm its lesson as taught by St Francis [184]. Elizabeth of Hungary restrains her childhood playmates from excessive song or laughter [*LHW*, 262]. She cares nothing for the privations of her widowhood [*GL*, vol. 6, 222], and actively seeks out poverty [*LHW*, 270–1]. She accepts all sufferings so that 'by patience she might possess her soul' [*GL*, vol. 6, 223], and, though during this time she has her patience sorely tried [*LHW*, 275], she accepts all with gladness [276]. She prays for poverty, patience, and constancy [280], and even urges her followers to submit meekly to all affliction and to welcome tribulation [281].

Elizabeth also seeks out suffering, and exemplifies the full range of late medieval virtues. She cares for the sick and diseased, ministering to their needs however repellent, searching for bodily corruption so that she might accept 'ful pacyently' the foulest air or stench [272]. On one singular occasion, she washes the face of one so diseased that no-one else will attend him [265–6]. Her confessor's tests of her resolve try her patience to its utmost, but she receives all

... wyth-out resystence
Of murmur or grocchyng,

remaining ever 'constaunte to pacyence' [280].

Patience remains a vital component of a saintly code recognised by all. Caxton's version of the life of St Margaret contains a final tag, itself a fixing device to label, 'know', and appropriate its subject. Of Margaret's many virtues, patience is particularly commended, and the reference is to her as a vessel 'full of the dread of God . . . and singular in patience' [*GL*, vol. 4, 71]. It is a virtue divinely, or hagiographically, ordained, its sealed, emotional control only permitted to break in contemplation of God. Thus, many saints weep as they pray, while the narrator of the life of Mary of Oignies speaks of her apparently confusing emotions. She is so patient and passive that when inwardly sad, she appears happy [*Prosalegenden*, 148], a knowledge which the omniscient biographer claims for himself.

Patience is associated not only with poverty but with silence, enclosure, withdrawal, and a closing down or concealment of emotion. Thus it is a key concept in the lives of those disguised and penitent women, remaining, in fact, the lesson of their texts. Marine is expelled from the monastery within which she is hiding. Nevertheless, she accepts this 'in great patience' [*GL*, vol. 3, 227], performs all 'patiently and devoutly' [228], and lives her life 'full patiently' [227] before being allowed to return on account of 'his humility and patience' [228]. Equally, Theodora's tale focuses upon her 'much patience' [*GL*, vol. 4, 51]. She is also expelled then readmitted because of her patient suffering [52], and is tormented by the devil, envious 'of her much patience' [51].

Yet, this highly complex series of tales also demonstrates a silent, emotional control used to confound others and provide a protective covering beneath which lies an undisclosed self-identity. Such a fissure similarly inadvertently reveals itself in the ambiguity of Chaucer's *The Clerk's Tale*, where Griselda's instinctive concealment of her self, a mimicry of desired female behaviour, exacts a heavy price.

As already seen, Griselda's meek demeanour comprises her holy virtue, and corresponds to male expectations of femininity. She works hard, cares for her father, is obedient, and full of 'vertuous beautee' [*IV(E)*, 211–31]. Her virtue is matched 'in chiere' and 'dede' [241] because it is her true self. However, as the tale progresses, this careful front is fractured. Though her self remains unchanged, and her behaviour compliant, her response confounds for it hides the real depth of her emotions. For the narrator, the delineation of this is merely a demonstration of her holy patience, but its subtext remains profoundly unsettling, simultaneously reiterating for the male the threatening mystery of 'woman', and asserting his power over a submissively obedient wife. Women in the audience might equally have recognised the deliberate or instinctive adoption of a behaviour which both protects and conceals, effectively resisting final knowledge or appropriation. Chaucer's comment, made through his fictional narrator, that Griselda's lesson is 'inportable' for wives to emulate, highlights that gap between theory and practice, authority and society, prompted by the impossible ideal of patience. What it also fails to acknowledge is the fissure inherent within any approximation to that ideal where it becomes a shield for those who have most to lose within a patriarchal world. It is the space within which the feminine in Griselda speaks and resists all that is ostensibly inscribed upon her.

The narrative pattern highlights the tensions within the notion of patience depicted by the writer. Its focus is upon 'chiere' or 'contenaunce', the outward sign which works in contrast to the secret, enclosed identity or 'corage' explored in chapter two. For the narrator, both demonstrate the virtue of patience. For the woman, they are separate but work in tandem in order to deceive and prevent access to knowledge.

Enclosed in Griselda's breast is a 'rype and sad corage' [220] much admired by Walter whose 'assays' are designed to test it. His constant search for proof of its alteration focuses upon 'countenaunce' or outward appearance. His eventual discovery that she remains 'ay oon in herte and in visage' [708–11] is itself an obfuscation, as will be seen, for Walter fails to recognise either the depth of Griselda's distress or her control over it. Thus, she remains 'ay sad and constant as a wal' [1047], a wall of patience imposed by her hagiographical text, a wall enclosing her within patriarchy, and a barrier wall behind which she conceals her self.

The pattern operates in conjunction with Griselda's speech and silence, discussed earlier, and seems a model of womanly behaviour. From the very beginning she speaks to Walter 'with reverence, in humble cheere' [298]. The oath imposed upon her is one of total allegiance in which she vows never to complain or contradict, either in word or deed, nor by 'frownyng contenance' [356]. This she obeys to the letter. Her discourse is mild, and her outward demeanour submissive.

Walter insists that she 'Shewe now youre pacience in youre werkyng' [495], a virtue put to the test with the apparent murder of her first child. Griselda remains unchanged in 'chiere or contenaunce' [499], and, like the holy symbol she is, 'as a lamb she sitteth meke and stille' while her daughter is removed [538]. Although Walter observes her closely, she remains 'evere in oon ylike sad and kynde' [602]. The same occurs after the birth of her son. The narrator rails against those husbands who needlessly torment 'Whan that they fynde a pacient creature' [623]. Walter urges 'Beth pacient' [644] and wonders that she is able to suffer all 'In pacience' [670]. Yet, she remains 'evere in oon so pacient', displaying no sign of emotion or care [677–8]. Walter is confounded by her, and can only contemplate 'Upon hir pacience' [688]. Again he watches, but nothing is revealed [708–11].

The cumulative effect of Griselda's perfect, mimetic display of the passive and patient female is profound. Brick by brick, she builds herself *into* her wall, and deceives the husband who represents patriarchy. Shamed by her apparent repudiation in favour of a new bride, she speaks only 'in pacience' [813]. Though others weep, her eyes remain dry [894–9], and, at home, 'this flour of wyfly pacience' merely waits [919]. Not a flicker in her 'contenaunce' or her 'face' recalls her previous high estate [920–4]. Instead, she sits 'ful of pacient benyngnytee' [929].

Recalled to the palace in order to prepare it for the wedding feast, she obeys 'with humble herte and glad visage' [949] greeting the guests 'With so glad chiere' [1016–17]. Finally, perceiving only 'hire pacience' and 'Hir glad chiere', Walter calls a halt to her suffering [1044–56]. Here, as already seen, she momentarily breaks down and struggles 'abaysed, from hire traunce' [1108]. For one brief moment, she discloses her self before, once again, donning her protective mimicry, quietly and meekly re-accepting her clothes and composing herself; she 'caught agayn hire contenaunce' [1060–110]. Griselda's mimesis deflects Walter's cruelty, and is a means of survival in a world whose rules she knows inside out. It enables her to protect herself and resist appropriation. It also permits her to undermine and subtly criticise that world, to turn back upon it all that it has imposed upon woman, and, thus, fracture its univocal assertion of power.

St Katherine

Once again, it is the life of St Katherine which offers the clearest example of a discourse at once holy ventriloquism and fissured subversion. In all versions of her *vita*, Katherine is permitted to mouth many points of theological doctrine, and to teach authoritatively in order to convert others. Those who listen to her are soon persuaded for 'With grete Ioye þis Maide prechede heom: of god and seinte marie' [*ESEL*, 97]. Confirming her holy worth, it is said that the Holy Ghost speaks within her [96]. Her preaching soon converts Athanasius [*GL*, vol. 7, 2] and other teachers [4]. She instructs her former adversaries as they await martyrdom, a fate inspired by their participation in a learned debate where her words are described as full of God's spirit [*LHW*, 186], and she herself as someone 'in whom the spirit of God speaketh' [*GL*, vol. 7, 21]. These philosophers are comforted for Katherine 'informed them diligently in the faith' [21]. Similarly, she 'began tó preach to the queen the joys of Paradise and converted her to the faith' [22], and later assures Maxentius's wife of her entry into Paradise, words that render the queen strong and confident [*LHW*, 196].

Katherine's dispute with the learned philosophers of her time provides many hagiographers with an excellent opportunity to clarify certain doctrinal issues, especially regarding the Trinity, the Immaculate Conception, the Resurrection, mortal and immortal Christ, and the soul and the body [*LKA*, 306–35]. Capgrave, in particular, 'quotes' Katherine at length in a defence not of herself but of the faith. All are said to have 'merueyled' at her eloquence [*LKA*, 314]. The account in Caxton tends not to record the actual details of her debate, but notes that 'she had disputed of many things' [*GL*, vol. 7, 18], and 'confounded their gods by open reasons' [20].

Thus, Katherine is transformed into a saint. Her important public trial centres upon her as a receptacle for the Word rather than an active, speaking

subject, while her subsequent suffering remains an example to all, an opportunity to retain the male writer's dominance as disseminator of the truth of all
Christianity as well as literary authority. Katherine, in the manner of all these
saints, prays for both patience and support in her hour of need [*LKA*, 299].
Sacred vessel of the divine, she is very firmly secured in her saintly place by one
narrator's additional, final comment elucidating the importance of this holy
woman, and her representation in theological debate. She is especially commended for her eloquence and reason, her 'sweet words in drawing the people
to the faith' and 'fair speech in preaching, as it appeared in her predications'
[*GL*, vol. 7, 29]. The narrative is similarly interrupted during a lengthy detailing of her young life in order to explicate the reasoning behind her refusal to
marry; unknown to Katherine, her heart was aflame with love of Christ [8].

Such a tight narrative framework attempts to suppress all that is transgressive
in Katherine's behaviour, but, as already demonstrated, her story remains
problematical. Probably the most important element of her *vita* is her confrontation with pagan law which directly leads to her martyrdom. However, inherent
within this clash is an attack upon social, familial, and political authority.
Katherine the saint rejects paganism, but, in the fissure beneath the text,
Katherine the woman confronts patriarchy. She speaks legitimately within this
world as a powerful queen, but also as an outsider by virtue of her femaleness
and saintly identity. As demonstrated in the previous chapter, Katherine's
assertion of a self which speaks through these spaces adds resonance to her
hagiographically allocated discourse.

As a young queen, whose family and subjects urge the safety of marriage, she
is initially reluctant to leave the protective space of her own interiority until she
realises

'My priuy counsell whech I hafe bor long
Now must it owte' [*LKA*, 88].

Katherine's concept of sovereignty is at odds with her social milieu. Her idea of
daughterhood is at odds with her family. Her notion of womanhood is at odds
with patriarchy, and it is here that the fissured text reveals itself. She thinks to
'hyr self a-lone' that she might be able to conceal her true identity, retain her
private vow of virginity, and compromise with her family and realm [89–90].

She appears to have an answer for all fears, declaring herself too young to
wed, or insisting on the use of prefects to enforce the law as her father did before
her [104–5]. The list of ideal qualities gradually unveiled before her – strength,
power, wealth, wisdom, royalty – is answered by a spouse so perfect that he
cannot exist except in the divine [162–7]. At the same time as this asserts
Katherine's saintly potential, it also confounds all worldly expectations. This
woman, who dares to speak out, inverts all laws and rules, challenges the fabric
of society by criticizing its accepted conventions. As such, she is thoroughly
perplexing.

Capgrave is not the only hagiographer to detail the dilemma of how

Katherine reconciles a public and a private identity, itself the source of her psychological dislocation as seen earlier. Once again, it is not what Katherine says but her ideally feminine response that prompts the fissure.

According to an account in Caxton's collection, initially her subjects' petition leaves her 'abashed and troubled in her courage', but she quickly recovers and, speaking 'with a sad cheer and a meek look', she begs them to turn from this 'to such matters as be requisite for the rule, governance, and universal weal of this realm' [*GL*, vol. 7, 5]. Her reply leaves all 'abashed of her words'. They attempt to remind her of her obligations. Her answers are humble, and made 'with a sad countenance' [6]. Insisting upon her perfect lover, Christ, 'she cast down her eyes meekly and held her still' [7]. She responds to further demands with 'a piteous sighing', and 'meekly' requests more time. The episode ends in 'great sorrow and lamentation' [8], with everyone saddened 'for they saw well that there was no remedy in that matter' [7].

Katherine wears the mask of the ideal woman, but, like Griselda, her appearance does not accord with either her heart or the import of her words. She speaks from within the world that made her, and accurately mimics all that is expected of her. Though her response is a feminised, ideal one, what she says is ultimately abhorrent to that world. The fact that she speaks at all, however carefully, is disturbing, while the content of her discourse is a quiet challenge to orthodoxy; her marriage *is* 'requisite for the rule, governance and universal weal' of her realm, but her dismissal of it both posits Christ as a higher authority and undermines masculine law. Even her mimesis, her meek demeanour, is a subversive strategy claiming a voice for the feminine that is whispered beneath the surface text.

Even more complex is the pattern at work when Katherine directly confronts the pagan Maxentius, and, hence, the masculine-dominated world. Capgrave, Caxton's version, and Bokenham all focus upon discourse itself, both verbal and non-verbal, in order to appropriate their subject and assert what is for them her only identity as a sacred vessel of the Word.

Katherine approaches Maxentius 'wyth ful sad visage' [*LKA*, 281], while her sweet words so soon begin to persuade others that he immediately regrets permitting her to speak at all [285]. Hence, he decides to call upon wise men to dispute with her once she has refused his offer of marriage, and, 'wyth sadnesse', declined to worship an idol made in her own image [290].

Her debate with the learned philosophers of her time is a vital ingredient of her story, one which goes far beyond the aggressive, masculine stance of all martyrs permitted, indeed required, by hagiographical tradition. Philosophy remains a masculine discourse. Its academic style is open only to an elitist few. Thus women are largely excluded from it, Irigaray even suggesting[33] that it is impossible for a woman to enter its arena as a woman. Thus Katherine mimics the outwardly submissive female, whilst her words, in a further mimesis of masculine philosophical discourse, challenge, confound, and refute the orthodoxy from which she speaks.

When Katherine first speaks to Maxentius, he is astounded [*LHW*, 178] by her words, and so 'much abashed' that he is unable to answer her until 'he was come to himself', when he declares: 'O Thou woman, suffer us to finish our sacrifice, and after, we shall give thee an answer' [*GL*, vol. 7, 18]. Further details of her ability to confound the masculine accumulate. Maxentius calls upon the support of his philosophers for 'in no manner he could resist her wisdom' [19] but is, again, left floundering as the weapon of their own logic is turned against them all; 'And when she had disputed of many things of the Incarnation of the Son of God much wisely, the emperor was much abashed and could not answer to her' until 'he was come to himself' [18]. His fear of her is reflected in the accusation made against her as 'a woman', a 'witche' [*LKA*, 375] who speaks with 'treccherous sotylte' [*LHW*, 181]. In an attempt to reduce her power, Maxentius speaks for the masculine world in his insistence that she is merely a mortal female, and,

> 'As we wel knowyn by experyence,
> We owe to yeuyn no credence
> On-to þi wurdys nere to þi speche' [181].

No authoritative experience has prepared him for her attack, and, thus, he can only accuse her of sorcery, pit his deceptive flattery against the frail words and weak will of woman, so that,

> With ful sotil langage on-to hir he sayde
> Alle [his] male-corage and his euele entent [*LKA*, 394].

On several occasions he offers marriage, promising to fabricate an idol of her, image of the ultimate patriarchal doll. Katherine mocks him 'with mery countenaunce', wonders how it might speak, move, or avoid the droppings of birds [352–3]; her jest conceals a criticism of woman's imposed immobility within the confines of a masculine-dominated world.

   In prison, the saint is described as 'sad' [287], but, from the moment she is brought into the public arena, she speaks 'with moost goodly chere' [308]. So powerful are her words that, once again, her audience is startled, stunned [311], and silent [320]. Other narrators echo Capgrave's words. Caxton's version records that fifty orators 'were abashed and wist not what to say' [*GL*, vol. 7, 20]. Masculine discourse, like masculine law, is unable to withstand this assault from within, despite Maxentius's earlier conviction that his philosophers could easily 'surmount a maiden well bespoken' [19]. Similarly quashed is his belief that Katherine will be vanquished by words rather than brute force [19–20].

   Maxentius introduces her to her adversaries with words echoing the hagiographer's intention. He says they come

> '. . . to don a luytel Maystrie,
> And for-to susteinen op heore lawe: þoru strencþe of clergie'
> [*ESEL*, 94].

Nowhere is this stricture more amply demonstrated than in Bokenham's version of Katherine's life with its constant reference to discourse. In the silence and solitude of her private chamber, Katherine hears a great noise as Maxentius orders all those in the city to sacrifice. She listens to

> The noyse of þe bestys & peplys cry,
> The voys of orgons & of dyuers menstralcy,

to sounds carried on the air [*LHW*, 176]. The world discloses itself, presses in on her, and calls upon her to participate within it, to forsake her marginalisation and speak publicly. Interestingly, she hears rather than witnesses what is effectively her invitation to martyrdom, a significance explored in the next section.

Katherine goes out, and mimics the style of male philosophers, not simply because she is the learned vessel of divine grace refuting ignorant heathen belief, but because she must make herself heard in a world recognising only its own masculine voice. So accurately do her first words parody this style that Maxentius is confused. Subsequently, she attempts to insert her own feminine voice into the dialogue, using the vernacular or plain, direct 'common speche' [177].

Maxentius marvels at her words [178]. He leaves her in order to sacrifice, and contemplate her threat, to prepare himself for a return battle [179]. He inserts a space between them, unable to cope with her transgression, for Katherine remains a profoundly unsettling resistance to masculine authoritative wisdom. At first, he rejects the use of violence as a means of restraining 'Hyr pompous language', a masculine discourse which she has appropriated for herself. He knows that he could torment her into silence but, foolishly, prefers debate [183]. Katherine's active participation in this is due to her command of masculine, philosophical discourse which she mimics in an open, public, male arena. Yet, she also makes this space her own, again interspersing her mimesis with her own feminine style:

> '. . . I ask leyser & space
> Myn entent pleynly for to declare,
> Wyth-owte rethoryk, in wurdys bare
> Or argumentatyf dysceptacyoun' [184].

Similarly, she later speaks to Maxentius's converted queen 'in wurdys pleyn' [189].

Katherine's holy discourse permits her terrifying transgression. Maxentius's demand 'be ye tunglees?' [185] is a redundant one. The fissure lies within her mimicry of masculine discourse, and occurs at the same time as Bokenham believes he has appropriated the words of his female subject, and made her mouth the divine. It continues as Maxentius tries to confront her as a man as well as a pagan. He offers wealth, prestige, an image of herself. He urges her to listen to him [187], and later begs her to allow his words to penetrate her heart [192]. Katherine's resistance is unwavering. Soon, the only way to impose masculine law upon her is to inscribe her body with the signs of masculine power. Under torture, she continues to scorn him, and, when he 'þese wurdys herd' [193], 'at þis wurd' he orders the instrument of her supposedly final torture [198]. When his own queen cries out in protest, he 'Wyth a loude voys' drowns her words [195]. Despite his apparently apologetic protestations to the contrary, Bokenham does exactly the same to a female saint whose voice, nevertheless, continues to insert itself into the blank spaces of his text, and whose instinctive mimesis both protects her and disrupts the univocal assertion of patriarchy.

Other voices: tears, melody, and angels

One of the most interesting aspects of *The Clerk's Tale* is its exemplification of masculine reliance upon the visual, upon an obsessive need to 'speculate' and appropriate. It is this route to knowledge which mirrors the visualisation of the divine so fundamental to Christianity, and is so different to the Judaic tradition of the faith with its focus upon the ear or the voice. That Griselda is finally conquered and reabsorbed into the masculine world, I do not doubt. She composes herself, and controls her emotions. Even her clothing advertises her status as Walter's wife. Her outward demeanour satisfies Walter but obscures his knowledge of her. Such reliance upon the visual leaves the male open to illusion, for Griselda's mimesis is deceptive, and, ultimately, transgressive. Her appearance so overshadows the ambiguous nature of her discourse that Walter fails to hear its full import. In contrast, Irigaray's exploration of the Judaic power of the voice posits the aural as a feminine space with the potential to fracture masculine reliance upon sight. It is this undercurrent of sound which opens up the texts of female saints' lives, and articulates other voices, speaking differently and undermining the patriarchal world.

A legitimate emotion of hagiography is a tearful display closely linked to the concept of patience, and, thus, an important validation of saintly worth. Mary of Oignies weeps copiously whenever she sees or hears of the Passion. Though she attempts to staunch the flow by concentrating upon the Godhead rather than Christ's humanity, she is usually unsuccessful [*Prosalegenden*, 137]. She cries almost continuously so that even the kerchiefs intended to cover her head remain perpetually damp. The author of her life cites a miracle as proof that her tears are divinely inspired, and, consequently, worthy. Embarrassed by a priest who requests that she weep more quietly when in church, Mary prays that he might learn she is unable to control this emotion. Later, taking mass, the priest is suddenly so swamped by his feelings that he is soaked by his own tears [138].

Here, the hagiographer demonstrates that such affective piety is to be commended. These 'womanly' tears, a sign of weakness in both sexes, are approved by God and their involuntary emission receives holy valency. Other saints similarly signal their own worth through such behaviour. Pauline 'wept so much that it seemed of her eyes a fountain', and even declares that a face ought to be tear-stained, for beauty is an affront to the commandments of God. In the same way, she urges that laughter should be replaced by weeping [*GL*, vol. 3, 4–5].

Clerical authority is also reinforced by the prevalence of saintly tears during the sacrament. Mary of Egypt weeps when Zosimus gives her the host, and Caxton's version notes 'How well that she had always wept and shed tears so abundantly that it seemed that she had lost her sight' [109]. Clare of Assisi also cries during such moments because it is then that she is closest to Christ. One miracle in particular exemplifies this. Unable to attend the Christmas service because of illness, she nevertheless hears the singing, and emotionally participates in the ritual. This, says the narrator, is due to divine grace [*GL*, vol. 6, 173–4].

Elizabeth of Hungary cries 'without changing of semblance' [216], and even appears glad:

> . . . þow she outward shewyd trystesse
> Yet of inward ioye she hadde habundaunce [*LHW*, 265].

Her weeping is also associated with her visionary powers. Once, in an attempt to explicate these mixed emotions, she tells how she 'saw' Christ, and was filled with joy. She wept as the vision disappeared, before being restored to gladness when informed that Christ will never forsake her [283–4]. Similarly, in Caxton's collection it is recounted that 'she had a special grace to weep abundantly tears, for to see celestial visions, and for to inflame the hearts of others to the love of God' [*GL*, vol. 6, 224].

Mary of Oignies also experiences a series of miracles alongside her tears. Examples are numerous but usually involve Christ. Some last for days at a time. She perceives Him as a tiny baby, a lamb, a dove, a pilgrim, a merchant, and a castrated ram with a star upon its forehead. At other times, vision matches location or occasion, so that in Bethlehem she sees the infant Christ, or, at Christmas, the child breast-fed by the Madonna [*Prosalegenden*, 172–5].

The visionary and ecstatic nature of female mystical experience has been well documented. Visionary experience, the motif of weeping, and the use of song combine to form an area largely exclusive to female hagiography, and its significance therefore deserves attention. The ecstatic, bypassing male clerical authority, may well have discovered a positive identification with the divine where the female saint speaks directly to God and is, in turn, answered. Admittedly, her visions are often, though not exclusively, subsequently interpreted by a male who appropriates, disseminates, and authorises her words. What is important, however, is that the male does not 'see' these visions himself, but, instead, relies upon the voice of a woman to articulate them and transform them into a reality he might share.

Similarly, holy tears are rearticulated by the masculine world, and offered as religious symbol. Alternatively, this representation is, at least partially, a false imposition, for their involuntary and uncontrollable emission stems from the chora, from an unarticulated, pre-Oedipal, and pre-language space. Tears, melody, visions, all speak of and from joy. Their very misarticulation by the masculine ensures that they remain firmly rooted in an aural, sensory, and experiential realm which is very different from the masculine validation of visual proof. Hearing rather than sight is privileged in those examples cited earlier, when Mary of Egypt fears the sound of her words might contaminate her listener [*GL*, vol. 3, 107], and when Christine spits her tongue at the provost thereby blinding him. [*LHW*, 84] As a man, he is unable to see what this feminine fissure asserts, while, conversely, Dorothy is only able to convert Theophilus by offering him tangible proof of Christ's garden [*GL*, vol. 7, 45]. Masculine hagiographers, excluded from this feminine perspective, impose their own discourse upon that which is ultimately outside language. As a means of articulating the holiness of their subject and rendering her visible to the world, it is highly successful. What it fails to embrace, however, is the humanity of its saint.

Interestingly, Bokenham comes very close to explicating this tension when he describes Mary Magdalene's copious tears as a display of penitence and 'meke obsequyousnesse'. He interprets them as a sign of contrition demonstrating the courage of her heart 'As þow she had vysd þis language' [*LHW*, 149]. Mary stands behind Christ and

> . . . wyth hir mouth outwardly
> To hym no wurde she dede expresse [ibid.].

Instead she weeps. In an effort to reclaim this experience for himself, as well as render her visible, the narrator, allocating her some words, quotes what is apparently in her heart, a knowledge to which he, the semi-divine male, has access. He has her tell Christ 'Y am a synnere' guilty of foul crimes, and in need of help [149]. Bokenham concludes with a narratorial intervention which seals both his interpretation and his appropriation:

> Lo, þus may we seen how euere mercyful
> God is, & synners ful besy to saue,
> By þis wumman in specyal [151].

Mary Magdalene's private thoughts remain unspoken except through her alternative voice, her tears, one which fractures the univocality of this phallocentric text.

In the same way, a series of male narrators claim that the female saint's song is divinely inspired. Cecilia is said to sing in her heart to God [*LHW*, 203; *VIII(G)*, 135–7]. During Katherine's vision of marriage to Christ, 'she could not speak', only 'hear' and 'see' in a dream-like manner [*GL*, vol. 7, 12]. She listens to a heavenly melody which so fills her with joy and sweetness 'that it cannot be expressed' [14]. Enclosed in an oven, Christine sings and praises the Lord [*LHW*, 79], while Mary Magdalene is so well sustained by a beautiful, heavenly melody that she has no need of God in her desert solitude [168].

Other holy women also exemplify this unusual experience. On her deathbed, Elizabeth of Hungary intones a melody so sweet that many request an explanation of its origin [*GL*, vol. 6, 226–7]. She recounts how in a vision she chorused with a bird calling her to heaven, and which flew in and out of her room [*LHW*, 286–7] in promise of liberation and joy. As she dies, many birds sing a delightful song, one of happiness, no funeral dirge [288]. Similarly, close to death, Mary of Oignies sings a high, sweet melody loudly and clearly, for a full three days. During this time, she also praises God, and sings of holy writ, for, according to her biographer, this song is divinely given [*Prosalegenden*, 178]. Towards the end she grows silent [180] before suddenly laughing and humming softly [183]. On other occasions she intones a wordless melody or mutters unintelligibly, often in rhyme or Romany [179]. Christina Mirabilis also choruses a sweet, angelic melody which the narrator explicates as divine teaching, similar to the manner in which this unschooled woman finds access to knowledge of Latin and holy writ. Interestingly, the sound of her song is not only produced in the usual manner but also stems from her breast [129].

This focus upon 'brest' or 'hert', an inner private space, symbolises its divine inspiration. Yet the breast, like the throat, is also the frequent target of male, pagan violence. It seems that here, in the fissures of these wounds, the body finds an alternative mode of expression; it is the feminine, the body itself which speaks. It speaks from the chora, from deep within, of a powerful joy, a private pleasure in the divine as well as in a personal, sensual enjoyment of feminine physicality. Often allied to direct communion with God in the form of visions, what is articulated in this unspoken space is confounding. What many women and some men might hear and acknowledge, those reliant upon the masculine and the visual cannot see. Thus, the masculine writer imposes a single valency upon such incidents; they are signs from God, a mark of holiness. In speaking for his subjects' revelatory experiences, the male hagiographer often attempts to close down the possibilities of interpretation, and articulate what is essentially resistant to classification, what cannot be articulated. Ultimately, however, he cannot seal the fissure.

Such a gap is similarly revealed in the association of saint and angel. The neuter or unsexed angel represents a space alternative to that of the phallus, and is a bridge between God and humans, between the two sexes. Love is the vehicle for crossing the divide while fluidity of exchange remains crucial.[34] The angel is both human and divine, male and female, mortal and immortal, corporeal and incorporeal. It moves easily between heaven and earth, its constantly metamorphosing shape recognisable to both men and women. The angel is an integral part of Irigaray's 'ethics of alterity', where she suggests that the (re)discovery of a 'self' for women is an open-ended, multiple experience. Alterity is the psychological meeting place of two genders. There, they might realise and accept the nature of the other's alterity. Here, is the possibility of mutual respect from autonomous and different beings, not the concept of androgyny so often associated with Kristeva or Cixous,[35] but an awareness that the sexes are not the same, and neither is dominant over the other.[36] Instead, each is able to open up to another's claims and needs, a mutuality witnessed in the image of the angel.

Such a theory greatly illuminates many female saints' lives. The presence of an angel is, of course, an index of holy worth. It is a messenger of the divine, a sign of the saint's alliance with Christ. The guardian angel supports, succours, protects, and, ultimately, leads the saint into Paradise. Yet there is evidence that its role is also one of mediator between the sexes as well as between human and God. It highlights the profound difference between masculine, purely visual faith and feminine, aural, sensual belief, the contrast between sight and sound, or scent, which the angel elides. Similarly, the angel's main occupation is to clothe, feed, or heal the tortured body. This it often does in the private space of prison or the chamber, itself the location of feminine identity, while its connection with the site of physical rupture (wounds as well as mouth) points to a vital 'feminisation' of hagiographical text. These sites are female or feminine fissures in themselves, and, thus, the angel's illumination is that of the subtext as well as the divine.

Many of these features become so inextricably bound together that it is often difficult to disentangle them. An imprisoned Katherine prays for help, and is rewarded by the comforting appearance of a bright angel foretelling victory in her debate when she will receive angelic protection [*LHW*, 183; *GL*, vol. 7, 20; *LKA*, 361]. Later, an angel destroys the horrific engine designed to kill her, scattering its pieces far and wide but sparing Christian onlookers [*LHW*, 194]. On another occasion, Maxentius's queen enters her prison, and, as the male writer imposes his own perception of the faith upon the text, she sees a vision of angels bathing Katherine's wounds [*GL*, vol. 7, 22]. Bokenham records how they were

> . . . ocupid wyth besy cure
> Hyr woundys for to heel & cure
> Wyt many a ful swete oynement
> Wych wer þan baum more redolent [*LHW*, 189].

For him, the scent of this holy balm indicates her great virtue, but its heady sweetness, the detailing of its ointment, is suggestive of a sensuous pleasure, of jouissance. The masculine voice struggles to remain dominant in other versions. One author cites the miracle of her bodily translation where, though the flesh has wasted, 'the bones were so compact and pure that they seemed to be kept by the cure of angels' [*GL*, vol. 7, 26]. While the narrator asserts a spiritual integrity demonstrated through the example of a physical incorruption for which he offers tangible, visual proof, the text's continued focus upon the female body fails to recognise that same body's significance.

This concentration upon corporeality is continued. Agnes is spared the brothel because an angel spread around her a band of light [*LHW*, 120]. Magdalene, whose own voice is termed angelic, is fed by angels who daily lift her closer to heaven [*ESEL*, 478]. An angel breaks Juliana's wheel, and heals her of those wounds already inflicted [*GL*, vol. 3, 49]. Dorothy is cast into prison where,

> ... by aungelys mynystracyoun
> Fed she was wyth heuenly consolacyoun [*LHW*, 131].

Her prayers are answered, and angels destroy a marble idol erected as monument to her own intransigence [132]. A gaoled Christine prays for aid, and suddenly perceives an angel who informs her that God has heard her and will not forsake her. For twelve days she receives no food until an angel brings her a loaf of bread. Others continue to feed her, and heal her wounds [64; 69]. Thus she is able to resist further torture, and finally sing with angels in her fiery furnace of immolation [*GL*, vol. 4, 96].

Though some of this remains to be explored in the final chapter, it is clear that much of this angelic succour takes place in private. The space is an interior (even domestic) one of furnaces and ovens, of feeding and caring for the sick. The angel mediates between saint and God, but, nevertheless, remains extremely close to the feminine. Its role borders on the maternal, and is focused upon the body. Though its nurturing is essentially spiritual, its relationship is open and cooperative. Close ally of the saint, the angel provides a neutral space for the evolution of an identity, at once both religious and personal.

Such neutrality is denied by the masculine textual voice which continues to assert its own gender above all others, to propose the angel largely as a male messenger of the divine. Irigaray's careful exploration of linguistics leads her to conclude that many grammatical constructions, particularly those of Romance languages, insert the masculine pronoun wherever there exists either a mixed plural or a neuter form.[37] In the same way, on the relatively rare occasion where a pronoun describes an angel, it is a masculine one. Such an insistence claims the angel, and, indeed much of religion, solely for the male. Chaucer's version of St. Cecilia's story tells how what is, in essence, *her* angel is male; 'He' might kill Valerian or else 'He wol yow loven as me' [*VIII(G)*, 155–61]. It is, however, Bokenham who is the greatest culprit in this respect despite his own patronising apologies to his exclusively female audience.

Of Christine's angel, he writes 'quod he' [*LHW*, 64], and of Anne's 'he vanysshed a-vay' once 'his ambacyat' had been accomplished [49]. Anne's angel is the same one [49; 51] which also appears to Joachim in the likeness of a young man [50]. The masculine pronoun is subsequently used throughout [50–3]. Cecilia's loving angel is, again, male in form: 'he wyl ben angry' or else 'he þe louyn as wel as me', and show 'to þe hys grace' [204–5]. Similarly, it holds garlands 'in hys hand' [208].

Yet feminine fissures continue to insert themselves into the text. As seen, Anne and Joachim share the same angel. Though it brings news of divine grace with its annunciation to both of their promised child, it also mediates between them providing an opportunity for these human lovers to articulate their individual despair [49]. It is the angel which, though 'kepere' of Joachim and servant of God, repeatedly urges him to return home [53]. In addition, it tells Anne how and where she might meet her beloved husband [54].

A similar reciprocity is established between Cecilia and Valerian through an angel which the latter is invited to share. She begs Valerian not to betray her counsel, and describes how, in return for the renunciation of his legitimate claim upon her body, he too might gain Paradise. It is an angel, not a husband, which is guardian of Cecilia's body, a fact emphasised in most versions. Chaucer notes,

> 'I have an aungel which that loveth me,
> That with greet love, wher so I wake or sleepe,
> Is redy ay my body for to kepe' [*VIII(G)*, 152–4].

Bokenham writes,

> 'An aungel of god a louere haue I
> Wych my body kepyth wyth greth jelusy' [*LHW*, 204].

Both detail how one unchaste touch will call down the angel's mighty vengeance [204; *VIII(G)*, 155–8], whilst restraint will evoke his love. In this way, in the powerful privacy of her own chamber, Cecilia reclaims her body for herself, a daring transgression which all accounts fail to perceive in their simplistic insistence upon her holy chastity.

Most versions insist upon the visual proof so vital to masculine experience, and this record of material evidence is transmitted via the text. Cecilia promises that, in return for Valerian's continence, the angel will 'shewen yow his joye and his brightnesse' [*VIII(G)*, 161]. In fact, Valerian insists upon it. He wishes to 'hym biholde' [164], to receive proof 'hym an aungel to be' [*LHW*, 205], for, if it is simply a man, then he will kill it. The reward for Valerian's obedience to her instructions is the sight of the angel, something she promises on several occasions. In Chaucer's account, she twice repeats that he will see it [*VIII(G)*, 170; 182], a vow similarly repeated in Bokenham [*LHW*, 205–6].

It is a materiality ostensibly reiterated when, after his conversion, Valerian returns to Cecilia's chamber where she waits, the angel beside her [*VIII(G)*, 219]. Her experience of this invisible angel is entirely different from that of either Valerian or his brother Tiburce, but she does not deny the validity of either. Instead, she uses the angel, who appears only in the first half of her story, to bridge the gap.

Thus, Valerian is rewarded with visual evidence of his rival, and achieves a mutuality with his wife which transcends sexuality. As promised, he sees one who will love him 'as weel as me' [*LHW*, 206]. The angel crowns them with roses and lilies, significantly giving the flowers first to Cecilia, and then to Valerian 'hir make' [*VIII(G)*, 224; *LHW*, 208]. They are informed that these garlands will never rot or lose their fragrance so long as their pact of chastity is maintained. This scent, later used to assert Tiburce's holy worth, is an unseen proof associated, therefore, with the feminine. Its valency so insinuates itself into the story that what is proclaimed is the positive value of an experience which is neither superior nor inferior to that of the male, but simply different. In this respect, the angel's significance is clear.

Bokenham describes the garlands as

> . . . of so swete redolence
> That neythyr baum ner frankencence
> Yaf so swete a flauour as dede tho [*LHW*, 208].

Such crowns, both are warned, can only be perceived by one as chaste as they; no other 'wight shal seen hem with his ye' [*VIII(G)*, 230]. When the angel grants Valerian his request to convert his brother, he prays that Tiburce might smell the garlands [256]. Entering Cecilia's chamber, Tiburce remarks upon the strong scent of flowers currently out of season [243–59], and is assured that he too might finally be able to perceive 'Whiche that thyne eyen han no myght to see' [255; *LHW*, 210]. Cecilia's subsequent preaching promises that, after a visit to Urban, he will find the grace to purchase the sight of the angel's face [*LHW*, 211], that his baptism will enable him the 'aungels for to se' [214]. Thus, Tiburce obeys her instructions

> '. . . so that thou mowe biholde
> The angels face of which thy brother tolde' [*VIII(G)*, 300–1].

Eventually, he becomes so holy

> That every day he saugh in tyme and space
> The aungel of God [355–6].

This is a fissure which proclaims its inherent sexual difference, and undermines a surface text intent only upon the masculine. What is clear is that, just as in the use of space before it, there exists within female hagiography a voice, often only semi-articulated, which speaks itself from the body, from the chora, from jouissance. Because it is spoken differently, its presence is a whispered one, but it remains no more nor less valid than the loudly proclaimed masculine one whose orthodox validation publicly asserts its authority, a univocality fractured and fragmented by that which cannot be ignored.

Notes

1 Reference to Authorised Version.
2 Millet and Wogan-Browne 1990:141; 143.
3 Petroff 1994: preface; 3–9. Her work explores the tensions inherent in such behaviour (see especially 163–77). She also suggests the possibility of discovering a personal speaking female self in the rhythms of alterity found in the relationship between Christ and the visionary female mystic (see 204–19).

4 Leclerc 1990: 74.
5 ibid. 75.
6 Kristeva 1986a: 153.
7 ibid. 153; 145.
8 Moi 1985: 140.
9 Research by De Francisio (1991) and Fishman (1980) cited in Coates 1993: 114; 122–3.
10 See Guberman 1996: 257–70, especially 269.
11 Jones, D. 1990: 243.
12 There is some evidence to suggest that women enjoyed the friendship of other religious women whether in the cloister or as part of a subculture of lay piety, some of which might have involved communal living, such as beguinage communities. The icons and symbols of feminine writing point to a shared experience of religion, while other feminine ritualised activities ensured that traditionally it was women who gathered in order to deal with birth and death. Ulrike Wiethaus suggests that women were able to define themselves in and through themselves. See her paper (1993) 'In search of medieval women's friendships – Hildegard of Bingen's letters to her female contemporaries', in Wiethaus 1992: 93–111.
13 Jones, D. 1990: 243–4; 246–7.
14 Simon the Pharisee is rebuked by Christ for suggesting that a real prophet would not suffer the touch of the sinful Mary Magdalene [*LHW*, 150]. Martha accuses her of idleness [152], while Judas Iscariot says that her use of precious oil to anoint Christ is wasteful [155]. More generally, she is known for the loss of her good name [148].
15 Anderson 1969: 7–19.
16 ibid. 32.
17 William Langland, D. Pearsall (ed.) 1978: 12.
18 ibid. Passus XV, 1–106.
19 ibid. Passus XVI, 1–372.
20 ibid. Passus XII, 1–246. See also notes to 15.
21 ibid. Passus XV, 161.
22 ibid. Passus XV, 164–5.
23 ibid. Passus XV, 254.
24 Late medieval concepts of patience were crucial but problematical, having moved away from notions of mere passive endurance of suffering and remaining closely linked to silence, hardship, equanimity, and poverty. Patience was understood to be both active and passive, an important part of *imitatio Christi*, well beyond the stoic acceptance of external events. Instead, texts such as Langland's *Piers Plowman* and the *Patience* poem, as well as Julian of Norwich's work, indicate that it is a transforming concept where, in imitation of Christ, sin and death are transformed into love and life, and patient poverty has the power to change humanity (see Schifforst 1978). See also Kirk 1978, Hanna 1978, and Baldwin 1990.
25 For an excellent summary of a feature which seems to have informed, or even defined, Anglo-American feminism in all its aspects, see Cameron 1990: 23–6.
26 Irigaray is especially scathing of this Freudian notion of frigidity posited as a psychical option for women in relation to the masculine world. For a woman to choose it, apparently involves a refusal of genital orgasmic pleasure. (According to Freud, vaginal rather than clitoral orgasm is a superior and more mature pleasure, a dichotomy long established as false.) For more on this, see Grosz 1989: 134–5.
27 ibid.
28 For further clarification, see Grosz 1989: 136–9 or Whitford 1991: 71–97.
29 Grosz 1989: 138–9.
30 See 'Cultural Strangeness and the Subject in Crisis', in Guberman 1996: 45–6.
31 Moi 1985: 143.

32 Whitford 1991: 72.
33 It is this view which, in part, was responsible for her mimetic essay *Speculum of the Other Woman*. For further details on the ways in which women have traditionally been excluded from this style of discourse, see le Doeuff 1989: 100–28.
34 Whitford 1991: 163–5.
35 Many people assume that, unlike Irigaray, these two advocate bisexuality or a dissolving of personal or sexual identity, as in the example of avant-garde writing or symbolic poetry. See Kristeva 1986: 145, and Moi 1985: 106–9. However, Cixous (1981: 245–64) denies that she aims for a specifically hermaphrodite or bisexual state, preferring instead that both sexes are located in one. Kristeva warns against fixing the feminine simply as different for, she suggests, the emphasis should be upon more not two, upon multiplication, with differences between women as important as differences between men and women, a concept that perhaps allies her more closely with Irigaray than previously thought (see Kristeva 1996: 43).
36 Grosz 1989: 140–6. Irigaray suggests that the angel might open up what is closed in terms of the world, identity, action, and history; all limits might be transgressed by the bodies of both men and women. When the angel and the body are found together, then love might unify the masculine and the feminine (see Irigaray 1991c: 173–4).
37 Irigaray argues that man gives his name to anything of value, and marks it as his own by the use of the male gender. Thus, God or the sun 'become' masculine, and the masculine pronoun takes precedence in the plural, the impersonal, or what appears to be neuter. The feminine plural is only used when describing women who remain among themselves. It is this, she believes, that ensures women are unable to subjectivise the world as their own (see Irigaray 1993: 30–5; 67–74).

4 Written on the body

There exists a fundamental tension at the heart of late medieval piety. On the one hand, an assertion of the Word through both pulpit and text promulgates the necessity of giving credence to what is spoken or written, and demands a need for faith. Yet there is a simultaneous emphasis upon material, tangible evidence which corresponds to the masculine desire to 'see' God. Eyewitness report, where the biographer's claim to have 'seen' events invokes masculine power and suppresses the feminine as well as invoking the power of the masculine gaze which appropriates the female, thus becomes invaluable. Equally important is the cult of relics, visual proof inscribed on the bodies of the virgin martyrs or upon Christ Himself, as well as miraculous intervention ensuring that corpses are seen to be incorrupt and angels embodied. Hagiographical tradition reflects this tension between blind faith and ocular evidence, between spiritual 'truth' and material proof.

Yet, within this genre is an intimation of a feminine alternative combining the two in a total experience of shared, empathetic suffering, a stress upon the physicality of Christ as well as female visionary or mystical experience during which the woman alone 'sees', touches, hears, feels. Though this experience is often articulated only by the male, the important point is that it exists and that the body is the vehicle of its expression.

The human body remains symbolic of culture, society, and theology; it is constructed through the symbolic itself. Its significance in the formulation of identity is witnessed during the Lacanian mirror stage when the young child, initially unaware of its body as an entity, moves from a sense of fragmentation to a realisation that it is also like others. The body is, thus, a site of significance and ambivalence, for it is both fragmented *and* unified. Irigaray focuses upon Christ's body as symbol, and, in particular, its openness, its holes and wounds. These orifices mirror the apertures of the female body, and, I would suggest, the fissures of a 'closed', authoritative, and masculine text. Irigaray maps female lack onto the masculine body thereby reclaiming that lack for women. Irigaray suggests that an attempt is made to close the gap of this fractured space at the same time as its lack is nurtured for, as seen in chapter two, it is in this infinite space that God and women might meet.[1]

Inevitably, a section concerning the body, about which much has already been written, moves between the two strands of female hagiography, virgin martyrology and the *imitatio Christi* of many historical holy figures including married saints. My focus is mainly upon the former, and incorporates notions of virginity and chastity, gender, Christ's body, the body itself, and an imitation of Christ which involves food, flagellation, and other bodily or mystical phenomena. My concern is with violence, whether that integral to the lives of the virgin martyrs or self-inflicted, and with the bodily emissions, blood, water, and milk, which link these two hagiographical strands. Firstly, however, it is necessary to map the significance or meaning of the body itself.

The physical body was viewed as the prison of the soul, hence a theological emphasis upon spirituality and chastity. Of great importance was the Pauline notion of a hierarchy where virginity was the most admired, followed by chaste widowhood, then marriage. A series of sexual taboos or proscriptions circumscribed the body, and jouissance was repressed.[2] Similarly, there existed an apparent dichotomy between the flesh and the soul, between woman and man. Both were believed to possess a rational soul, but the male was thought superior to woman who represented the border between body and soul, the fissure within which boundaries might be erased, for she especially was, even physically, open to corruption and concupiscence. The female's transgressive role as Eve also ensured that she remained more credulous and inferior in reasoning. Biologically too the male's supremacy was established with the woman as the passive auxiliary of his sperm. According to Aquinas, all that was required was the inner space of the mother's womb, the morally weaker vessel that was woman.

Acceptance of a simplistic binary system – male/female, soul/body, spirit/flesh, figurative/literal – may well demand a reinscription, however. Lochrie's tracing of a theological development stemming from St Augustine and resulting in a representation of woman as flesh rather than passive body – a fissure dividing human from divine Will, a site of disruption requiring control – is a persuasive one. She argues that it lead to a gendered psychology of sin and an insistence upon a notion of *integritas* designed to repress and seal this fissured boundary, flesh, a concept refusing to acknowledge the liberatory possibility of that same boundary as a site of potential subversion.[3] This emphasis upon the notion of *integritas*, a stance later softened in a move towards psychological rather than actual bodily virginity, permeated medieval culture.[4] Without doubt, though at least some of the literature encoding these ideas might have been ambivalent or open to alternative readings, its intention was to impose an ideal, to circumscribe the female body as well as female behaviour.

The opposition between male and female was, however, a far less clear-cut distinction than might be expected, and here the influence of Bakhtin's depiction of 'classical' and 'grotesque' bodies is particularly resonant.[5] The 'classical' body is usually masculine, closed, hermetic, static, homogeneous, and associated with high culture, with Latin, with a disembodied spirituality. It is authoritative and invested with power. In contrast, the 'grotesque' body is feminine, open, heterogeneous, composed of gaps, orifices, offshoots (the open mouth, genitals, breast, belly, nose, phallus), apertures, and disproportion. It exceeds its own limits in pregnancy, childbirth, dying, eating, drinking, in copulation, and defecation. If the 'classical' is linked to male hagiographers' attempts to close their texts, then the 'grotesque' is often reflected in the lives of the female saints themselves, and in the tenets of this study. The body of the female saint is itself the site of these two contesting discourses, and her story subverts or dissolves its tensions at the same time as it juxtaposes and so highlights them.[6]

In a similar way, gender boundaries themselves were not fixed, but were part of a continuum where the male was the paradigm and the female less than perfect.[7] It was recognised that there was an opportunity to make identity via a body which was also vulnerable to attack and fragmentation. Thus, a series of images and icons of corporeal wholeness and personal unity existed alongside those of fragmentation and dismemberment. A belief that the person was the body led to a desire to hide decay, to prepare fragments for the reassembling which would occur on Judgement Day, and to demonstrate a moral integrity through the physical.[8] Hence, the punishment fragmenting the bodies of virgin martyrs was realigned in the depiction of their intact and incorrupt corpses, while this tension was reflected in later medieval saints' lives in the practice of contemplating the wounds of Christ.

If women saw themselves as matter rather than gender, then they were especially saved via the physical, human matter associated with the crucified Christ.[9] Such tensions and ambivalences were particularly sited in Christ's body, focus of spiritual and temporal authority. They were reflected, too, in images of a feminised or dual-gendered Christ whose body became an arena of struggle, constructed by a series of paradoxes: it was both human and divine, exclusive and inclusive, 'classical' and 'grotesque'. An iconographical focus upon mouth, blood, and wounds revealed what Camille describes as 'an eroticised, gender-bending and penetratable body open to flows and fluid desires, that signalled danger in other lesser bodies.'[10] Christ's body was the site of both sacred and profane, a private and public resource, and a body politic, while its bodily margins (wounds) indicated a place where systems might be simultaneously created and destroyed, ruptured and renegotiated. It also served as text, publicly marked and inscribed, demonstrating the workings of power but also how 'different regimes of marking construct male and female bodies differently within the culture.'[11] The multivalent and permeable symbol of Christ's body became a particular focus of female spirituality.

Thus, the female body is reflected in the body of Christ. Open and fissured, it is as threateningly disruptive as the fissures of the hagiographical texts examined here. Through its gaps and orifices, the female body articulates its own unique experience. Beneath the masculine voice of her life story, with its insistence upon a univocal and authoritative experience, is an alternative, hidden feminine voice relating how 'My body flows with the vast rhythmic pulsation of life.'[12] It is through the hagiographical text's very focus upon the violence of the tortured body, upon breasts, blood, and other fluids, that the female saint speaks herself and declares her own identity as both saint and woman.

Imitatio Christi: the site of the abject

The late medieval focus upon the body is amply demonstrated through a pattern of affective piety involving food, scourging, disease, paramystical phenomena, and a body so 'sealed' that it no longer excretes or menstruates. These areas have been extensively explored elsewhere. Many have noted its particular application to female saints, and its subversive possibilities.

Caroline Walker Bynum's influential work on food suggests that the provision and preparation of it, eating, feeding others, and fasting might have formed part of a control of self, and an assertion of identity.[13] In feeding others, yet abstaining themselves, as well as ingesting the suffering of others by consuming bodily corruption such as scabs or pus, women became God-like through the experience of illness or starvation, metamorphosed flesh into spirit, and manipulated a body said to be a source of pollution yet transformed into a positive symbol beyond a simplistic notion of hysteric or anorexic.[14] Women, too, might be said to become Christ by 'eating' Him in the eucharist, which also allowed them to bypass male clerical authority.[15]

Many holy women used their own bodies, and an ideal of purity, as a dynamic opposing their own flesh, and deliberately exposed it to pain, self-inflicted violence, or the unclean (illness and disease) in order to test the power of their own purity over the forces of corruption. This type of *imitatio Christi* focuses upon Christ's body both as a vehicle inscribed by pain and an agent whose suffering is experienced by another. Pain became part of a spiritual process of renewal, and, for many female mystics, its experience was said to lead to a deepening of love of God, exemplified through a devotion to the crucified Christ's wounds.[16] Many believe that though suffering leads to salvation, it also liberates women from the very physicality within which they are rooted, elevates rather than rejects the material, and offers a challenge to existing systems.[17] As Elizabeth Robertson suggests, the holy woman comes to an understanding of God, and, I would suggest, herself, through the very physical world in which she is immersed via the body, the domestic, through blood.[18]

Kristeva's notion of abjection also has important implications here. She describes the abject as the time and space between, inside, and outside the body, the space between the self and other, on the very threshold of language, the stable and symbolised self. For the self and its subjectivity to become defined and unified requires the expulsion of all that is improper, unclean, or disorderly, of that which cannot be fully dissolved or expelled but, instead, hovers at the borders, remaining a threat to the psychic and social unity of the subject. It is the recognition of this threat that leads to the sensation of abjection, and any attempt to avoid its abyss, or 'the hole into which the subject may fall when its identity is put into question'[19] involves 'the paradoxically necessary but impossible desire to transcend corporeality.'[20] The abject is only held at bay via a series of taboos designed to preserve the integrity of the body's boundaries. These taboos incorporate food, bodily waste and fluids, disease, and a focus upon blood, sign of sexual difference, demonstrated in proscriptions concerning incest, menstruation, and blood itself. The child must abject (reject) the mother in order to create its own space. It is a condition at once repellent yet necessary, both revealing the existence of a speaking 'I', yet threatening its identity.[21]

The concept of abjection is closely allied to mystical experience[22] but also links with much of the preceding work of this book. It embodies those very taboos against the flesh which ward off the abject but also constrict and suppress a feminine voice. It remains inextricably bound with the formulation of identity. By inverting taboo, revelling in what is abject and forbidden, the female saint might overcome it. She both acknowledges and accepts the way in which the abject helps to construct her self, and this applies whether she deliberately seeks it out or inflicts it upon herself, or whether she chooses the pains of martyrdom. It is linked too to the permeability of body boundaries, with the openness of the 'grotesque', and a perverse form of jouissance where the saint revels in *all* aspects of her own body.

On the one hand, hagiographical texts promulgate the notion of the 'classical' sealed and homogeneous body invested with authority, whose borders are firm, outline secure, and whose wholly incorrupt materiality offers itself as relic, proof of sanctity, and visual evidence of a holiness confirmed by both spiritual and physical integrity. Similarly, emphasis upon the miraculous confirms the female body as a passive vessel worked upon by the divine.

As Margaret is beheaded, onlookers are presented with ocular proof of her sanctity for they witness her soul, embodied as a milk-white dove, carried aloft by angels [*MF*, 202]. Similarly, all see Katherine's body transported to Mt Sinai by angels who give her a royal burial [*LHW*, 200], while, when her corpse is translated though the flesh has rotted, 'the bones were so compact and pure that they seemed to be kept by the cure of angels' [*GL*, vol. 7, 26]. Mary Magdalene instructs the priest who relates her story to prepare bishop Maximin for her death. The latter goes to the oratory as told and there he sees her carried away by angels who hold her aloft in the air [*LHW*, 171]. She dies only after receiving the sacrament from Maximin, a detail also confirming the role of the cleric. This orthodoxy is similarly outlined in the carefully recorded translation of Margaret's corpse [*LHW*, 27–37], and the way in which a monk, praying to St Katherine, receives a relic, the joint of one of her fingers [*GL*, vol. 7, 27]. Caxton's version of Katherine's *vita* relates how the narrator prays for her to act as 'advocatrice in all our needs bodily and ghostly' [30]. Mediatrix between humanity and heaven, the saint's corpse is instrument of this function. It also has the power to affirm belief on behalf of the wider Christian community. Thus, Winifred's shrine is the site of numerous holy miracles, like those cured by drinking the water with which her bones were washed [*MF*, 180–1]. From Katherine's bones flows healing oil [*GL*, vol. 7, 27; *LHW*, 200], and from Mary Magdalene's corpse 'A ful redolent odour' which lasts for days and heals many [*LHW*, 171]. Similarly, when Elizabeth of Hungary dies, a marvellous 'odour of solace' emanates from her body [288]. The burial sites of Agnes and Margaret offer up many miracles [127–8; 32; 37], while Agatha's tomb is highly revered, not least when the flow of lava threatening the town is halted after her veil is placed in its path [242].

Yet, this intercessory role has a double valency simultaneously reducing the female saint, and intimating a powerful alternative. As already seen, several saints pray as they die, urging grace for all those who recall, read, recount, or simply possess their stories. Dorothy prays for those who recall her story, particularly women in childbirth [134; *GL*, vol. 7, 46], as does Margaret [23; *MF*, 202]. Here, it is not solely the written word that is privileged, but an alternative experience based upon an oral, aural, tactile, and physical presence. Enmeshed within this is a general assertion that the body is the focus of personal, lived, experienced faith. This body is not totally incorruptible and does not denote simply pure spirituality. Instead, it breaks up, is dismembered, and leaks fragrance. The virgin martyr's body is fragmented and mutilated, while other saints are racked by pain or corrupted by disease. Paradoxically, in death, bodily parts are unified and rendered whole. The body is closed, a homogeneous representative of a masculine world. Yet, almost immediately, it is once again the site of the abject, is blurred and splintered, is identified by its relics or fluids, associated with milk, oil, blood, with not the ocular but the olfactory; thus the corpse becomes creative and life-affirming.

A similar multiplicity is located in the healing and feeding miracles so prevalent in this genre. Angels feed Christine and heal her wounds [69] before later saving her from drowning in the sea [70]. An imprisoned Dorothy is fed so well by angels, 'wyth heuenly consolacyoun,' that 'she was nothing appaired.' [*LHW*, 131; *GL*, vol. 7, 43] Katherine tells her tormentor that she was fed daily by angels [192; *LKA*, 361], that a dove gave her 'meat celestial' [*GL*, vol. 7, 22]. One biographer insists that Mary Magdalene needed no food or water in the desert 'because our Redeemer did do show it openly, that he had ordained for her refection celestial, and no bodily meats' [*GL*, vol. 4, 83], while Bokenham notes

> In body & soule she fede was so wele
> þat of bodyly food she nedyd no dele [*LHW*, 168; *ESEL*, 478–9].

Similarly, Mary of Egypt survives her desert penitence for she was 'nourished of spiritual meat of the word of our Lord' [*GL*, vol. 3, 108].

Here, the holy valency of these miracles is clarified. Capgrave even interrupts his life of Katherine in order to explicate it more fully. He notes her miraculous feeding, referring to other sources mentioning that she is fed by a dove. He also indicates Augustine's teachings concerning the desert fathers and their food miracles, suggesting that it is the Holy Ghost which nourishes these saints, and adding

> She was fed – that haue we of treuthe;
> If god had lefte hir in soo bitter bale
> With-outen comfort, it had ben grete reuthe [*LKA*, 368–70].

Yet, other examples highlight the abject. Elizabeth of Hungary contents herself with simple bread and gross meats, except when in public for she never humiliates her husband or neglects her position, but, instead, handles and serves food exactly as she ought to. Bokenham cites the example of how, exhausted after a long journey, she will take only black bread moistened with a little water, in her private desire to push to the limits her concept of her self [*LHW*, 268–9]. Elizabeth of Spalbeck will only eat if forced, and then only a few spoonfuls of milk. She strives to seal her body totally, to revel in the abjection this demands; she speaks no evil, while from her mouth there is no spittle or moisture, or 'mater of vnclennes fro hir nese-þirles' [*Prosalegenden*, 118]. Mary of Oignies refuses food [162] but craves the sacrament [175]. When she is buried, it is seen that she is so frail and wasted through fasting and illness, that her backbone clings to her womb, and her bones protrude [183]. Mary of Egypt eats only herbs [*GL*, vol. 3, 108]. Pauline makes her young nuns fast in order to break 'their fleshly desires' [3], while she herself refuses fish, milk, eggs, and meat [6]. Genevieve fasts every day except Sundays and Thursdays when she eats barley bread and beans. She is eventually warned by her bishop to be less abstemious, and so eats more [290]. Clare fasts three times a week and drinks nothing until she, too, is ordered, by St Francis, to take at least one and a half ounces of bread per day [*GL*, vol. 6, 164]. As she dies, she again refuses all food, for a total of twelve days, and later she is seen to have been greatly enfeebled by her strict penance [179; 183].

Though such excesses were recognised as special signs of holiness, the Church itself was against them. However, such behaviour was highly significant as woman 'became' what she was said to be, sealed herself within her own corrupt flesh, became a silent, non-excreting, non-menstruating, non-sexualised body. She both escaped the limits of her flesh and immersed herself in it, investing it with a power almost exclusive to women. It is a paradox witnessed in the stripping away of flesh which renders her both near-invisible woman-other and highly visible female saint. It is seen, too, in Mary of Egypt who initially appears to Zosimus to be a man's shadow flat on the ground, [*ESEL*, 265], and, later, a ghost [266; *GL*, vol. 3, 106]. Similarly, after returning to the forest in later life, the occasional sighting of Christina Mirabilis is interpreted as the seeing of a phantom or spirit [*Prosalegenden*, 131], while the mere sight of her shadow instils terror in the observer [131]. As spirit rather than flesh, the holy woman also renders herself invisible and immaterial in order to gain a fresh identity and find a voice.

Others immerse themselves in abject corruption symbolising their spiritual worth, and also exploring a fragile sense of self. Elizabeth of Hungary cares for a servant suffering from a skin disease so appalling that none will touch him. She, however, lances his boils, releases the pus, cuts his hair, and wipes his face [*LHW*, 265–6]. She also regularly visits the hospitalised sick or poor, never flinching from a stench so repugnant that everyone else turns away [272].

More generally, there exists a focus upon privation and pain demonstrated in the filthy rags or animal skins that cover the hair shirt worn by Mary of Oignies

[*Prosalegenden*, 147], or the thin, simple coat which Clare of Assisi wears regardless of the weather [*GL*, vol. 6, 164]. It is said by her male narrator that Mary regularly whips herself in order to conquer lechery [*Prosalegenden*, 166], also a practice of Elizabeth of Hungary who mortifies her own flesh, and, in private and in her husband's absence, orders her maids to beat her violently, again to suppress lust [*LHW*, 268]. She also permits herself to be stripped and beaten by her confessor in humble atonement for disobedience [267]. Elizabeth of Spalbeck scourges herself between the ages of five and twenty, proof of her virginity according to Dan Philip of Clarevalle, her original biographer [*Prosalegenden*, 108]. Elizabeth is also famed for her bodily re-enactment of Christ's Passion. In a trance, she dramatises each separate moment from the time of His capture, when she walks up and down striking her cheeks, hitting her head on the ground, and grinding her fists in her eyes, to the crucifixion itself when she adopts a similar, frozen posture [107; 108].

That such details affirm an especial sanctity is not in question. The masculine voice of the biographer emphasises that Elizabeth of Spalbeck, for example, behaves in this bizarre manner because her body is a text written upon by men for the benefit of a holy community, where she 'figures and expones not allonly Cryste, but Cryste crucifyed, in hir body, and also þe figuratyf body of Cryste, þat is holy chirche' [118]. Her actions stem from 'a priue vertue of god' [108].

At the same time, however, Elizabeth's body reinscribes a masculine text. Her body speaks its own suffering femininity by sharing the experience of Christ's tortured humanity. She gains a voice and an identity, albeit apparently only holy. In particular, she elevates female-as-flesh and, through the pain associated with the experience of being a woman, is liberated. This association is a physical pain exemplified in childbirth, or an emotional one associated with loss, with lack, with invisibility. As seen in chapter two, it is a freedom demonstrated by Christina Mirabilis's literal immersion in the domestic, in interior or feminine space, and its obverse, her ascent to a heaven, symbolised by treetops, roofs, and steeples [122–3]. Attempting to contain her, her family lock her in a cellar, but she picks a hole in the wall through which her spirit might escape. She is tied to a tree and fed like a dog, her struggles to escape causing her back and shoulders to fester. She represents all that is feminine, sealed and subordinated within the masculine, symbolic world. Yet, within that same space she remains holy and admired [124].

The body and, in particular, its fluids and emissions, becomes the site of this positive and celebratory reinscription and affirmation of human spirit. Its distinctions are permeable and liable to dissolve, exemplified in Christina's trances where her body whirls so fast that her limbs are indistinguishable. She also whips herself with thorns so that she is continually covered in blood [123], while her dry virginal breasts nourish her with milk and oil with which she anoints her wounds [124]. An explicit allusion to the Virgin Mary [121] ensures that, once again, the masculine writing voice confirms the religious significance of such events, but its complex symbolisation cannot be so easily reduced. Elizabeth of Spalbeck achieves notoriety for the stigmata on her hands, feet, and sides which bleed each Friday, while these same stigmata, together with her eyes and fingertips, bleed on the hour as she 'enacts' Christ's Passion [107; 114].

Here, the 'grotesque' body with its offshoots, its breasts, its wounds, its fissures, its leaking fluids of blood, milk, and oil, rearticulates itself. As will be demonstrated in this final section, it speaks of pain and suffering but it also tells of joy, of an alternative feminine experience derived from an awareness of woman's own, different body.

Torture and violence: the rhythm of blood

Medieval thought viewed all bodily emissions as a bleeding, a menstruation, regardless of biological sex, a concept exemplified in slippery representations of Christ's body as a nurturing and lactating one. This lack of polarisation tended to lead towards either a blurring or the insertion of distinctions.[23] It is the latter which is a particular feature of female hagiography and, more especially, virgin martyrology where saints remain beautiful despite horrendous physical torture, their incorrupt bodies reflections of the soul's glory and unusual bodily events an expression of that soul. Once again the body, particularly an intact virginal one, provides access to the divine.[24]

Such bodies are marked by violence, whether perpetrated by a male, pagan representative of the law, or self-inflicted where the pattern of representation is slightly different. Those historical saints who scourge and mutilate themselves gain power by reinscribing their own bodies, making them bear the marks of spiritual authority by acting upon them, writing them as text, in the role of both torturer and victim. Thus, they reappropriate power and authority and speak themselves in their construction or explication of culture.[25] More generally, Irigaray suggests that violence and identity go hand in hand, are mediated by God. Religion turns the violence of a community inside out, and so what is sacrificial also has its corollary in fertility.[26] The saint is a sacrificial victim opposing and diluting the male threat of violence, surrendering her body to Christ yet also making her own identity. It is a process exemplified through violence, in the significant morphology of blood, breasts, and bodily emissions.

Hagiographical tradition demands that virgin martyrology emphasises the sexual torture of its saintly victims. Sadism is the rite of passage preceding salvation, and sanctity is achieved precisely because the woman risks her holy virginity. Thus, a sometimes titillating emphasis upon nakedness, upon pain, demonstrates how that virginity is threatened, and how *all* might triumph over the body. That this emphasis might also arouse its audience is a bonus, for then the male writer can instil guilt and shame,[27] emotions ensuring that readers and listeners are doubly vulnerable to the text's Christian 'message'.

The biographer notes the male abuse of the saintly female body, grabs for himself the right to speak her faith, and leaves her self untouched. The male takes pleasure in looking at her, in the sadistic pains with which she is inscribed. Yet she herself remains intact and unfragmented. She sings, she speaks in her 'alternative' voice, her flesh actually resisting his intentions and his world.

Jocelyn Wogan-Browne argues for a similar re-reading of this material.[28] She notes its holy valency where the outer husk of the body is stripped in order to reveal its inner or spiritual meaning but suggests that such a 'theatre of punishment' resists 'the anatomising and consuming gaze of narrators and courtly lovers in lyric and romance'[29] which is replicated in the ambivalent stance of a biographer who is both voyeur and participant in a process of textual dismemberment.[30]

She identifies a narrative subcode which includes a stress upon visual outline, unique to female saints, as they are stripped, bathed in their own blood, surrounded by fire or marked by a contrast between red and white. It is a bodily integrity which defines the Christian community, and encodes anxieties concerning heresy as well as establishing social and cultural boundaries.[31] I would further suggest that what is refuted is masculine ocular proof. Nothing harms or penetrates her body; she continues to sing, laugh, cry, to confound a more literal minded male, as suggested in earlier chapters. Perhaps, more importantly, the pattern of torture permits a resistant reading.

A common form of torture in female hagiography is burning, itself a medieval punishment for heresy. Wogan-Browne suggests that the fire intended to destroy the holy virgin is reinscribed as the fire of baptism or the flames of the Pentecost.[32] The saint is unfailingly preserved in the flames, whilst the cruelty of such torment is highlighted by the *Early South-English Legendary* narrator of the life of Cecilia who records the pity of weeping onlookers:

> 'Allas', þei seyde, 'þat þis ʒongge þing, þus fair a creature,
> Schal nou lese hit ʒongge lif, ʒ deye' [*ESEL*, 495].

Miracles accumulate throughout a range of stories. Cecilia is placed in a bath of flames where she remains cool and free from pain [*VIII(G)*, 521]. Agnes is cast into a furnace where the flames divide, preserving her within this path while those watching are burnt to death [*LHW*, 124]. A naked Agatha is laid on a bed of hot shards and coals, while Dorothy remains unharmed in a vessel of hot oil which anoints her like sweet balm [131; 239]. Juliana has molten lead heaped on her head, and, when this fails, is immersed in a pot of the same substance [*GL*, vol. 3, 46; 49]. Hot oil is thrown over Lucy [*LHW*, 255] before her naked body is thrown into a fiery furnace [*ESEL*, 105]. Faith is stripped and tied to a brass bed beneath which is a continually stoked furnace. There she is turned as if on a spit [85], while the flames lick so high up the sides that all cry out against her tormentor [*LHW*, 102]. She is saved by the dew from a dove's wings which extinguishes the fire, and heals her wounds [104].

Attention is drawn to the outline of a whole and incorrupt body, to that same body's naked vulnerability protected by the fire of faith. However, the details of the fire symbol also indicate the presence of a voice speaking beneath the saintly one, beneath the masculine text. As demonstrated earlier, woman is associated with interiority, itself an open-ended and multiple concept. She is closed and constricted in the inner spaces which contain her: vessels, pots, beds, baths.

Yet, these same containers are familiar, domestic ones, part of the daily experience of the female who uses fire (and oil) as fuel both for warmth and cooking,
who fills pots, roasts and turns meat, bakes in ovens. This world is immediately
recognisable and holds no fear. Within its creative fertility, she is secure in a
collective identity as woman *and* saint. Within it, she sings her own unique
song and deflects a masculine brutality. Christine's father lashes her to an iron
wheel, its circular shape symbolic of femininity, beneath which he builds a fire,
but he cannot harm her [*LHW*, 68]. Later she is immersed in a vessel of boiling
oil [74] whose destructive threat is inverted for there she sits as if

> . . . in a full fresh herbere
> Amoung flourys lyne & amoung grene gras [75].

When the furnace is lit, she remains calm, 'rocked as a child in a cradle' [*GL*,
vol. 4, 96]. Burning coals are heaped on her head while a third prefect shuts
her in an oven where, for three days, she sings with angels, and marks her
forehead with a cross [*LHW*, 79]. She emerges unscathed from this feminine
environment,

> . . . as shynyng was
> As is þe sunne in his degre,

and still articulating her alternative song [80].

Both fire and ritualised beating are spiritually cleansing. A physical and
moral integrity is exemplified in the wholeness of a virginal body resistant to
fragmentation, penetration, and dismemberment, and is miraculously
preserved from earthly corruption in a manner recalling the Assumption of the
Virgin Mary. Mirk details how she was brought into Paradise by a band of
angels, with great joy, and surrounded by a heavenly melody for Christ so loved
her that He refused to allow her body to decompose. Thus she is to be sought in
heaven and not on earth [*MF*, 225].

The virginal body becomes patriarchal text, is marked as holy by the male
biographer. During Katherine's desert vision, it is said that 'she was entered
into the body of the church' [*GL*, vol. 7, 12]. Similarly, during Margaret's
defiance of Olibrius she is made to declare that her body will soon be in
Paradise, and that she welcomes death [*LHW*, 16]. She informs a weeping
crowd that such earthly purgatory guarantees her immediate heavenly reward
[177], adding 'this cruel torment of my flesh is salvation of my soul' for no man
has power over the latter [*GL*, vol. 4, 68]. Refusing to surrender despite her
torments, Margaret's holy sacrifice is clarified in her comment that

> '. . . if I of my flesh shuld haue mercy,
> My soule perysh shuld' [*LHW*, 18].

Similarly, Agatha welcomes her torture as if receiving good news or
discovering buried treasure, insisting that her soul needs to be cleansed in this

way prior to entering Paradise, just as grain is separated from chaff [233]. Katherine too parrots the voice of the male narrator when she reminds how beauty fades and bodies rot while, in contrast, martyrdom promises immortality [*LKA*, 379]. In Caxton's version of the life of Dorothy, the masculine voice asserts itself through an appendix explicating the religious *exemplum* contained in the torture to which she submits through the grace of Christ 'for whose love she took on her these great and sharp torments' [*GL*, vol. 7, 45].

A threatening female sexuality is also deflected by the holiness these lives describe. Sanctity asserts itself as Agnes, sent to a brothel as punishment, is surrounded by a light so bright that every man is blinded by it. Miraculously, she receives a white smock with which to cover and preserve her virginal body [*LHW*, 120]. Similarly, Lucy's faith is so firmly entrenched that she is literally unmoved by all attempts to drag her into a bordello [253]. Her resistance to both temptation and assault is clarified in her reply to Pascas:

> 'þe more þat mi bodi a-ȝein mi wille: here defouled is,
> þe clenore is mi mayden-hod: and þe more mi mede, i-wis' [*ESEL*, 104].

She cannot be corrupted without her soul's assent, and, even if he causes

> '. . . by force þe integryte
> Of my body to be reft fro me',

her soul remains defiant [*LHW*, 252]. She has no fear of torture for she loves Christ, and yields her entire body to Him [*ESEL*, 103]. Another account indicates that if she is forcibly ravished, her 'chastity' is, in fact, doubly strengthened [*GL*, vol. 2, 134].

However, beneath the sanctimonious voice of these patriarchal dolls, a fissure is revealed. The series of tortures detailed in female hagiography are highly sexualised, emphasising naked white bodies and sadistic ritualised beatings, many focused upon breasts. The virgin martyr's body is an elevated ideal unbreached by either childbirth or the loss of her hymen. Instead, her body is penetrated by vicious, sharp, and phallic torture implements designed to lacerate and shred her skin. That ultimately she remains unfragmented is testament to her faith; she literally embodies the lesson of her biographer's text.

So, inflamed by lust, Olibrius viciously attacks Margaret. She prays continuously as

> They rent hyr flesh on euery syde
> So dispetously [*LHW*, 18].

She is menaced by a dragon, symbol of both evil and sexuality, and a terrifying corporeal presence which Bokenham describes in detail [19]. She is suspended upside down and beaten, first with rods, and then with 'iron combs to rend and draw her flesh to the bones' [*GL*, vol. 4, 68]. Similarly, Dorothy is hung on a gibbet, whipped, and torn [*LHW*, 132] then hung upside down, her body ripped by hooks and her breasts burnt [*GL*, vol. 7, 44]. Later, her face is beaten in with staves [*LHW*, 133].

A further example is Christine, enclosed in a tower by her own father at the start of her fourteen-year persecution by three separate judges. Her refusal to sacrifice results in her being beaten until her tormentors are weary [65; *GL*, vol. 4, 94], before she is suspended from a gibbet and her flesh torn [68]. Her father details her punishments demanding that she is drawn by iron hooks and that her limbs are broken and torn from her body [*GL*, vol. 4, 95]. A second prefect beats her with rods, and parades her through the streets, naked and with her head shaved, displaying to the world his possession. Katherine too is stripped, whipped, and imprisoned [*LHW*,188]. There, she is beaten with scorpions [*GL*, vol. 7, 22; *MF*, 276]. She is attacked 'Soo dispitously that shame it was to see', and most people turn away in horror [*LKA*, 376]. Her engine of torture, the Katherine wheel, an instrument that some describe in graphic detail [*LKA*, 380], is razored so that 'she might be horribly all detrenched and cut in that torment' [*GL*, vol. 7, 23].

Barbara, taken before a judge who is overwhelmed by lust, is stripped, beaten with bullwhips, and her flesh rubbed with salt. Subsequently, she is stretched between two forked trees, beaten in the kidneys with staves and in the head with a mallet. Lamps also scorch her sides, and, later, she is dragged through the streets for all to see [*GL*, vol. 6, 202–3]. Juliana's provost is similarly maddened by desire when her father, having severely beaten her, hands over to him her naked body. Spurning his advances, she is cruelly thrashed with iron rods before being suspended by her hair [*GL*, vol. 3, 45–6].

Many saints are stabbed, often in the throat, as seen earlier, in an effort to silence them. The penetrative instrument used to inflict this damage parallels the phallus, itself associated with entry into the symbolic world where the predominant discourse is a masculine one. It is through this, and other tortures, that the pagan tormentor is, yet again, seen to be representative of patriarchy. His intention is to appropriate the virginal body as his own. Invariably smitten by the beauty of his victim, he is incensed by her refusal of him, and determined to rupture her *integritas*. Thus, his weapons penetrate her, his gaze consumes her, and his torture seeks to fragment her. Capgrave's interruption, railing against a Maxentius who intends 'Thi virgynal body to destroye and shende' [*LKA*, 381], gallantly protects his vulnerable subject, Katherine. At the same time, it serves to highlight the function of patriarchy which is to subsume the female.

Yet the female resists, and in ways beyond the scope of the holy. Her corporeality remains intact for her soul, her faith *and* inner self, refuse to accept the imposition of the masculine. After twelve days in prison, Katherine is

. . . bryhter of ble
And of colour fressher in euery wyse [*LHW*, 191].

Her incorrupt wholeness is in defiance of the words of those onlookers, agents of patriarchy, who regard her as unnatural, asking

> . . . What woman are ye that soo despyse youre age
> Youre body, youre beute þat ye sette at nought? [*LKA*, 376].

Capgrave, like most biographers, is implicated in the masculine process of destruction; his mask is that of sympathetic protector, but his real focus is the sight of a lovely body. He tells how the crowd bewail the fate of Katherine's beautiful body, adding 'It is soo reent, зoure skyn is al to-tore', and 'Youre white skyn' shall be ripped [376; 377].

It is emphasis upon the masculine that is subverted within the fissured text. Katherine's circular wheel speaks of a cyclic and domestic continuity and opposes the linear, phallic rods, swords, and whips associated with male, pagan tormentors. The angel breaks that wheel, and saves her. Similarly, Juliana is strapped to a wheel drawn by four horses 'so that all the body was tobroken in such wise that the marrow came out of the bones, and the wheel was all bloody'. This wheel too is fractured by an angel which then renders her whole and sound [*GL*, vol. 3, 49]. Agnes is protected in the brothel by a miraculous blinding light which deflects and dissolves a masculine insistence upon the visual. Lucy cannot be dragged to a whore-house. Both resist the appropriation of their bodies, and assert an identity outside a sexual one as virgin or whore, an element witnessed elsewhere in these stories.

In return for repudiating the provost's advances, Dorothy's face is smashed in [*LHW*, 133]. Though an imposed identity as sexual temptress, as beautiful woman, is countered in the destruction of her voice and her loveliness, her true identity remains intact, for the following day she is more lovely than ever [*GL*, vol. 7, 45]. Similarly, Lucy's body is assaulted and fragmented. Yet, despite a sword thrust into her throat, she continues to speak 'not wythstondying þat greuous wounde' [*LHW*, 256]. Of course she speaks of Christ, but, equally, she asserts her own feminine identity through the fissure of her bodily wound. In the same way, flesh 'speaks' when Christine spits her tongue at her tormentor[33] and blinds him [84], and also when she throws her own flesh back at her father, denying his claim upon her, and asserting the rights both of her self and the mother [68].

The female body is used to articulate identity in other ways. Agnes is paraded through the city streets where

> . . . so naked so heo was i-bore
> þat ech man scholde i-seon hire derne limes [*ESEL*, 182].

Her hair hides her shame, preserves her holy worth, and negates the power of a masculine gaze which recognises nothing beyond the literal and the superficial. She asks how she might be humiliated when *all* woman are like this [182]. Here, she highlights a natural sexual difference as well as recalling a pre-Lapsarian innocence. Similarly, Agatha dissolves sexual tension by reminding of a common humanity as well as that difference. She greets St Peter, disguised as an old man and sent to heal her wounds, in a manner echoing Irigaray's notion of alterity. Though initially protesting her modesty, she admits that she is so disfigured that no man could ever be tempted by her [*LHW*, 236]. Another version declares that 'my body is defeated by the torments', and, so, feels no sexual shame [*GL*, vol. 3, 36].

Identity is also articulated through the body of Christine. Her third tormentor calls for a snake charmer to bring his venomous serpents and kill her. The sexual symbolism is obvious, but, instead, the snakes kill their owner [*LHW*, 81–2]. They lick Christine's feet, while adders 'wound them about her neck and licked up her sweat' [*GL*, vol. 4, 96], revelling in this body of Eve. They

> . . . heng up-on hir pappys also
> Lyk smal infauntys wych kun no wykke [*LHW*, 81].

This innocent image dissolves woman's sexual transgression as Eve, recalls the domesticity of the maternal, and reinscribes the female body with a creative and generative power enhanced by the fact that Christine resurrects the snake charmer [81–2].

Undoubtedly, this is a power whose driving force is holy, and which is primarily articulated by the controlling masculine voice of the narrator, but its 'secret', open-ended subtlety contains a multiplicity of implications. Saints like Cecilia, Margaret, Dorothy, Katherine, and Juliana can only be killed when they are beheaded. It is a form of death reminiscent of an aristocratic form of torture with the head as a prize, as in the story of John the Baptist. What is made evident is a distinction between the thinking, rational, 'male' head, and a grosser, sensual body. By separating the two, woman is reduced to a fragmented materiality, and is effectively silenced. At the same time, her body serves as text. Thus Winifred is beheaded in revenge for the preservation of her virginity. She is resurrected by the holy hermit, Beuno, who, before a large crowd, pronounces a sermon and places her head back with her body [*MF*, 178; *GL*, vol. 6, 129–30]. 'Masculine', clerical authority is privileged.

However, a spring wells up from Winifred's head, while she herself speaks 'hole and sownde as sche was before' [*MF*, 178]. Her flesh, too, has generative properties, and it is her fragmented flesh, her wound, which speaks. Though pagan-patriarch and male narrator are intertwined in a process imposing a masculine rationality at the expense of the feminine, their success is undermined by a female body whose faith and selfhood are experienced *through* that body, in a sensual and affective manner unaffected by physical assault.

The mutilation of female breasts features strongly in these saints' lives, and it is this aspect in particular which opens up the hagiographical text. Frantzen suggests that the symbol operates as a model of holiness which conflates the male and the secondary female under God. Women are saved by becoming 'manly' and transcending the body. Thus, breasts are not a sign of sexual identity, but a non-gendered aspect of human and holy worth.[34]

Undoubtedly, the intention of the male writer is to signal the sanctity of his subject. Agatha's 'words' highlight this when she insists that, despite the loss of her breasts, inside is 'my soule al hool wyth-ynne'. It is this which enables her to 'fostre & susteyne' her wits and faith [*LHW*, 234]. Similarly, Christine tells her final tormentor

> 'Syth, þou my pappys a-weye doost rase,
> In tokyn of clennes of uirginite,
> Lo, mylk for blood þere-out doth pase' [83].

The saint's body, virginal and breastless, remains a source of spiritual nourishment.

Yet, this common and cruel breach of the 'grotesque' body has a validation beyond the holy, one which relates to the signification of the tormentor not just as pagan but as male, representative of patriarchy. The mutilation functions as a positive and celebratory indication of the feminine; located in the corporeal fissures of its wounds are portents of resistance and disruption. It is a multiplicity witnessed in the medieval devotion to Christ's body, and, particularly to His open 'female' wound, His bleeding heart, His breast, a permeable bodily orifice which might be described as 'a vast vagina-like object of desire'.[35] The female breast *is* a marker of sexual difference, and any attack is a sexual assault upon the virginal, female body. It is also an attempt to obliterate feminine identity, an identity asserted through a cultural representation of woman *as* woman as well as mother. Wearing masculine dress, Eugenia is brought before her father-judge, accused of fornication. Her only defence is to reveal her breasts, offer herself as vulnerable daughter, yet also assert her sense of self [*GL*, vol. 5, 124].

During the Lacanian mirror stage the son reluctantly turns from the mother when he realises her difference, and aligns himself with power, with the masculine. When the pagan-patriarch orders the removal of the virgin martyr's breasts, his attack is upon the mother, normally regained as masculine property in the sex act. These men invariably lust after their victims who always repudiate them. Their attack is a double revenge against maternal and female loss, a reminder of masculine power, for man both gives and withdraws the privilege of marriage and the privileged shelter of motherhood, something amply demonstrated in Chaucer's *The Clerk's Tale*. They destroy what, in fact, they love, and assert a difference in which the female is subordinated. Thus, Barbara and Christine lose their breasts [*GL*, vol. 6, 203; vol. 4, 97], while part of Dorothy's torture is the instruction that

> . . . hyr pappy vnpetously
> Wyth feerbrondys brent [*LHW*, 132].

Maxentius's queen is punished for her defence of Katherine by having her breasts pulled off [*LKA*, 387]:

> . . . wyth forkys of yryn ful cruelly
> Hyr brestys þei rent from hyr body [*LHW*, 196].

Quincian demands that Agatha's breasts are removed from her body [*GL*, vol. 3, 35]. Using blunt pincers, his men tug at her breasts 'Ful boystously'. Red-hot firebrands burn her breasts to cinders before they

> . . . wyth yirnene forkys out rent
> The flesh þer-of.

Finally, Quincian orders that her breasts be hacked off and thrown away [*LHW*, 234].

It is Agatha's response that rearticulates a reading of those events. Several versions cite a confrontation in which she directly recalls the maternal, and implicitly demands an acknowledgement of the debt owed to the mother. She accepts her breasts as a sign of sexual difference, but calls for a recognition of her identity as a female person, not merely a sexualised object. She asks

> '. . . hast þou no shame
> A-wey to kuttyn that on thy dame
> Thou dedyst soukyn for þi fostryng
> Ere þou koudyst etyn?' [234],

a comment echoed in Caxton's collection [*GL*, vol. 3, 35], and the *Early South-English Legendary* which notes 'Ne hastþov no schame in þine heorte: defoul; þus ani man þat lyme þat þov þi moder of soke: and þe hath forth i-brouȝt?' [*ESEL*, 195].

What is highlighted is a creative, generative female body which negates the destructive implications of a masculine act of violence, and extends beyond the holy. Textual fissures speak of a sensual pleasure, of breasts that men *and* women 'didst suck in thy mother' [*GL*, vol. 3, 35]. Ultimately it is a different, feminine identity and a maternal power that are asserted, for the virginal body remains unbreached, unfragmented, Agatha's wounds healed by St Peter [*LHW*, 236–7].

The multivalency of the female body is similarly exemplified through its permeability. It is both open and closed. It contains fissures and orifices through which bodily fluids are spilled. In religious terms, blood purges and is redemptive, an idea embodied in affective devotion to Christ's nurturing and 'female' body. Many saintly miracles involve blood (stigmata, bleeding Host) or other emissions such as milk, itself regarded as twice-cooked blood. Some believe that events and miracles like this were exclusive to female saints.[36] Because gender imagery was fluid, all bleeding, however trivial, was viewed as significant and as feminine. The female body was simultaneously weak and corrupt, and fertile and generative.[37]

Elizabeth Robertson's explorations of the *Ancrene Wisse* and Julian of Norwich's *Showings* begin from an examination of medieval medical constructions of woman. She argues that this provides a vocabulary with which female mystics described their own somatic experiences.[38] Some of her findings are relevant here. She indicates that women were regarded as fundamentally excessively moist *and* cold, requiring a heat provided by the male which made them sexually voracious. As women were inferior in both body and soul, so feminine religious experience was expressed via that physicality in celebration of an erotic, sexualised and corporeal body (Christ). When the female mystic contemplated Christ's blood, she contemplated her own in redemption of her own fleshliness and excess moisture. Central to this experience were blood and tears[39] ideas also fundamental to Irigaray.

I would agree that all bodily emissions remain significant symbols expressing holy female devotion, but also offer an opportunity to celebrate the female and her experience, and resist the fixed, authoritative notion of her as exclusively holy. Once again, it is a sense of identity which is called into question. Blood, milk, and tears form part of a saintly code recognised and accepted by all. It is blood which unites *all* female saints; the virgin martyrs bleed as a result of male-inflicted torture and other saints through self-inflicted punishment or paramystical events. It is also blood which unites all women.

Feminine experience of blood remains fundamentally different from that of the masculine. For the latter, blood signifies death, and a fear of it leads to a series of taboos warding off the abject including menstruation or the bodily emissions of childbirth. Such proscriptions focus upon the female so that her body is never open to her, never fully belongs to her.[40] Instead, women are bought with their own blood. It is token of virginity, and the virginal woman is a prize, protecting the patrilinear blood line. As a new bride, woman surrenders her blood, her body, her identity in exchange for the status of wife and, usually, mother when her fluids, blood, and pain, even her milk, are given up for the pleasure of providing an heir whom she will ultimately 'lose'. During pregnancy, she does not bleed at all. What happens is that man cuts off woman from her own blood, mark of her difference and, in part at least, site of her identity.

Nowhere is the process better exemplified than in Chaucer's holy women, Custance and Griselda; their role as both embodied ideal and articulated, resistant practice has been fully explored in previous chapters. It is seen, too, in virgin martyrology where the pagan-patriarch has his victims beaten until his power is apparent to all. The blood flows in token representation of the loss of virginity and surrender to the male. A naked Agnes is assaulted until the crowd witnesses

> . . . rede blod orn a-doun: on hire limes so ȝwite.
> Fairore ne miȝte no-þing [be]: þane was þat ilke blod
> On hire limes þat weren so ȝwite [*ESEL*, 184].

Those observing the punishment meted out to Katherine's royal defender note how

> The blood in the veynes with the mylke ryse;
> Al rent and ragged and blody was shee [*LKA*, 387],

while Margaret's cruel beating ensures

> That lyk as watyr in a ryuer
> So ran hyr blood owt plenteuously [*LHW*, 16].

It forms a river so wide that even Olibrius, its instigator, is repelled, and unable to watch the 'Blood rennyng owt so gret plente' [18]. The amputation of Christine's breasts releases milk not blood [83; *GL*, vol. 4, 97]. Katherine is scourged until her blood gushes, while later she is beheaded, her neck described as so fair and white [*LKA*, 358; 400]. She, too, 'bleeds' milk [401; *GL*, vol. 7, 25] in a flow as wide as a lake [*LHW*, 200].

The holy woman, whether virgin martyr or historical saint, sacrifices her body in exchange for sanctity. Her blood is milk, redemptive and nourishing, symbol of her spirituality. Yet the emission is also a form of menstruation unique to the saint. Denied expression of the joys of her body, she revels in its life-force, in blood, deliberately placing herself at the site of the abject. Its rhythm is unfailingly regular. Torture makes her bleed, she makes *herself* bleed, she weeps, she participates in a ritual of paramystical phenomena, she spills her fluids in the creative pain of 'childbirth'; this is the menstrual cycle of the saint.

It is the sign of the fertility of a generative, female body where the feminine experience of blood is a celebratory one. The loss of virginity is a rite of passage perhaps leading to actual birth. Its metaphorical loss ensures the glory of heavenly reward. Either way, it is part of a process regenerating the self. Blood holds no fear for women for it is part of their *lived* experience. In touch with the cycle of her own body, the female saint remains close to her self. Thus, once again, images designed to affirm the immortality of the Christian sacrificial body also articulate a positive resistance to the masculine. Even the virgin martyr remains whole and intact, the rhythm of her blood speaking of the creative possibilities of a joyful life. Her blood is a river, a lake, it is milk. All that is fragmented is a masculine text.

Notes

1 For further clarification of the notions of 'desire' and 'lack' see Stockton 1994: 34–5; 50–1.
2 For further details see le Goff 1988: 93–107 but especially 95–6.
3 See Lochrie 1991: 15–27.
4 This area has been extensively researched. See Prusak 1974; Ruether 1974; McLaughlin 1974: See also John Bugge (1975) who traces the theological development of notions of chastity as does T. J. Heffernan (1988: 235–55). Jocelyn Wogan-Browne also offers a history of this development (1994: 166–73 in particular). Within the same paper, she also presents a resistant reading of this notion, arguing that the widespread dissemination of a literature of virginity went beyond the theological, and sometimes offered women a choice; free of men, they gained 'a paradoxical version of autonomy and self-fashioning at once empowering and disabling' (ibid. 71). More generally, see Millet and Wogan-Browne 1990.
5 See Bakhtin 1984: 19–30. More generally chapters five and six remain useful.

6 Such an activity also occurs in the discourse of medieval female mystical writing. On this topic, see Finke, 1993: 29–44 but particularly 35–9, as well as chapter three of Petroff 1994: especially 56–93. For a more general description of Bakhtin's two bodies see Finke 1993: 35–9 and Beckwith 1993: 44, as well as Bakhtin 1984: 26 for a description of the 'grotesque' body.

7 See Evans 1994: especially 116–18; also Rubin 1994: 101–11.

8 See Bynum 1992: 239–98 but especially 290–6.

9 See Bynum 1992: 119–50.

10 Camille 1994: 77.

11 Evans 1994: 125.

12 Leclerc 1990: 77.

13 See Bynum 1987: especially 90–215; 270.

14 See Bell (1985), a study of some female saints, where it is suggested that food abstinence was an individual female response to woman's place within patriarchy. Though interesting, Bell's work tends to emphasise hysteria or psychological illness, which detracts from the saint's achievements, ignores how an individual also has a collective identity, and, generally, neglects *how* these women become holy.

15 Eucharistic devotion has been extensively covered elsewhere, and, because of its close association with mysticism, I am omitting it. See, however, Rubin (1991) for a full discussion of eucharistic devotion and spiritual food. See also Bynum (1987: 47–77; 216–35), as well as her paper 'Women Mystics and Eucharistic Devotion in the Thirteenth Century', (1991: 119–50).

16 The idea of a pure body as a dynamic is explored by Jo Ann McNamara (1993: 15). Sarah Beckwith (1993) explores the shifting symbolisation of Christ's body while Ellen Ross (1993) examines female mysticism. Devotion to Christ's body is traced by Miri Rubin (1991: 302–6).

17 See Robertson 1991. Her exploration of an Old English version of St Margaret suggests that the subversive response of the saint's body is typical of much female hagiography. See also Bynum (1987: 246–57), as well as some work on Margery Kempe: Sarah Beckwith (1986) and (1993), C.W. Atkinson (1983: 129–56), and Lochrie (1991).

18 Robertson 1991: 286.

19 Grosz 1989: 72.

20 ibid. 72.

21 See E. Grosz's commentary (1989: 71–78) upon Julia Kristeva's 'The Powers of Horror'. See also McAffee (1993) and Moi (1985:170; 1986: 238–9) where she discusses Kristeva's discourse of love based upon knowledge of the concept of abjection, site of the first efforts of a 'self' to separate from the mother.

22 See Karma Lochrie 1991b: 128–32 in particular.

23 For further ideas concerning this, see Bynum 1991: 202–24.

24 ibid. 234–5.

25 See Finke 1993: 40–2.

26 The clearest explanation I have found is in Whitford (1991: 145–7).

27 See Heffernan 1988: especially 276–83.

28 Wogan-Browne (1994) examines what she terms a 'theatre of punishment' in virgin martyrology as part of an explanation of how literature of virginity might have spoken to women.

29 Wogan-Browne also notes that the pagan and courtly gaze are the same. Each desires to possess, but the female saint looks back, negates the power of this stare, and renders the masculine world 'incoherent'. It is witnessed too in the way it is metaphorically 'dishevelled and fractured on the body of the virgin' (ibid. 178; 175).

30 ibid. 175.

31 ibid. 177.

32 ibid. 179.

33 The idea of the body 'talking', or providing a site of resistance, is not new. See, for example, Burns 1993. Basing her study on Irigaray, she explains how the female body, or more specifically the vagina, 'answers' the male. By repositioning the female, and citing her body as a centre of knowledge and thought, traditional binary oppositions are dissolved.

34 Allen J. Frantzen examines Old English hagiography, and, in particular, the stories of Agatha, Eugenia, and Euphrosyne in Aelfric's *Lives Of The Saints*. Agatha, for example, loses her breasts for, according to Frantzen, her identity as a woman is less important than her faith. Consequently, she 'becomes' a man before being restored to womanhood (see Frantzen 1993: especially 462–7).

35 Camille 1994: 77.

36 Bynum (1991) 'The body of Christ in the later Middle Ages: a reply to Leo Steinberg': 101–2.

37 ibid.: 116–17.

38 Robertson 1994: 142–67.

39 ibid. 146–50. See also Lochrie (1991: 8 in particular) who explores the way Margery Kempe finds entry into her own mystical text via tears (and laughter). Lochrie also notes the valency of tears as part of a model of compassion seen in medieval drama depictions of the Virgin Mary and Mary Magdalene, a model debated by medieval theology and found in conjunction with the image of Christ's suffering body as book, a book 'read' by the Virgin herself plus those who have compassion for Him. Thus tears make the spectacle of a reading of the body of Christ.

40 Leclerc 1990: 78.

Conclusion
Song of the saint

This study has been concerned with the interplay between the sexes and their separate discourse revealed through the texts of later medieval female hagiography. To dismantle existing systems or deny the power of these literary texts, the authoritative masculine control of their predominant voice, has never been my intention. Rather, my aim has been to explore the ways in which this voice, with its idealisation of saint and 'woman', its circumscription of feminine behaviour, is undercut by other, concealed, and *different* voices. It has been based upon a search for fissures in the text, an attempt to open up what is unsaid, to multiply and compound perspective, to reveal shadows, echoes, hidden space. For, without doubt, there exists both a masculine and a feminine voice, each equally important, each, without the other, essentially reductive. As Cixous writes,

> Just as the one is not without the other,
> The one cannot be *thought* without the other.[1]

In order to make sense, not just of these textual lives, but of the lives of ordinary men and women throughout the ages, both voices must have their say. As Irigaray tells 'man', 'you will hear nothing of women as long as you are bending them thus to your will', for when this occurs 'woman' 'has learned at least this much from your wisdom: when the other does not hear you, it is better to be silent'.[2]

Undoubtedly, the predominant discourse belongs to the male writers of female saints' lives, even where individual characteristics and different audiences partially detract from its univocality. These biographers speak in two ways – as authoritative, literary poets or clerics, and as men, representative of patriarchal law. Both aspects inform their choice of controlling narrative framework. The intention of the hagiographical text is to confirm the sanctity of its subject, to render visible the saint, 'relic' of a wider Christian community, and this is achieved in a variety of ways.

Firstly, there exists a saintly code recognised by all, and conforming to a repetitive pattern. Virgin martyrs are located in time, place, history with an emphasis upon patriarchal, pagan genealogy. Their love of Christ leads to a confrontation with a male representative of the law, a series of opportunities to recant, violent and sexualised torture, and subsequent martyrdom. Historical saints, or holy women, are again located in the symbolic world, emphasised as holy despite their tender years, and praised for those ideal qualities directly matching the virtues of late medieval piety.

Secondly, religious allusion or even direct comparison, usually to the Virgin Mary, indicates holiness while all apparently independent action is described as heavenly intervention. Words and knowledge stem from the Holy Ghost, and images of interiority confirm the female saint as the vessel of the Christian Word. Her humanity is largely ignored as a process of nomenclature and labelling constrict her, reducing her to 'saint', 'blessed virgin', or 'holy'. Finally, the masculine is asserted through an emphasis upon patrilinear and textual dissemination which cites other authorities, and explicates miracles or points of doctrine.

Thus, the female's identity is solely saintly. Her lesson is clarified by the writer, her experiences and knowledge (of God *and* self) appropriated by him, her transgressive behaviour diluted and reinscribed. He allocates her words and disseminates her fragmented life. Holiness closes her lips through the very act of writing; she surrenders her flesh and sacrifices her self.[3] The biographer also speaks as a man, and, consequently, it is masculine experience which is privileged as superior. Her body is a text marked by him. Interruptions profess his chivalry, itself a patronising mask. An ideal of womanhood is promulgated emphasising meekness, mildness, patience. His subject is merely man's other, receptacle of faith and masculine authority, and thus she is sealed within the tower of his text just as she is in life, a process demonstrated in the words of Cixous:

> It was a question of my whole life. He was pulling it to pieces, I wasn't living it . . . And all in praise of his fictions, he was annihilating my reality.[4]

There remain, however, some fundamental questions to be raised. When medieval woman heard this voice did she recognise herself, or, rather, did she see herself reflected in a distorting hall of mirrors? As she was constantly told that she was nothing, invisible, a void filled only by Christ or children, corrupt matter, weak flesh, sexual temptress, and informed how she should behave, her identity was fragmented into a huge and complex jigsaw, where no single piece tells the full story or authoritatively defines her as this or that. Somewhere too, there were other voices different from and resistant to masculine univocality. These are the voices to be found in the fissures of the text, in the gap between theory and practice so well articulated in Chaucer's Custance and Griselda, and in the role of the hagiographical angel, symbol of alterity, and bridge between men and women, women and God.

For there is also a feminine experience contained within these texts. It is articulated differently, often through the body and its fissures, but, neverthe-less, what is indicated is the presence of a speaking 'I' that is 'woman'. The same symbols that reveal this are also invested with spiritual and holy meaning, are the vehicle of authorial intention. What has so far been neglected is their multiplicity of meaning where several voices, masculine, feminine, and holy, speak simultaneously.

It is seen in the use of space, a series of oppositions involving high and low, physical and psychological, exterior and interior, where images of containment (including the maternal), enclosure, and imprisonment are associated with the feminine. Yet, these dichotomies are dissolved as these same images multiply and expand. Some apparently constricting space is, in fact, liberating: the feminine shape of Katherine's garden, the domestic and familiar continuity of ovens, baths, pots, and barrels. Some is deliberately chosen as in the example of Griselda's metaphorical wall, an interiority which both protects her and confounds her tormentor. Divided and separated by men, women, in fact, continually transgress their boundaries in a fluidity of exchange denoted by the resonant representation of the anchoritic window or open doors, archways, the window of a 'phallic' tower. It is seen too in the myth of Persephone, separated from her mother when she winters in Hades, each cut off from the self as well as the other, but where the daughter represents both inside and outside, continually crossing and recrossing the frontiers of her own marginalised world.[5]

The female also reclaims her body, and with it her voice, through a textual focus upon a shifting pattern of images or details, upon a song of joy or semi-articulate sounds, often with angels, upon an open or cyclic description of movement or events, as in the lives of Katherine and Chaucer's Custance, and upon rhythms and shapes, again circular or open, such as the body, a garden, the wheel, wounds, or sexual orifices, and containers like furnaces or barrels. Each condemnatory mention of sexual delight simultaneously affirms jouissance, while a general emphasis upon the sensual and experiential nature of women's affective piety, each detail of touch or scent, suggests creativity and life, negating a masculine insistence upon the ocular. At the same time, what is intended to invoke the destruction, dismemberment, or simple subordination of female flesh – fire, penetrative torture, the loss of breasts or blood – points to a life-affirming and celebratory power. Female flesh is surrendered to the divine presence for 'the heavenly kingdom is at hand only when the flesh has been stripped away',[6] yet it reinscribes itself through the very violence it bears, speaks itself through its own wounds, fissures, and emissions, especially blood and tears, while a focus upon the abject and taboo enables a revelling in all aspects of materiality and corporeality, be it blood, flesh, disease, corruption, or pain.

There is an emphasis, too, upon the maternal, not simply the privileged shelter allocated by the male, but something more open-ended recalling maternal debt, dissolving patrilinear genealogy, and emphasising not only the pain of children but their pleasure too. It is here, in particular, that ideals concerning feminine behaviour are manipulated, where the holy woman speaks and acts with exemplary obedience, yet quietly asserts herself and inverts expectations. Women like Custance and Griselda speak from within that same world which circumscribes them, covertly resisting it, and using their own knowledge of it to make known their own experiences.

Irigaray writes,

> Nearly all women are in some state of madness: shut up in their bodies, in their silence, and their 'home'. This kind of imprisonment means that they may live their madness without it being noticed.[7]

The voice of the masculine writer seeks to close his controlling text and authoritatively silence his female subject. Yet, it is a text often marked by fissures, sites of disruption. Within that space a feminine voice is heard, and what it articulates is its own identity. What also surfaces is this 'madness', a sense of isolation, a fear of existing nowhere except in its own head. The voice of the feminine is the multiplicity of Irigaray's 'two-lips'. When Agatha tells Quincian that she will always love Christ, 'And wyth my lyppys to hym clepe & calle' [*LHW*, 238], it is a saintly identity which is imposed. Beneath it, her own fissured sex speaks itself, engages in the struggle facing all women which is to move 'from the inside to the outside of themselves, to experience themselves as autonomous and free subjects'.[8] The female subject of hagiographical texts is at once saint, idealised woman, man's other – all possibly false, imposed identities. She also has a social self as wife, mother, daughter, virgin, whore, which is no less important. Equally, she has a true, personal, individual identity unique to her alone, largely unspoken, plus a collective identity as a woman articulated through the fissured text, and through her own body. She may be all, some, or even none of these but what is important is to recognise the possibilities, to hear beneath the univocality of the masculine another discourse, another harmony, 'the incantation that moves, troubles, sings – of the impossibility of clearly saying anything, that says everything'.[9]

Here is another story desperate to be heard in conjunction *with* the other for only then will a fuller picture emerge, a voice that is neither better nor worse than that other but which speaks itself and the saint differently. It is the muffled voice of the feminine which warns,

> But I am coming back from far, far away. And say to you: your horizon has limits. Holes even.[10]

Notes

1 Cixous 1994b: 8.
2 Irigaray 1991: 39.
3 ibid. 166–7.
4 Cixous 1994: 79.
5 Irigaray 1991: 112–17.
6 ibid. 177.
7 Irigaray 1990: 94.
8 Irigaray 1993: 48.
9 Irigaray 1991: 96.
10 ibid. 4.

Bibliography

Primary Texts

Anderson, J. J. (ed.) (1969) *'Patience'. (Middle English Poem)*, Manchester: Manchester University Press.

Bokenham, Osbern, M. S. Serjeantson (ed.) (1938) *Legendys of Hooly Wummen*, EETS OS 206.

Capgrave, John, Carl Horstmann (ed.) (1893) *The Life of St. Katherine of Alexandria*, EETS OS 100.

Capgrave, John, J. J. Munro (ed.) (1910) *Lives of St. Augustine and St. Gilbert of Sempringham, and a sermon*, EETS OS 140.

Caxton, William, F. S. Ellis (ed.) (1900) *The Golden Legend – or Lives of the saints as englished by William Caxton*, volumes 2–7, London: Dent.

Chaucer, Geoffrey, L. D. Benson (ed.) (1988) *The Riverside Chaucer*, 3rd edn, Oxford: Oxford University Press.

D'Evelyn, C. and Mill, A. J. (eds) (1956) *The South-English Legendary*, vols 1 and 2, EETS OS 235; 236.

Gorlach, M. (ed.) (1976) *An East-Midland Revision of the 'South-English Legendary'*, Middle English Texts 4, Heidelberg: Carl Winter.

Hamer, R. (ed.) (1978) *Three Lives from the 'Gilte Legende'*, Middle English Texts 9, Heidelberg: Carl Winter.

Herzfeld, G. (ed.) (1899) *An Old-English Martyrology*, EETS OS 116.

Hodgson, P. (ed.) (1944) *The Cloud of Unknowing and the Book of Privy Counselling*, EETS OS 218.

Horstmann, C. (ed.) (1885) *Prosalegenden* (anonymous Middle English lives of Elizabeth of Spalbeck, Mary of Oignies, Christina Mirabilis), *Anglia*, 8.

Horstmann, C. (ed.) (1887) *Early South-English Legendary*, EETS OS 87.

Langland, William, D. Pearsall (ed.) (1978) *Piers Plowman, the C-text*, Exeter: University of Exeter Press.

Meech, S. B. (ed.) (1940) *The Book of Margery Kempe*, EETS OS 212.

Mirkus, Johannes (John Mirk), T. Erbe (ed.) (1905) *Mirk's Festial: A Collection of Homilies*, EETS ES 96.

Nevanlinna, S. and Taavitsainen, I. (eds) (1993) *St. Katherine of Alexandria – The Late Middle English Prose Legend in Southwell Minster MS7*, Cambridge: D. S. Brewer, Finnish Academy of Science and Letters.

Raymond of Capua, trans. G. Lamb (1960) *The Life of St Catherine of Siena*, London: Harvill Press.

Saint Gregory of Nyssa, *The Life of Saint Macrina*, trans. V. W. Callahan (1967) *Fathers of the Church*, 58, Washington, DC: Catholic University of America Press.

Simmons, T. F. (ed.) (1878) *The Lay Folks' Mass Book*, EETS OS 71.

Skeat (ed.) (1881) *Aelfric's 'Lives of the Saints'*, EETS OS 76; 82 and OS 94; 114.

Talbot, C. H. (ed., trans.) (1987) *The Life of Christina of Markyate: a twelfth century recluse*, Oxford: Clarendon Press/Oxford University Press.

de Voragine, Jacobus, *The Golden Legend of Jacobus de Voragine*, trans. G. Ryan and H. Ripperger (1941) London: Longmans, Green & Co.

Wynkyn de Word, Whiteford, P. (ed.) (1990) *The Myracles of Oure Lady*, Middle English Texts 23, Heidelberg: Carl Winter.

French feminists: primary texts

Cixous, H. (1981a) 'Sorties', trans. A. Liddle, in E. Marks and I. Courtivron (eds) *New French Feminisms: an Anthology*, Brighton: Harvester.

—— (1981b) 'The Laugh of the Medusa', trans. K. Cohen and P. Cohen, in E. Marks and I. Courtivron (eds) *New French Feminisms: an Anthology*, Brighton: Harvester.

—— (1994a) 'Angst' in S. Sellers (ed.) *The Hélène Cixous Reader*, London: Routledge.

—— (1994b) 'Holocauste' in S. Sellers (ed.) *The Hélène Cixous Reader*, London: Routledge.

—— and Clément, C. (1986) *The Newly Born Woman*, trans. B. Wing, London: University of Minnesota Press.

Hermann, C. (1981) 'Women in Space and Time', trans. M. R. Schuster, in E. Marks and I. Courtivron (eds) *New French Feminisms: an Anthology*, Brighton: Harvester.

Irigaray, L. (1985a) *Speculum of the Other Woman,* trans. G. C. Gill, Ithaca, NY: Cornell University Press.

—— (1985b) 'The mechanics of fluids', trans. C. Porter and C. Burke, in L. Irigaray *This Sex Which Is Not One*, Ithaca, NY: Cornell University Press.

—— (1985c) *This Sex Which Is Not One*, trans. C. Porter with C. Burke, Ithaca, NY: Cornell University Press.

—— (1985d) 'This sex which is not one', trans. C. Porter, in L. Irigaray *This Sex Which Is Not One*, Ithaca, NY: Cornell University Press.

—— (1985e) 'When Our Lips Speak Together', trans. C. Porter, in L. Irigaray *This Sex Which Is Not One*, Ithaca, NY: Cornell University Press.

—— (1990) 'Women's exile: interview with Luce Irigaray', trans. C. Venn, in D. Cameron (ed.) *The Feminist Critique of Language: a Reader*, London: Routledge.

—— (1991a) *Marine Lover of Friedrich Nietzsche*, trans. G. C. Gill, New York: Columbia University Press.

—— (1991b) 'Questions to Emmanuel Levinas', in M. Whitford (ed.) *The Irigaray Reader*, Oxford: Basil Blackwell.

—— (1991c) 'Sexual Difference' in M. Whitford (ed.) *The Irigaray Reader*, Oxford: Basil Blackwell.

—— (1991d) 'The bodily encounter with the Mother', trans. D. Macey, in M. Whitford (ed.) *The Irigaray Reader*, Oxford: Basil Blackwell.

—— (1991e) 'Women–Mothers, the silent substratum of the social order', trans. D. Macey, in M. Whitford (ed.) *The Irigaray Reader*, Oxford: Basil Blackwell.

—— (1993) *je, tu, nous – Toward a Culture of Difference*, trans. A. Martin, London: Routledge.

—— (1996) *I Love To You: Sketch for a Possibility Within History*, trans. A. Martin, London: Routledge.

Kristeva, J. (1981a)'Oscillation between power and denial', trans. M. A. August, in E. Marks and I. Courtivron (eds) *New French Feminisms: an Anthology*, Brighton: Harvester.

—— (1981b) 'Woman can never be defined', trans. M. A. August in E. Marks and I. Courtivron, (eds) *New French Feminisms: an Anthology*, Brighton: Harvester.

—— (1982) *Powers of Horror: an Essay on Abjection*, trans. L. S. Roudiez, New York: Columbia University Press.

—— (1986a) 'About Chinese Women', in T. Moi (ed.) *The Kristeva Reader*, New York: Columbia University Press.

—— (1986b) 'Freud and Love: treatment and its discontents', in T. Moi (ed.) *The Kristeva Reader*, New York: Columbia University Press.

—— (1986c) 'Stabat Mater', in T. Moi (ed.) *The Kristeva Reader*, New York: Columbia University Press.

—— (1986d) 'The system and the speaking subject', in T. Moi (ed.) *The Kristeva Reader*, New York: Columbia University Press.

—— (1986e) 'Women's Time', in T. Moi (ed.) *The Kristeva Reader*, New York: Columbia University Press.

Leclerc, A. (1990) 'Woman's Word', trans. C. Duchen, in D. Cameron (ed.) *The Feminist Critique of Language: a Reader*, London: Routledge.

General Bibliography

Aers, D. (1980) *Chaucer, Langland, and the Creative Imagination*, London: Routledge and Kegan Paul.

—— (1983) '*Piers Plowman* and problems in the perceptions of poverty: a culture in transition', *Leeds Studies in English* NS 14: 5–25.

—— (1986a) *Chaucer*, Brighton: Harvester.

—— (ed.) (1986b) *Medieval Literature: Criticism, Ideology, and History*, New York: St Martin's.

—— (1986c) 'Reflections on the Allegory of the Theologians: ideology and *Piers Plowman*', in *Medieval Literature: Criticism, Ideology, and History*, New York: St Martin's.

Arthur, K. (1998) 'Equivocal subjectivity in Chaucer's *Second Nun's Prologue* and *Tale*', *Chaucer Review* 32: 215–31.

Atkinson, C. W. (1983) *Mystic and Pilgrim: the Book and the World of Margery Kempe*, Ithaca, NY: Cornell University Press.

Bakhtin, M. M. (1984) *Rabelais And His World*, trans. H. Iswolsky, Bloomington, IN: Indiana University Press.

Baldwin, A. P. (1990) 'The triumph of patience in Julian of Norwich and Langland', in H. Philips (ed.) *Langland, the Mystics, And the Medieval English Religious Tradition*, Cambridge: Brewer.

Beckwith, S. (1986) 'A very material mysticism: the medieval mysticism of Margery Kempe', in D. Aers (ed.) *Medieval Literature: Criticism, Ideology, and History*, New York: St. Martin's.

—— (1993) *Christ's Body: Identity, Culture, and Society in Late Medieval Writings*, London: Routledge.

Bell, R. M. (1985) *Holy Anorexia*, Chicago: University of Chicago Press.

Bell, S. G. (1989) 'Medieval women book owners: arbiters of lay piety and ambassadors of culture', in J. M. Bennett, E. A. Clark, J. F. O'Barr, B. A. Vilen and S. Westphal-Wihl (eds) *Sisters and Workers in the Middle Ages*, Chicago: University of Chicago Press.

Bennett, J. M. (1988) 'Public power and authority in the medieval English country-side', in M. Erler and M. Kowaleski (eds) *Women and Power in the Middle Ages*, London: University of Georgia Press.

—— (1989) *Sisters and Workers in the Middle Ages*, Chicago: University of Chicago Press.

Benstock, S. (ed.) (1988) *The Private Self: Theory and Practice of Women's Autobiographical Writings*, London: Routledge.

Blake, N. F. (1972) *Middle English Religious Prose*, London: Edward Arnold.

Blumenfeld-Kosinski, R. and Szell, T. (eds) (1991) *Images of Sainthood in Medieval Europe*, Ithaca, NY: Cornell University Press.

Bolton, B. (1976) 'Mulieres Sanctae' in S. M. Stuard (ed.) *Women in Medieval Society*, Philadelphia, PA: University of Pennsylvania Press.

Brown, P. (1981) *The Cult of the Saints: its Rise and Function in Latin Christianity*, London: University of Chicago Press.

Brundage, J. A. (1989) 'Prostitution in the medieval canon', in J. M. Bennett, E. A. Clark, J. F. O'Barr, B. A. Vilen and S. Westphal-Wihl (eds) *Sisters and Workers in the Middle Ages*, Chicago: University of Chicago Press.

Bugge, J. (1975) *Virginitas: an Essay in the History of a Medieval Ideal*, The Hague: Martinus Nijhoff.

Burns, J. E. (1993) 'This prick which is not one: how women talk back in Old French fabliaux', in L. Lomperis and S. Stanbury (eds) *Feminist Approaches to the Body in Medieval Literature*, Philadelphia, PA: University of Pennsylvania Press.

Butler, J. (1993a) *Bodies That Matter: on the Discursive Limits of Sex*, New York: Routledge.

—— (1993b) 'The Body Politics of Julia Kristeva', in K. Oliver (ed.) *Ethics, Politics, and Difference in Julia Kristeva's Writing*, London: Routledge.

Bynum, C. W. (1984) *Jesus As Mother: Studies in the Spirituality of the High Middle Ages*, Berkeley, CA: University of California Press.

—— (1987) *Holy Feast And Holy Fast: the Religious Significance of Food to Medieval Women*, Berkeley, CA: University of California Press.

—— (1991) *Fragmentation and Redemption: Essays on Gender and the Human Body in Medieval Religion*, New York: Zone Books.

Cameron, D. (1985) *Feminism and Linguistic Theory*, London: Macmillan.

—— (ed.) (1990) *The Feminist Critique of Language: a Reader*, London: Routledge.

Camille, M. (1994) 'The image and the self: unwriting late medieval bodies' in S. Kay and M. Rubin (eds) *Framing Medieval Bodies*, Manchester: Manchester University Press.

Clasby, E. (1979) 'Chaucer's Constance: womanly virtue and the heroic life', *Chaucer Review* 13: 221–33.

Coates, J. (1993) *Women, Men, and Language: a Sociolinguistic Account of Sex Differences*, 2nd edn, London: Longman.

Coletti, T. (1993) 'Purity and danger: the paradox of Mary's body and the en-gendering of the infancy narrative in the English Mystery cycles' in L. Lomperis and S. Stanbury (eds) *Feminist Approaches to the Body in Medieval Literature*, Philadelphia, PA: University of Pennsylvania Press.

Constable, G. (1995) *Three Studies in Medieval Religious and Social Thought*, Cambridge: Cambridge University Press.

Dinshaw, C. (1989) *Chaucer's Sexual Poetics*, Madison, WI: University of Wisconsin Press.

le Doeuff, M. (1989) *The Philosophical Imaginary*, trans. C. Gordon, London: Athlone.

Douglas, M. (1970) *Natural Symbols: Explorations in Cosmology*, London: Barrie and Rockliff.

Doyle, P. M. (1974) 'Women and religion: psychological and cultural implications' in R. Ruether (ed.) *Religion and Sexism: Images of Woman in the Jewish and Christian Traditions*, New York: Simon and Schuster.

Dronke, P. (1984) *Women Writers of the Middle Ages*, Cambridge: Cambridge University Press.

Duby, G. (1978) *Medieval Marriage: Two Models from Twelfth Century France*, trans. E. Forster, Baltimore, MD: The Johns Hopkins University Press.

Edwards, A. S. G. (1994) 'The transmission and audience of Osbern Bokenham's *Legendys of Hooly Wummen*' in A. J. Minnis (ed.) *Late Medieval Religious Texts and Their Transmission*, Cambridge: Brewer.

Elliot, A. G. (1987) *Roads to Paradise: Reading the Lives of the Early Saints*, Hanover and London: University Press of New England.

Elshtain, J. B. (1982) 'Feminist discourse and its discontents: language, power, and meaning', in N. O'Keohane, M. Z. Rosaldo and B. C. Gelpi (eds) *Feminist Theory: a Critique of Ideology*, Brighton: Harvester.

Erler, M. and Kowaleski, M. (eds) (1988) *Women and Power in the Middle Ages*, London: University of Georgia Press.

Evans, R. (1994) 'Body politics: engendering medieval cycle drama', in R. Evans and L. Johnson (eds) *Feminist Readings in Middle English Literature: the Wife of Bath and all her Sect*, London: Routledge.

Evans R. and Johnson, L. (eds) (1994) *Feminist Readings in Middle English Literature: the Wife of Bath and all her Sect*, London: Routledge.

Finke, L. A. (1992) 'Mystical bodies and dialogics of vision' in U. Wiethaus (ed.) *Maps of Flesh and Light: the Religious Experience of Medieval Women Mystics*, Syracuse, NY: Syracuse University Press.

Frantzen, A. J. (ed.) (1991) *Speaking Two Languages: Traditional Disciplines and Contemporary Theory in Medieval Studies*, Albany, NY: State University of New York Press.

—— (1993) 'When women aren't enough', *Speculum* 68: 445–71.

Gallop, J. (1988) *Thinking Through the Body*, New York: Columbia University Press.

Georgianna, L. (1981) *The Solitary Self: Individuality in the Ancrene Wisse*, Cambridge, MA: Harvard University Press.

Gilmartin, K. (1979) 'Array in the *Clerk's Tale*', *Chaucer Review* 13: 234–46.

Gilson, E. (1940) *The Mystical Theology of Saint Bernard*, trans. A. H. C. Downes, London: Sheed and Ward.

Glasscoe, M. (ed.) (1992) *The Medieval Mystical Tradition in England*, Exeter Symposium V, Cambridge: Brewer.

—— (1993) *English Medieval Mystics: Games of Faith*, London: Longman.

le Goff, J. (1988) *The Medieval Imagination*, trans. A. Goldhammer, Chicago, ILL: University of Chicago Press.

Goodich, M. (1985) 'Ancilla Dei: the servant as saint in the late Middle Ages' in J. Kirshner and S. Wemple (eds) *Women of the Medieval World: Essays in Honour of John H. Mundy*, Oxford: Basil Blackwell.

Grosz, E. (1989) *Sexual Subversions: Three French Feminists*, London: Allen and Unwin.

—— (1990) *Jacques Lacan: a Feminist Introduction*, London: Routledge.

Grudin, M. P. (1989) 'Chaucer's *The Clerk's Tale* as political paradox', *Studies in the Age of Chaucer*, 11: 63–92.

Guberman, R. M. (ed.) *Julia Kristeva Interviews*, New York: Columbia University Press.

Hanna III, R. (1978) 'Some commonplaces of late Medieval patience discussions: an introduction', in G. Schifforst (ed.) *The Triumph of Patience*, Orlando, FL: University Presses of Florida.

Hansen, E. T. (1992) *Chaucer and the Fictions of Gender*, Berkeley, CA: University of California Press.

Harding, W. (1993) 'Body in text: *The Book of Margery Kempe*' in L. Lomperis and S. Stanbury (eds) *Feminist Approaches to the Body in Medieval Literature*, Philadelphia, PA: University of Pennsylvania Press.

Heffernan, T. J. (1988) *Sacred Biography: Saints and Their Biographers in the Middle Ages*, Oxford: Oxford University Press.

Hirsh, J. C. (1989) *The Revelations of Margery Kempe: Paramystical Practices in Late Medieval England*, New York: E. J. Brill.

Howell, M. C. (1988) 'Citizenship and Gender: Women's Political Status in Northern Medieval Cities', in M. Erler and M. Kowaleski (eds) *Women and Power in the Middle Ages*, London: University of Georgia Press.

Jehlen, M. (1982) 'Archimedes and the paradox of feminist criticism', in N. O'Keohane, M. Z. Rosaldo and B. C. Gelpi (eds) *Feminist Theory: a Critique of Ideology*, Brighton: Harvester.

Johnson, L. (1994) 'Reincarnations of Griselda: Contexts for the *Clerk's Tale*' in R. Evans and L. Johnson (eds) *Feminist Readings in Middle English Literature: the Wife of Bath and all her Sect*, London: Routledge.

Jones, A. R. (1986) 'Writing the body: toward an understanding of l'écriture féminine', in E. Showalter (ed.) *The New Feminist Criticism: Essays on Women, Literature, and Theory*, London: Virago.

Jones, D. (1990) 'Gossip: notes on women's oral culture', in D. Cameron (ed.) *The Feminist Critique of Language: a Reader*, London: Routledge.

Karras, R. M. (1989) 'The Regulation of Brothels in Later Medieval England' in J. M. Bennett, E. A. Clark, J. F. O'Barr, B. A. Vilen and S. Westphal-Wihl (eds) *Sisters and Workers in the Middle Ages*, Chicago: University of Chicago Press.

Kaplan, C. (1990) 'Language and Gender' in D. Cameron (ed.) *The Feminist Critique of Language: a Reader*, London: Routledge.

Kay, S. and Rubin, M. (eds) (1994) *Framing Medieval Bodies*, Manchester: Manchester University Press.

Kieckhefer, R. (1984) *Unquiet Souls: Fourteenth Century Saints and their Religious Milieu*, London: University of Chicago Press.

Kirk, E. D. '"Who suffreth more than God?": Narrative Redefinition of Patience in *Patience* and *Piers Plowman*' in G. Schifforst (ed.) *The Triumph of Patience*, Orlando, FL: University Presses of Florida.

Kirshner, J. and Wemple, S. F. (eds) (1985) *Women of the Medieval World: Essays in Honour of John H. Mundy*, Oxford: Basil Blackwell.

Kolodny, A. (1986) 'A map for rereading gender and the interpretation of literary texts', in E. Showalter (ed.) *The New Feminist Criticism: Essays on Women, Literature, and Theory*, London: Virago.

Kolve, V. A. (1984) *Chaucer and the Imagery of Narrative –The First Five Canterbury Tales*, London: Edward Arnold.

Kowaleski, M. and Bennett, J. M. (1989) 'Crafts, gilds, and women in the Middle Ages', in J. M. Bennett, E. A. Clark, J. F. O'Barr, B. A. Vilen and S. Westphal-Wihl (eds) *Sisters and Workers in the Middle Ages*, Chicago: University of Chicago Press.

Labarge, M. W. (1986) *Women in Medieval Life: a Small Sound of the Trumpet*, London: Hamish Hamilton.

Little, L. K. (1978) *Religious Poverty and the Profit Economy in Medieval Europe*, Ithaca, NY: Cornell University Press.

Lochrie, K. (1991a) 'The language of transgression: body, flesh, and word in mystical discourse' in A. J. Frantzen (ed.) *Speaking Two Languages: Traditional Disciplines and Contemporary Theory in Medieval Studies*, Albany, NY: State University of New York Press.

—— (1991b) *Margery Kempe and Translations of the Flesh*, Philadelphia, PA: University of Pennsylvania Press.

Lomas, P. (1973) *True and False Experience*, London: Allen Lane.

Lomperis, L. and Stanbury, S. (eds) (1993) *Feminist Approaches To The Body In Medieval Literature*, Philadelphia, PA: University of Pennsylvania Press.

Lucas, A. (1983) *Women In The Middle Ages: Religion, Marriage, and Letters*, Brighton: Harvester.

Lynch, K. L. (1988) 'Despoiling Griselda: Chaucer's Walter and the problem of knowledge in the *Clerk's Tale*', *Studies in the Age of Chaucer* 10: 41–70.

McAffee, N. (1993) 'Abject strangers: towards an ethics of respect' in K. Oliver (ed.) *Ethics, Politics, and Difference in Julia Kristeva's Writings*, London: Routledge.

Machan, T. W. (ed.) (1991) *Medieval Literature: Texts and Interpretation*, New York: Binghampton, Medieval and Renaissance Texts & Studies.

McLaughlin, E. C. (1974) 'Equality of souls, inequality of sexes: woman in medieval theology', in R. Ruether (ed.) *Religion and Sexism: Images of Woman in the Jewish and Christian Traditions*, New York: Simon and Schuster.

McNamara, J. A. (1985) 'A Legacy of Miracles: Hagiography and Nunneries in Merovingian Gaul' in J. Kirshner and S. Wemple (eds) *Women of the Medieval World: Essays in Honour of John H. Mundy*, Oxford: Basil Blackwell.

—— (1991) 'The need to give: suffering and female sanctity in the Middle Ages', in R. Blumenfeld-Kosinski and T. Szell (eds) *Images of Sainthood in Medieval Europe*, Ithaca, NY: Cornell University Press.

—— (1992) 'The rhetoric of orthodoxy: clerical authority and female innovation in the struggle with heresy', in U. Wiethaus (ed.) *Maps of Flesh and Light: the Religious Experience of Medieval Women Mystics*, Syracuse, NY: Syracuse University Press.

Mann, J. (1991) *Geoffrey Chaucer*, London: Harvester.

Manning, S. (1979) 'Chaucer's Constance: pale and passive', in E. Vasta and Z. P. Thundy (eds) *Chaucerian Problems and Perspectives*, Notre Dame: University of Notre Dame Press.

Margherita, G. (1993) 'Originary fantasies and Chaucer's *Book of the Duchess*', in L. Lomperis and S. Stanbury (eds) *Feminist Approaches To The Body In Medieval Literature*, Philadelphia, PA: University of Pennsylvania Press.

Marks, E. and de Courtivron, I. (eds) (1981) *New French Feminisms: an Anthology*, Brighton: Harvester.

Martin, P. (1990) *Chaucer's Women: Nuns, Wives and Amazons*, Basingstoke: Macmillan.

Meale, C. (ed.) (1993) *Women and Literature in Britain 1150–1500*, Cambridge: Cambridge University Press.

Millett, B. (1993) 'Women in no-man's land: English recluses and the development of vernacular literature in the twelfth and thirteenth centuries', in C. Meale (ed.) *Women and Literature in Britain 1150–1500*, Cambridge: Cambridge University Press.

Millett, B. and Wogan-Browne, J. (eds) (1990) *Medieval English Prose for Women: selections from the Katherine group and Ancrene Wisse*, Oxford: Clarendon.

Minnis, A. J. (ed.) (1994) *Late Medieval Religious Texts and Their Transmission*, Cambridge: Brewer.

Moi, T. (1985) *Sexual/Textual Politics: Feminist Literary Theory*, London: Methuen.

—— (ed.) (1986) *The Kristeva Reader*, New York: Columbia University Press.

—— (ed.) (1987) *French Feminist Thought: a Reader*, Oxford: Basil Blackwell.

Morse, C. (1985) 'The exemplary Griselda', *Studies in the Age of Chaucer* 7: 51–86.

Neel, C. (1989) 'The origins of the Beguines', J. M. Bennett, E. A. Clark, J. F. O'Barr, B. A. Vilen and S. Westphal-Wihl (eds) *Sisters and Workers in the Middle Ages*, Chicago: University of Chicago Press.

Nielsen, H. B. (ed.) (1981) *Hagiography and Medieval Literature: a symposium*, Odense: Odense University Press.

Oliver, K. (ed.) (1993) *Ethics, Politics, and Difference in Julia Kristeva's Writing*, London: Routledge.

O'Keohane, N., Rosaldo, M. Z. and Gelpi, B. C. (eds) (1982) *Feminist Theory: a Critique of Ideology*, Brighton: Harvester.

O'Mara, V. M. (1992) 'From print to manuscript: *The Golden Legend* and British Library Landsdowne MS 379', *Leeds Studies in English* NS 23: 81–104.

Owst, G. R. (1926) *Preaching in Medieval England: An Introduction to Sermon Manuscripts of the Period c. 1350–1450*, Cambridge: Cambridge University Press.

Park, T. (1992) 'Reflecting Christ: The role of the flesh in Walter Hilton and Julian of Norwich', in M. Glasscoe (ed.) *The Medieval Mystical Tradition in England*, Exeter Symposium V, Cambridge: Brewer.

Petroff, E. E. (1994) *Body and Soul: Essays on Medieval Women and Mysticism*, Oxford: Oxford University Press.

Pickering, O. S. (1994) 'The outspoken *South-English Legendary* poet' in A. J. Minnis (ed.) *Late Medieval Religious Texts and Their Transmission*, Cambridge: Brewer.

Powell, S. (1991) 'John Mirk's *Festial* and the pastoral programme', *Leeds Studies in English*, NS 22: 85–102.

Prusak, B. (1974) 'Woman: seductive siren or source of sin?', in R. Ruether (ed.) *Religion and Sexism: Images of Woman in the Jewish and Christian Traditions*, New York: Simon and Schuster.

Raybin, D. (1990) 'Custance and history: woman as outsider in Chaucer's *Man of Law's Tale*', *Studies in the Age of Chaucer* 12: 65–84.

Reames, S. L. (1980) 'The Cecilia legend as Chaucer inherited it and retold it: the disappearance of an Augustinian ideal', *Speculum* 55: 38–57.

—— (1991) 'Mouvance and interpretation in late medieval Latin: the legend of St. Cecilia in British breviaries', in T. W. Machan (ed.) *Medieval Literature: Texts and Interpretation*, New York: Binghampton, Medieval and Renaissance Texts & Studies.

Roberts, P. B. (1985) 'Stephen Langton's *Sermo de Virginibus*', in J. Kirshner and S. Wemple (eds) *Women of the Medieval World: Essays in Honour of John H. Mundy*, Oxford: Basil Blackwell.

Robertson, E. (1991) 'The corporeality of female sanctity in *The Life of St. Margaret*', in R. Blumenfeld-Kosinski and T. Szell (eds) *Images of Sainthood in Medieval Europe*, Ithaca, NY: Cornell University Press.

—— (1993) 'Medieval medical views of women and female spirituality in the *Ancrene Wisse* and Julian of Norwich's *Showings*' in L. Lomperis and S. Stanbury (eds) *Feminist Approaches To The Body In Medieval Literature*, Philadelphia, PA: University of Pennsylvania Press.

Ross, E. (1992) '"She wept and cried right loud for sorrow and for pain" – suffering, the spiritual journey, and women's experience in late mysticism', in U. Wiethaus (ed.) *Maps of Flesh and Light: the Religious Experience of Medieval Women Mystics*, Syracuse, NY: Syracuse University Press.

Rubin, M. (1991) *Corpus Christi – the eucharist in late medieval culture*, Cambridge: Cambridge University Press.

—— (1994) 'The person in the form: medieval challenges to bodily "order"' in S. Kay and M. Rubin (eds) *Framing Medieval Bodies*, Manchester: Manchester University Press.

Ruether, R. R. (ed.) (1974a) *Religion and Sexism: Images of Woman in the Jewish and Christian Traditions*, New York: Simon and Schuster.

—— (1974b) 'Misogynism and virginal feminism in the fathers of the Church', in R. Ruether (ed.) *Religion and Sexism: Images of Woman in the Jewish and Christian Traditions*, New York: Simon and Schuster.

Salter, E. (1962) *Chaucer – 'The Knight's Tale' and 'The Clerk's Tale'*, London: Edward Arnold.

Schibanoff, S. (1994) '"Taking the gold out of Egypt": the art of reading as a woman', in R. Evans and L. Johnson eds. *Feminist Readings in Middle English Literature: the Wife of Bath and all her Sect*, London: Routledge.

Schiffhorst, G. J. (ed.) (1978) *The Triumph of Patience*, Orlando, FL: University Presses of Florida.

Schulenburg, J. T. (1989) 'Women's monastic communities 500–1100, a comparative survey of Britain, France, Belgium: patterns of expansion and decline', in J. M. Bennett, E. A. Clark, J. F. O'Barr, B. A. Vilen and S. Westphal-Wihl (eds) *Sisters and Workers in the Middle Ages*, Chicago: University of Chicago Press.

Sellers, S. (ed.) (1994) *The Hélène Cixous Reader*, London: Routledge.

Showalter, E. (ed.) (1986) *The New Feminist Criticism: Essays on Women, Literature, and Theory*, London: Virago.

Spacks, P. M. (1988) 'Female rhetorics' in S. Benstock (ed.) *The Private Self: Theory and Practice of Women's Autobiographical Writings*, London: Routledge.

Stanbury, S. (1993) 'Feminist masterplots: the gaze on the body of the *Pearl's* dead girl', in L. Lomperis and S. Stanbury (eds) *Feminist Approaches To The Body In Medieval Literature*, Philadelphia, PA: University of Pennsylvania Press.

Stockton, K. B. (1994) *God Between Their Lips: Desire Between Women in Irigaray, Bronte, and Eliot*, Stanford, MT: Stanford University Press.

Strohm, P. (1992) *Hochon's Arrow, the social imagination of fourteenth century texts*, Princeton, NJ: Princeton University Press.

Stuard, S. M. (ed.) (1976) *Women in Medieval Society*, Philadelphia, PA: University of Pennsylvania Press.

Suleiman, S. R. (ed.) (1985) *The Female Body in Western Culture: Contemporary Perspectives*, London: Harvard University Press.

Thompson, A. B. (1991) 'Narrative art in the *South-English Legendary*', in *Journal of English and Germanic Philology* 90: 20–30.

Vasta, E. and Thundy, Z. P. (eds) (1979) *Chaucerian Problems and Perspectives*, Notre Dame: University of Notre Dame Press.

Warner, M. (1976) *Alone of All Her Sex: the myth and the cult of the Virgin Mary*, London: Weidenfeld and Nicolson.

Weisl, A. J. (1995) *Conquering the Reign of Femeny: Gender and Genre in Chaucer's Romance*, Chaucer Studies XXII, Cambridge: Brewer.

Whitford, M. (1991a) *Luce Irigaray: Philosophy in the Feminine*, London: Routledge.

—— (ed.) (1991b) *The Irigaray Reader*, Oxford: Basil Blackwell.

Wiethaus, Ulrike (ed.) (1992) *Maps of Flesh and Light: the Religious Experience of Medieval Women Mystics*, Syracuse, NY: Syracuse University Press.

Wilson, K. M. (ed.) (1984) *Medieval Women Writers*, Manchester: Manchester University Press.

Wogan-Browne, J. (1991) 'Saints' lives and the female reader', *Forum for Modern Language Studies* 27: 314–32.

—— (1994a) 'The Virgin's Tale', in R. Evans and L. Johnson (eds) *Feminist Readings in Middle English Literature: the Wife of Bath and all her Sect*, London: Routledge.

—— (1994b) 'Chaste bodies: frames and experiences', in S. Kay and M. Rubin (eds) *Framing Medieval Bodies*, Manchester: Manchester University Press.

—— (1994c) 'The apple's message: some post conquest hagiographic accounts of textual transmission', in A. J. Minnis (ed.) *Late Medieval Religious Texts and Their Transmission*, Cambridge: Brewer.

Index